"Norman's analogy that reason is the mind's immune system for combating bad ideas is astonishingly enlightening and productive. His analysis of reason as an essentially social process fills out the picture and adds great depth."

—Michael Tomasello, author of *Becoming Human*
and *A Natural History of Human Thinking*

"Andy Norman's *Mental Immunity* is the perfect vaccine for the mind-viruses infecting our culture: alternative facts, fake news, and conspiracy thinking, to name a few. How can so much irrationality exist in an age of rationality, and what can we do about it? Norman's tools for inoculating minds should be taught to everyone, from students to senators. A masterful treatise."

—Michael Shermer, publisher of *Skeptic* magazine and
author of *The Moral Arc* and *Heavens on Earth*

"With torchlight and spade, Andy Norman digs into the roots of mass irrationality and plants the seeds of wisdom. Read *Mental Immunity*, and you'll gain the power to ward off mind-viruses, become a smarter version of yourself, and help heal our damaged cultural immune system."

—Clay Farris Naff, member, National Association of Science Writers

"I cannot overemphasize how timely and important Andy Norman's book is. He has taken on the daunting task of enchanting us into an appreciation of reason. His writing is lively, creative, and playful, while its all-important focus never wavers. This is just the book for our confusing, chaotic times."

—Rebecca Goldstein, MacArthur Fellow
and author of *Plato at the Googleplex*

"This book thoroughly explains our topsy-turvy world. It explains what I see on TV and informs how I watch the news. Without being expressly political, *Mental Immunity* sheds more light on modern politics than any treatise from left, right, or center. The charming, simple, and intelligent narration carries ideas that can change the world."

—Eric Lotke, author *2044* and *Making Manna*

"*Mental Immunity* was written for the moral uncertainty of our times. Andy Norman illuminates the intersection between science and philosophy, and his thoughtful, fascinating theory guides us toward the better angels of our nature. The most important book you will read this year."

—Brian Hare and Vanessa Woods, authors of *Survival of the Friendliest*

"An epidemic of irrationality grips our nation, and we're waking to the need for a science of mental immune health. In *Mental Immunity*, Andy Norman launches the science of cognitive immunology, and shows how we can inoculate ourselves and each other against mind-parasites. A thrilling expedition on an emerging scientific frontier."

—Dennis Trumble, author of *The Way of Science*

"*Mental Immunity* is a gem. Andy Norman takes us on an exhilarating ride—one destined to change the way we think about reason and faith, science, and religion. If you're concerned about the state of unreason in our current society, read this book. Public philosophy at its finest."

—Lee McIntyre, author of *Post-Truth* and *How to Talk to a Science Denier*

"Andy Norman offers a promising strategy for protecting us against dangerous beliefs that go viral and infect whole swathes of the population. *Mental Immunity* is a fine example of philosophy at work to solve real social problems."

—Peter Singer, Ira W. DeCamp Professor
of Bioethics, Princeton University

"QAnon, religious extremists, and the Trump cult; unreason is a defining problem of our age. In this book, Andy Norman delivers a provocative answer. Drawing on philosophy, psychology, and the social sciences, he outlines an engaging and ambitious program for a new science of cognitive immunology. Let us hope that his plan succeeds."

—Katherine Stewart, author of *The Power Worshippers*
and *The Good News Club*

"Many lament declines in critical reasoning, respect for evidence, and civil discourse. Some have tried to understand how that happens. Andy Norman proposes how we might do something about it. His model of reasoning as a distributed cultural immune system provides constructive ways to enhance our ability to think clearly and learn from one another."

—Joseph Rouse, author of *Articulating the World*

"Nearly every page contains something interesting and valuable: a clear summary of an important idea, a thought-provoking anecdote, or a challenge to some aspect of conventional knowledge. A mind-bending reading experience that will help you think straight!"

—Bart Campolo, host of the *Humanize Me* podcast
and coauthor of *Why I Left / Why I Stayed*

"Andy Norman's thought-provoking book comes at just the right time—when the failure of reasoned public debate threatens the very future of the country."

—Jeffrey Tayler, author of *Topless Jihadis*

# Mental
# Immunity

# Mental Immunity

Infectious Ideas,
Mind-Parasites,
and the Search
for a Better Way
to Think

## Andy Norman

With a Foreword by Steven Pinker

HARPER WAVE

*An Imprint of HarperCollinsPublishers*

HarperCollins books may be purchased for educational, business, or sales promotional use. For information, please email the Special Markets Department at SPsales@harpercollins.com.

FIRST EDITION

*Designed by Nancy Singer*

Library of Congress Cataloging-in-Publication Data has been applied for.

ISBN 978-0-06-300298-2

21 22 23 24 25  LSC  10 9 8 7 6 5 4 3 2 1

To all those without whom
the arc of history wouldn't bend.
Especially Heidi, without whom not.

*See how elastic our stiff prejudices grow, when love comes to bend them.*

—HERMAN MELVILLE

# Contents

## PART III: Antibodies and System Failures

## PART IV: Inoculating Minds

# Foreword by Steven Pinker

Andy Norman's *Mental Immunity* comes in the wake of two disasters of the twenty-first century—the Covid-19 pandemic, and the presidency of Donald Trump—and connects them, though not with the familiar linkage of Trump's disastrous mishandling of the government's response to the pandemic. No, Norman suggests that the pandemic may have morals for the mystery of how a paragon of irrationality—defiant of truth, science, expertise, and constructive discourse—could have attained the presidency with the support of almost half the American public. The morals are that bad ideas are like an infectious disease, and our best safeguard is to boost our mental immune systems.

Certainly every thinking person alive in this century has a mystery to explain: how, in an era blessed with unprecedented resources for reasoning, the public sphere is infested with so much fake news, conspiracy theorizing, and "post-truth" rhetoric.

There are, to be sure, theories on why irrationality flourishes. According to a growing conventional wisdom in social sciences and the media, the human being is portrayed as a caveman out of time, poised to react to a lion in the grass with a suite of biases, blind spots, fallacies, illusions, and fundamental errors. (The Wikipedia entry for cognitive biases lists almost two hundred.) Though I am a prominent advocate of evolutionary psychology, I don't sign on to this cynical picture of our species. Hunter-gatherers—our ancestors and contemporaries—are not nervous antelopes but cerebral problem solvers. And a list of the ways in which we are stupid cannot explain why we're so smart: how we discovered the laws of nature, transformed the planet, lengthened and enriched our lives, and articulated the rules of rationality that people so often flout.

While I agree that the environment that shaped our minds did not select for modern instruments of rationality like statistical formulas and datasets, I think it's better to think of that environment as the backdrop to most of human life, right up to the present. The benchmarks of rationality come from academic philosophy, science, and mathematics. These were never a part of people's lived experience, and for most people, still are not. When people deal with problems that are closer to their personal reality, they are not as benighted as the media would suggest. In getting to work and raising their kids, most people execute feats of rationality that outthink our best artificial intelligence software.

So how could otherwise rational people believe that Hillary Clinton ran a child sex ring out of a pizzeria, or that jet contrails are made of mind-altering drugs dispersed by a secret government program? The standard answers from philosophy, probability theory, and cognitive psychology—blunders in critical thinking like affirming the consequent, misunderstandings of chance like the Gambler's Fallacy, cognitive biases like Base-Rate Neglect—provided little insight.

In his other writings, Norman has convincingly refuted the idea that human reasoning evolved to serve some non-rational function like besting our social rivals in arguments. We really are equipped, he says, with rational faculties that, when healthy, align our collective beliefs with reality.

What, then, makes the rational animal so irrational? Here, Norman explores the vulnerability of all complex systems to infection by agents with their own ultimate goals. Some of them are small organisms that infiltrate our tissues and cells. But some of them are small ideas that infiltrate our brains.

As this book goes to press, the news is dominated by two events that, by the lights of this book, align into a poetic coincidence. Within days of each other, the first safe and effective vaccine against Covid 19 was announced, and the winner of the 2020 American election became apparent. No one should savor this week more than Norman, because his book sent to press that week argues that it's the equivalent of a vaccine we must deploy if we are to keep future infections of bad ideas at bay.

—*Steven Pinker*
*Johnstone Family Professor of Psychology*
*Harvard University*
*Author of* How the Mind Works *and* Enlightenment Now

# Tree of Life,
# Seeds of Death

*Those who can make you believe absurdities
can make you commit atrocities. —Voltaire*

I pulled open the glass outer door of the Tree of Life synagogue and went in to retrieve my son. It was a crisp fall day in Pittsburgh, and Kai—then about four—attended day care in the now-infamous house of worship. Kai hugged his friends goodbye, took my hand, and we walked outside. By the curb sat the family car, my wife at the wheel. Kai liked the challenge of climbing up and into his car seat, so I waited as he made his ascent. He completed the maneuver and smiled up proudly. I buckled him in. "How was school, buddy?" I asked. "Good," he replied. "We met God."

Heidi shot me an astonished look. I returned it, and slid into the passenger seat. "Holy cow!" I said. "Can we hear the story?" Kai was matter-of-fact: God came in, talked to his teacher, and gave him a high five. Then he left. Really, Dad, it was no big deal. Later, we made inquiries, and his teacher told a different story. Apparently, the synagogue's bewhiskered rabbi had dropped in to say hello. His teacher introduced him as a "man of God," and Kai, who knew God to be bearded, had connected the dots.

Years later, a deranged ideologue named Robert Bowers parked his car where Heidi had parked ours. He got out, reached into his trunk, and pulled out a semiautomatic rifle. Then he threw open the synagogue's glass outer door, entered the sanctuary, and began shooting. People he'd never met began dying. Panicked congregants barricaded doors; others phoned for help. Sirens wailed and law enforcement scrambled to the scene. Screaming "All Jews must die!" Bowers turned his guns on the arriving officers. He wounded two and retreated into the very annex where my kids attended "school."

Within the hour, a SWAT team arrived. A firefight ensued, and Bowers took a bullet. Trapped and bleeding, he finally surrendered. Police took him into custody and medics rushed in to tend victims. Sadly, eleven of my neighbors were beyond helping. It was the deadliest attack on Jews in America's history.

Bowers was taken to a nearby hospital. There, he received care from incomparably better human beings, many of them Jews.

I count myself lucky to have grown up in Squirrel Hill, the neighborhood where all this took place. Some say Squirrel Hill was the inspiration for *Mister Rogers' Neighborhood*, the nurturing fictional world created for public television. (The show's gentle host—the late Fred Rogers—lived close by.) Now, our neighborhood—Mr. Rogers' neighborhood—is the site of a horrific hate crime.

When Bowers began shooting, my family was out of harm's way. Kai's teacher and rabbinical "God" were also safe: they'd left the congregation years before. God himself? I have no idea where he was. I was mere blocks away, developing a vaccine for extremism.

## A Plague of Ideologies

We learn about tragedies like these, come together in grief, and resolve "Never again." Then, seeking remedies, we ask questions. How can people do such unspeakable things? We try to fathom the thinking behind such acts, find ourselves baffled, and label it "unthinkable."

Words like *unthinkable* serve to express our horror, but they also smack of denial. For evidently, people *do* think such things. Some go so far as to plan them. Apparently, a sufficiently disordered mind can speak the unspeakable and find sense in the senseless. There's a dreadful phenomenon at work here, and so far, it has defied our best efforts at comprehension. Examine it carefully, and you'll find something genuinely anomalous—something we can't explain with existing frameworks.

Yet explain it we must. For similar forms of derangement are cropping up everywhere. Extremist worldviews, conspiracy thinking, and hyper-partisan politics spread like cancers online. Mass shootings, terror bombings, and hate crimes occur almost daily. In recent years, we've seen culture wars erupt, zealous fundamentalisms make a comeback, and toxic nationalisms gain strength. In 2017, American *Nazis* marched openly through the streets of Charlottesville, Virginia chanting "Blood and soil!" and "Jews will not replace us." Why is this happening? Why again, and why now? Evidently, something quite fundamental is amiss. But what? And how in the world do we fix it?

I want to develop a novel understanding of these phenomena— and with it, an overlooked approach to addressing the problem. The approach centers on an unsettling idea: bad ideas are mind parasites— pathogens that quite literally "infect" minds. Happily, minds have immune systems: operations that keep bad ideas at bay. Sadly, these systems don't always perform well. Sometimes, bad ideas overrun them and thoroughly disorder minds. In fact, a mind's defenses can collapse under certain kinds of stress.

Especially the kind of stresses *ideologies* subject them to.

This is a book about the mind's immune system—its marvelous capacity to protect us from many of the bad ideas out there, and its glaring failure to protect us from divisive ideologies. It's about how mental immune systems work, why they often fail, and how we can strengthen them against failure. It's also about *cultural* immune systems—the things cultures do to prevent bad ideas from spreading—and why these systems are also prone to collapse. That epidemic of unreason we're witnessing today? It's rooted in a cultural immune disorder.

Interpreting our situation in immunological terms sheds an uncanny light on our "post-truth" predicament. It highlights root causes and suggests novel remedies. It opens the door to a more systematic approach to controlling the spread of bad ideas: one based on the realization that mental immune performance can be enhanced. I think this approach will help us achieve something a century's worth of critical thinking instruction has thus far failed to accomplish: "herd immunity" to ideological contagion. By patiently inoculating willing minds, we can prevent deadly outbreaks of unreason.

## Untold Story

Scientists have done a lot in recent years to expose a root cause of our dysfunctional politics. The psychologist Jonathan Haidt summarizes the research in his best-selling book *The Righteous Mind*.[1] His conclusion? Our brains have a kind of tribal architecture. As he puts it, we're "groupish" creatures: beneath the level of conscious awareness, our thinking is bent by the need for tribal solidarity. Passionate loyalty to an in-group "us" makes it hard to think in a fair-minded way. When an out-group "them" is made to seem threatening, our thinking becomes especially bent. Demagogues and propagandists exploit these vulnerabilities: they stoke judgment-warping fears and manipulate their own loyalists.

Robert Bowers was a textbook case. A staunch conservative, he became a follower of aggressive right-wing media. He consumed online propaganda, embraced a militant Christian identity, and viewed the mainstream media as a big conspiracy. He came to trust the delusional claims of white supremacists. Then, in October 2018, several hundred Hispanic refugees began a long march for the US border, hoping to gain asylum. America's president saw a political opportunity and cast them as an invading mob. Online, conspiracy theorists alleged that American Jews were orchestrating an "invasion." Apparently, Bowers was unequipped—or disinclined—to question this narrative. Within days, he snapped. On a website for extremists, he posted a message that speaks to the depths of his derangement: "I can't sit by and watch my people get slaughtered . . . I'm going in." He then loaded his weapons and headed for Mr. Rogers' neighborhood.

Bowers failed to question ideas central to his identity. He became deranged, and others paid the price. He is not alone in this: billions of us make similar—if less lethal—mistakes: we fail to ask basic questions, embrace self-serving beliefs, and saddle others with the costs. As I will show, the garden-variety irresponsible thinking of otherwise decent people paves the way for extremism. This is a huge problem for humanity—and always has been. But now, with Internet connectivity, it has become an existential threat. Climate denial alone could do us in, and that's just the tip of the iceberg. Only the iceberg of irresponsible thinking isn't melting: it's growing.

I study psychology because I want to understand how thinking goes haywire. For a time, I thought that references to the brain's tribal architecture sufficed as an explanation. I came to realize, though, that they can't be the whole story. We all have brains with the same basic architecture; why then do some *but not others* shoot up synagogues? Why is humanity sometimes more tribal, and sometimes less? Why do people exhibit different levels of susceptibility to divisive ideologies? Evidently, biological constants interact with cultural variables in ways that make a difference. And here's the thing: the variables are the very thing prevention efforts must vary. They're our levers: the things we must adjust to solve the problem. We need to understand them. So what's the rest of the story?

We know that Bowers' moral sensibilities had been scrambled. We also know that *ideologies* had a hand in the scrambling. In this book, I'm going to use the term *ideology* to mean a system of ideas that doesn't serve its human hosts well—a system of ideas that is infectious, dysfunctional, harmful, manipulative, or stubbornly resistant to rational revision. (Later, I'll elaborate on this definition; for now, it's enough to see that Bowers appears to have contracted several.)

Ideologies in this sense have enormous power to disorder minds. Like demagogues, they exploit mental vulnerabilities. For thousands of years, ideologies have spread like diseases, warping worldviews, inciting violence, and wreaking havoc on human prospects. They've destabilized magnificent civilizations. They've sustained oppressive orthodoxies. They've divided peaceful societies, provoked devastating wars, and unleashed genocidal furies. History is a living, breathing testament to this truth: outbreaks of ideological thinking end in tragedy. Yet we still lack the kind of understanding that would allow us to prevent such outbreaks. This must change.

As we'll see, an ideology can hijack a mind without any help from a propagandist. In fact, demagogues rise to power in populations where ideological rigidity has *already* taken root. This is true, for example, of the America that elected Donald Trump: as pundits are fond of saying, his electoral victory was merely a symptom. To understand the disease, we must grasp how ideologies circumvent common sense, take up residence as belief, and alter the way people think.

## Mental Malware

Ideas can induce minds to help them—the ideas—proliferate. For example, successful memes impel millions to repost them online. Salacious rumors get gossips to share them. Evangelical convictions inspire the faithful to proselytize. Propaganda induces its victims to propagate it. Conspiracy theories captivate minds and get them to infect other minds. The basic point is simple and uncontroversial: ideas can spread despite being false, delusional, or destructive.

Nor do ideas always serve the best interests of the minds that host them. In fact, they can be actively harmful. Take the idea that Allah wants you to don an explosive vest and kill infidels. An idea like that can destroy the mind that harbors it. You'd think host immolation would be a losing strategy for an idea, yet this one manages to spread even so. How? When a successful suicide bomber inspires copycats, one copy of the idea is obliterated, but other copies take its place in the larger meme pool. Individual hosts prove expendable. Think about it. In cases like this, bad ideas *use people* to proliferate. And garden-variety bad ideas are relevantly similar: host the idea that smoking cigarettes is cool and you're likely to pay a price—even as you're infecting others with the idea.

We like to think of ideas as things that answer our beck and call: that we have agency and they don't. But this is a simplistic conceit, as the phenomenon of viral "memes" makes clear. The fact is, bundles of information frequently take on a life of their own. And the language of agency is useful for understanding the complex and sometimes lifelike behavior they exhibit. Viruses don't think, but they manipulate host cells. In fact, experts attest that they trick cells into serving their—the virus's—"interest" in spreading. In the same way, an idea can trick a mind into serving its "interests."[2]

Bad ideas have all the properties of parasites. Minds *host* them, the way bodies host bacteria. When bad ideas spread, they *replicate*—copies are created in other minds. An idea can even induce its host to *infect* other minds, just as the flu virus can induce an infection-spreading sneeze. Finally, bad ideas are harmful almost by definition.

I'll spell out what I mean by "bad idea" soon enough; for now, just note three things. First, an idea can benefit its host—by comforting or inspiring, say—but still be bad in the sense of false. Second, an idea can be *short-term beneficial* but *long-term harmful*: by delivering a satisfying jolt of righteous indignation, say, but causing us to say things we regret. Third, an idea can *benefit its host* while *harming others*—say, by inducing him or her to swindle. Such ideas can rightly be called bad even when they're beneficial in some limited sense.

Many today have an almost allergic reaction to frank talk about bad ideas. We think: "Who am *I* to say that so-and-so's idea is bad?" Then we abstain from judgment and congratulate ourselves for our tolerance. This is a culturally conditioned reflex, and it's not serving us well. Here's the truth: it's up to *us* to filter out bad ideas. As we'll see, avoiding such work is an indefensible form of responsibility avoidance. We need to call out problematic ideas, just as we call out problematic behaviors.

Bad ideas *are* parasites. Not "analogous to parasites" or "metaphorical parasites" but *actual* parasites. Philosophers have shown that the concept of mind-parasites has theoretical integrity, and scientists are waking to the implications.[3] Public health officials are describing the spread of misinformation about the coronavirus as an "infodemic."[4] Scholars are publishing peer-reviewed articles about how to "inoculate" minds against misinformation.[5] Think tanks are exploring the idea of "cognitive immunity."[6] Science never turns on a dime, but on this question, it's begun to change direction.

We nonscientists need to wake up too. We pretend that, to a first approximation, mental contents are inert—that *what* we think doesn't affect *how* we think. We ignore the fact that ideas can seduce, addict, confuse, disorient, and derange. We suppress the knowledge that beliefs can compromise our ability to think in clear and impartial ways. (Beliefs of an identity-defining sort turn out to be especially problematic.) We half acknowledge that irresponsible believing causes enormous harm, but continue to treat belief formation (and identity formation) as utterly discretionary—a purely private affair. This neglects what is rapidly becoming undeniable: our minds are networked, susceptible, and easily unhinged. And mind-parasites are real.

Pathogens spread through populations, compromising the health of plants and animals. Malicious software spreads across the Internet, interfering with the proper functioning of computers. And bad ideas spread through social networks, interfering with the proper functioning of minds. These—all three of them—are facts. But we've come to grips with only two of the three.

Compare humanity's response to these three facts, and the need for a scientific revolution becomes clear. Case one: biologists have learned that viruses hijack cellular machinery to replicate. They study how viruses accomplish this, then medical professionals translate the resulting understanding into clinical interventions: everything from vaccines to virotherapy. If you haven't suffered recently from measles or mumps, chicken pox or smallpox, you can thank the specialists who safeguard this dimension of public health. Biology and medicine have answered the call.

Case two: network security specialists study malware—computer viruses, digital worms, Trojan horses, and the like. These "white hat" hackers puzzle out how digital parasites work, then use the resulting knowledge to develop countermeasures. From antivirus software to sound security protocols, we rely on the work of such specialists to keep our computer networks healthy. ("Healthy," of course, here means "functioning well.") If your computer behaved well today, you can thank network security professionals; they too have answered the call.

So why is there no science of *mental* immunity? Why aren't we putting mental immune systems under the microscope, and learning about *their* vulnerabilities? Why aren't we doing more to mitigate the mischief that mental malware makes?

The answer has nothing to do with the relative value of the affected systems. Medicine is a trillion-dollar industry because bodily health matters. Much the same is true of cybersecurity: we spend billions on it because we need our computers to function well. But the well functioning of our minds is every bit as important. Our computers are significant to us, but in the end, they're mere means—things we use and ultimately discard. (Some speak in similar ways about our bodies—as if they were mere vehicles for our minds.) By contrast, our minds are ends in themselves. They matter quite directly. Surely our concern for the quality of mental experience is the only reason we attach significance to anything. Mattering is *rooted* in minds.

So why don't we protect our minds with a science of mental immunity? Perhaps the concept of mental malware touches a nerve. Perhaps our pride is blinding us to the truth: ideas are constantly rewiring our brains—and for better or worse, remaking our minds.

## Cognitive Immunology

The expression "bad idea" doesn't have to mean "idea I happen to dislike." If used carefully, it can point to salient features of reality: the idea's actual logical and causal properties, say, or its tendency to subvert human interests. These are properties that diligent, objective inquiry can expose. As for the expression "mental immune system," it may not pick out a discrete chunk of matter, but that in no way implies that these systems aren't real. Mental immune systems *do* exist, but we must learn to see them for what they are. This book will show you how.

I envision a discipline that seeks to understand and enhance mental immune function—the things minds do to shed bad ideas. I call it "cognitive immunology." Cognitive immunologists will examine the properties of ideas—both logical and causal—and identify ideological pathogens; they'll comprehend how bad ideas infiltrate minds and devise strategies to prevent their spread. They'll puzzle out how healthy minds use reasons to remove bad ideas, and grasp why unhealthy minds cease reasoning in this way. And its applications will help rid us of false, unjustified, senseless, and dysfunctional beliefs—among them those that "suppress" our mental and cultural "immune response" to other bad ideas!

The science I envision will be both pure and applied: it will diagnose *and* it will treat. It will be based on evidence and informed by theory, but also guided, like its namesake, by a hard-to-define notion of health. Note that, so described, cognitive immunology is not free of value commitments: it unapologetically values function over dysfunction. This makes it analogous to medicine. Cognitive immunology can be every bit as scientific as the immunology that serves biological health.

There's a science here, waiting to be born. In fact, it's stirring. Cognitive scientists have concluded that "systems of misbelief may evolve into full-fledged mind-parasites"—that "viruses of the mind [really do] exist."[7] The concept of mind parasites is clearing up historical mysteries, like the rapid spread of witchcraft beliefs in early modern Europe.[8] Scientists at Princeton and MIT have founded a Network Contagion Research Institute. Self-described "inoculation theorists" are finding ways to combat science denial.[9] For my part, I'll show that mental immune systems are as real as the body's immune system. And that's just the beginning; the cognitive immunology revolution is coming.

Imagine a world where cognitive immunologists design interventions—"immunotherapies"—that restore mental immune health. Where mental immune "boosters" and "mind vaccines" prevent epidemics of partisan thinking. Where people think more clearly, reason more collaboratively, and change their minds when reasons show them to be in the wrong. Imagine reason-giving dialogue flourishing and breaking down ideological barriers. Imagine "fixed" mindsets unfurling, like flowers freed from frost.

Can we build such a world? The prevailing pessimism answers no. Read on, though, and you're apt to reach a different conclusion. Wisdom enthusiasts have time and again built comparatively enlightened worlds; and now, we have the tools to build another. In fact, we can put an end to the ideological corruption of minds. A new Enlightenment awaits—provided each of us does our part.

## Pre-Expedition Briefing

This book contains ideas, stories, and arguments selected for their immune-boosting power. You'll meet an idea that has liberated billions from ideological shackles. You'll try on an attitude that protects minds from premature closure. You'll learn how reasons work, and how you can reason more capably. Finally, I'll explain how you can update your brain's operating system for life in the Internet age.

The rest of this introduction amounts to a pre-expedition briefing. Think of it as a map of some challenging conceptual terrain. Or a compass you can use to get your bearings. After consulting it, you might want to customize your journey. If you like, skip to the chapters that most directly address your concerns. I ask only that you bring three things: grit, an explorer's mentality, and a little team spirit.

The book has four parts. Each will answer basic questions about mind parasites and mental immune systems: what they are, how they work, and how to deal with them. Earlier parts are designed to impart the habits of mind needed to master later parts. They're meant to scaffold what some call "higher order" thinking. Together, they chart a path to robust mental immune health.

Part I will introduce the basic concepts of cognitive immunology and equip you to use them. This should heighten your sensitivity to bad ideas. The world's most capable thinkers notice things that others miss; the immunology frame can help you *feel* the importance of these things—and thereby think more capably. The result is a kind of first aid kit for a culture in immune distress.

The rest of the book will delve into cognitive immunology's philosophical foundations. It will challenge you to think deeply about core concepts. Sadly, the concepts that regulate the contents of our minds—concepts like *good idea*, *bad idea*, *faith*, *science*, and *reasonable*—aren't doing the job. They leave us vulnerable to morally disorienting ideas and fail to induce the kind of wisdom our world needs. It's high time for an upgrade; to replace them, though, we need to wrestle with some tough questions.

Part II will explore the question "What makes good ideas good, and bad ideas bad?" We'll examine two answers, each leading to an influential "ethics" of belief. One focuses on an idea's "downstream" benefits and ends up endorsing certain kinds of faith. This view prevails in the world of religion. The other emphasizes "upstream" evidence. It prevails in the world of science and proves disruptive to faith-based attitudes. We'll learn from both proposals, as each contains a piece of a larger truth. Grasp this compound truth, and you'll see that both religious and secular worldviews bring something to the table. And your ability to spot mind parasites will grow.

In Part II, we'll also look at how cultures and subcultures regulate belief. The subculture of science, it turns out, does a particularly good job of it. We can learn a lot, then, by reverse-engineering science. Doing this reveals a pivotal fact: the common idea that each of us has a right to our opinion is busy compromising mental immune systems. I then develop treatments modeled on immunotherapy and show how we can use them to reduce our susceptibility to bad ideas.

In Part III, I put the mind's immune system under the microscope. This allows us to identify the "antibodies" of the mind. This yields new answers to ancient philosophical questions. Questions like: "What *are* reasons, exactly?" and "How do they work?" Reasons, it turns out, are like levers—we use them to pry loose some ideas and shoehorn others into place. Ideally, we use them to align beliefs with conditions in the world—that is, to seek truth. But we also need them to align our beliefs with other beliefs: to reconcile our attitudes, commitments, and feelings. Importantly, groups use reasons to forge and repair *shared* outlooks.[10] All these kinds of alignment are important, for they impact both individual and collective well-being. But sometimes, they work at cross-purposes. Believe purely in order to belong, for example, and your thinking can become evidence-resistant. Stay on this path, and your worldview can come unhinged.

The big idea of Part III is that reasons function properly only in the presence of a fulcrum-like social norm. This norm tells us that we must *yield* to good reasons—to change our minds and behavior in the face of them. I call this norm "reason's fulcrum" because without it, reasons can't do their jobs. It's the beating heart of all dialogue, all reasoning, all science, all problem-solving, and much learning. It's utterly fundamental to civilized existence. When we don't submit to better reasons but instead cling to, say, identity-defining beliefs, we damage this norm. When we make a habit of this, thinking comes unhinged: unmoored from the objective considerations that might otherwise anchor it. This makes us susceptible to dangerous ideas. When entire cultures abuse this norm, a pivotal social expectation wanes, and eventually, epidemics of unreason run riot. Mere anarchy is loosed. This is the deep story of why our culture is in disarray. The discovery points to a promising way to inoculate minds against ideological contagion.

In Part IV, I show that our conceptions of reasonable belief are like the mind's gatekeepers. In a sense, they're the brain's antivirus "software." By upgrading these conceptions, we can boost mental and cultural immune health. And here we uncover a startling truth: *the prevailing understanding of reason's requirements—the one our culture "preinstalls" in most of us—is busy compromising mental immune function all over the globe.* Put differently, a misleading picture of responsible belief is holding us back: it excuses irresponsible believing and disrupts our reason-giving practices. This prevents us from resolving deep differences of opinion and confounds efforts to forge consensus about the things that matter most. It frustrates our search for wisdom, and alienates us from deep sources of meaning and purpose. Finally, I develop an immune-boosting alternative: a standard of reasonable belief that inoculates minds against the worst kinds of infection.

I hope the book inspires you to become an advocate of responsible cognition. Not a *preacher* of responsible thinking but a *practitioner* of it. Someone who upholds the norms of accountable talk and, by so doing, makes everyday conversations extraordinary. When I speak of each of us doing our part, that's what I have in mind. In this way, you can be a difference-making contributor to the cognitive immunology revolution.

# Mental Immunity

Most men would rather deny
a hard truth than face it.

—Tyrion Lannister, *Game of Thrones*

# CHAPTER 1

# Beyond Critical Thinking

### Why existing approaches are failing us

In pursuit of knowledge, something new is
learned. In pursuit of wisdom, something
old is unlearned. —*Med Jones*

In the hit film *Ghostbusters*, a crack team of "paranormal researchers"
launches a poltergeist removal business. The start-up struggles until
an outbreak of troublesome spooks causes demand for its services to
spike. Suddenly, the ghostbusters are local celebrities, lionized for
their expertise. Then a minor character has the gall to question head
ghostbuster Peter Venkman. Playing an unflappable Venkman, Bill
Murray blinks politely and summons an indulgent smile. He then
delivers one of the great lines in movie history: "Back off, man," he
says, "I'm a scientist."

Like Venkman, I want to deliver an unconventional diagnosis.
And yes, I'd like it to be memorable. Unfortunately, I'm in no position
to "pull a Venkman." For one, I'm no scientist; I'm a philosopher, and
that gives me roughly half the street cred of your average paranormal
researcher. For another, my medium—the written word—doesn't

permit me to append a confident smile. You'll have to manage, then, with my unadorned words: Trust me, I'm a philosopher.

Doesn't land the same way, does it?

Know this, though: we philosophers have been incubating sciences for a hundred generations. Most of the established sciences were once our jurisdiction: physics, biology, economics, linguistics, psychology— all of these were once branches of "natural philosophy." In each case, entrepreneurial philosophers hatched a particularly useful way of look- ing at things, and philosophy spun off another science. That's where fledgling sciences come from: philosophy's science incubator. Seri- ously: storks have nothing to do with it.

I hope to deliver an infant science in these pages. It's been gestat- ing for a long while. (Long enough to rule me out as the father.) I've nurtured it for years, and I, among others, feel it quickening.[1] The idea is to study the way healthy minds fight off bad ideas, and work out better ways to strengthen mental immune systems.

In my next chapter, I'll define key concepts and establish the sci- entific credentials of cognitive immunology as I envision it. First, though, I want to frame the emerging science as the natural evolu- tion of an ancient quest. I mean Western philosophy's twenty-five- hundred-year hunt for wisdom: the multigenerational effort to get *Homo sapiens* to live up to its prideful name. (*Homo sapiens* is Latin for "wise human.") By framing cognitive immunology as an advance- ment of this quest, I mean to motivate a particularly broad concept of mental parasite, and an especially useful concept of mental immunity. If we put cognitive immunology on the right conceptual foundation, we can do more than merely survive our "post-truth" predicament; we can substantially mitigate ancient forms of folly.

## The Art of Bad Idea Removal

The *Ghostbusters* soundtrack included a catchy theme song with a rousing chorus: "Who you gonna call? Ghost-BUS-ters!" The song reached number one on Billboard's Hot 100, the music industry's official ranking of best-selling tunes. The song doubled as the fictional start-up's marketing jingle, and in the film, the marketing campaign becomes a runaway success. Disembodied beings would wreak havoc, and leave surfaces covered with slimy green ectoplasm. Panicked citizens would remember the lyric and place the call. Then a brash team of gadget-wielding ghostbusters would deploy to do what they did best: trap and remove troublesome spirits.

If philosophy had a competent marketing department, it might release a similar jingle. (I'm told focus groups liked "Who you gonna call? MYTH-bus-ters!" But Legal nixed it, citing trademark concerns.) Imagine troubled consumers of bad ideas making "the call," and question-wielding philosophers deploying to the scene of each outbreak. There, we could do what we do best: trap and remove troublesome ideas. And clean up ideological slime.

My point is this: "myth-busting" is a pretty good description of what we philosophers do. So is "bad idea removal." This is a key premise in my overall argument, so allow me to render it plausible.

For starters, it's right there in the name: "philosopher" means "lover of wisdom." (The word comes from the Greek words *philia*, meaning love, and *sophia*, meaning wisdom.) Mere yearning for wisdom, though, is not enough to make you a philosopher: to earn the title, you must *seek* it. But how does one seek wisdom? Where do you look? The answers are embedded in the epigraph to this chapter. There, the sage economist Med Jones observes that "in pursuit of wisdom, something old is unlearned." The implication is that we *gain* wisdom by *losing* our misconceptions—that wisdom consists not in the *presence* of something good but the *absence* of something bad. Combine these facts and you get a preliminary argument for my considered view: to a large extent, philosophy is about removing bad ideas.

Philosophy is in some ways a giant scavenger hunt for something elusive. Doing it can feel like groping around in the dark. If I'm right about wisdom, though—that it amounts to a kind of absence—this shouldn't surprise us. For wisdom, then, would not be the kind of thing one can "find" all at once—not in any way that might conclude the hunt. The space of possible misconceptions is a limitless darkness, so we build wisdom by patiently casting light into shadow after shadow, and incrementally refining our flawed maps of what truly matters. Join the hunt and help keep darkness at bay, but don't imagine that we can flip on the lights and behold wisdom in all its glory. It doesn't work that way.

Many credit an amiable curmudgeon named Socrates with launching Western philosophy. He did it by wandering the streets of Athens, engaging people in conversation. (This was four hundred years before Jesus launched the world's most successful religion—by delivering sermons.) He—Socrates, I mean—took a humbler approach: he'd invite people to share their ideas on important topics, then guide them through the process of *testing* those ideas. He wielded questions with exceptional skill and left people humbled yet newly mindful. He compared his art to midwifery, implying that he helped others give birth to healthy ideas, but his real gift lay in exposing "false" and "unhealthy" ideas.[2] He developed an idea-removal method that skilled thinkers admire to this day.

I refer, of course, to the famed Socratic method. Later, we'll see how this method strengthens mental immune systems, and apply the principles of cognitive immunology to enhance it. In this way, we can confer next-level mental immunity.

Exposing other people's bad ideas can get you in a heap of trouble. That's how Socrates met his end: his philosophical demonstrations embarrassed small-minded Athenians. They then charged him with heresy, won a conviction, and gave him a fatal dose of hemlock. In a way, he was martyred for the cause of bad idea removal.

He was not the last to sacrifice for the admirable absence we call wisdom. Hypatia of Alexandria—an extraordinary philosopher—was flayed alive by religious zealots for the sin of teaching. Benedict de Spinoza sparked the philosophical awakening we call the Enlightenment, and suffered excommunication. Thomas Hobbes challenged the orthodoxies of his day and was hounded into exile. Galileo, arguably the father of modern science, was sentenced to house arrest, his books banned by religious authorities. Thomas Paine, whose trenchant critiques helped spark the American Revolution, went on to question religious dogmas, only to die penniless and despised. Bad idea removal can be a tough business.

Even today, philosophers are about as popular as dentists. I often attend lectures at the University of Pittsburgh's Center for the Philosophy of Science, which brings in a steady stream of hugely accomplished scholars. Once, over a beer, a guest of the Center—an eminent scientist—confided that he dreaded philosophers' questions. He worried that such questions might expose deep flaws in his work and knew other scientists with similar worries. Even within the academy, philosophers are feared.

They shouldn't be. Philosophy isn't rocket science. It doesn't require great intelligence. You don't need a fancy degree to do it, or even a lab coat. All you need is that tangle of neurons that sits between your ears and a willingness to focus your attention in a certain way. In fact, you can learn the basics in about ten minutes and be reaping the rewards by lunchtime. Just rearrange some mental furniture and create a little space for idea-testing. Then drop into the "idea lab" from time to time and conduct the occasional thought experiment. Use questions and reasons to test ideas, and pay close attention to what happens. Do this for a while, and you'll discover that there are a *lot* of bad ideas out there. In fact, many pose as good ones and get away with it. To my way of thinking, philosophizing is mostly just paying attention to the problematic features of ideas and helping others appreciate the drawbacks of becoming overly fond of them.

To unlock philosophy's deepest benefits, of course, you need to practice. It's like anything else: mastery takes time and effort. But don't be deterred: you can philosophize whenever you have an un-distracted minute, and the relevant habits of mind can form quickly. In no time, you'll be flagging limiting assumptions and identifying half-baked beliefs. With a bit more practice, you'll be dismantling shabby arguments and warding off dysfunctional expectations. And over time, your onboard "nonsense detector" will grow more sensitive. As we'll see, the practice activates the mind's immune system, conferring an important kind of immunity.

Philosophical idea-testing is also good clean fun. It can spice up the blandest topic and enliven conversation. Many find that it frees them to explore fascinating realms of possibility; others say it reveals hidden depths of meaning. For me, it's all of the above: wonder in-ducing, freeing, and meaning-conferring. It's an invigorating habit of mind—a kind of existential tonic.

Philosophy is more art than science. Universities classify it as a "humanities" discipline, and one of the "liberal arts." But make no mistake: philosophy has always had scientific aspirations. Socrates' star pupil—a young playwright named Plato—admired the rigor of mathematics, and dreamed of transplanting it into ethics and polit-ical philosophy. Spinoza built a surprisingly modern system of eth-ics, complete with axioms, proofs, and theorems. Hobbes argued for a science of morals and anticipated a science that emerged in just the last few decades.[3] Immanuel Kant and John Stuart Mill each developed a semi-scientific approach to distinguishing right from wrong. David Hume and A. J. Ayer tried to purge philosophy of less-than-scientific metaphysical speculation. Philosophy may *be* the art of bad idea removal, but from the beginning, it has tried to *become* a science.

As I see it, philosophy has always been quasi-scientific. For when we philosophers examine assumptions, we treat them as hypotheses. We *test* them. Skilled philosophers do a handful of simple things well. We ask questions, suspend judgment, and examine arguments carefully. We set aside considerations that prove to be irrelevant, try to appreciate the considerations that really *are* relevant, and notice when such inquiry indicates a need to modify our convictions. This isn't exactly science, but it *is* an important kind of hypothesis-testing. And often, it reveals misplaced confidence.

During the scientific revolution, "natural philosophers" discovered that they could use experimentation and observation to weed out problematic factual claims. A distinction arose between natural philosophy and philosophy proper, and the two kinds of idea-testers worked out a division of labor. "Natural philosophy" got a new name—"science"—and philosophy hung on to its core business: the business of examining concepts, running consistency checks, and testing value judgments.

Philosophy continues to encompass *ethics*—the effort to develop our understanding of right and wrong—and *epistemology*, the subdiscipline devoted to understanding how we know things. The latter is of special relevance to this inquiry, for epistemologists study how reasoning, evidence, and learning work. Where psychology limits itself to describing how cognition does *in fact* work, though, epistemology embraces its original mandate to find *better* ways of conducting our cognitive affairs. By long historical precedent, epistemology is a normative (or values-clarifying) enterprise, so for a long time, it's been denied the mantle of science. But none of this changes the essential fact: for thousands of years, epistemologists have dug up insights that can strengthen mental immune systems. Epistemology is cognitive immunology in embryo.

I'm an epistemologist by training. I study how reasoning works. Science, inquiry, and dialogue all fascinate me, so for thirty years, I've tried to figure out what makes them tick. Along the way, I've managed to shed a little light on the evolutionary origins of human reasoning, and clarify the structure of fruitful dialogue. Most of all, though, I like to awaken the impulse to ask questions. This work has led me to a surprising conclusion: the art of bad idea removal is on the verge of becoming a science.

## Four Experiments

Cognitive immunology arrives at a key moment in history, where traditional approaches to controlling the spread of bad ideas are failing us badly. No doubt social media and disinformation campaigns are important parts of our moment's backstory; but so, too, is this: philosophy's efforts to promote wisdom have time and again fallen short of expectations. In what follows, I want to describe a few of these efforts and explain why they failed. I think this will underscore the need for cognitive immunology, and motivate others—you included—to help develop and apply it.

In my telling of the tale, philosophy has inspired several attempts to summit "Mount Wisdom." The oldest centers on the concept of *reason*. It has ancient origins, so I call it "antiquity's epistemology expedition." The second centers on the notion of *faith*, and rose to prominence in the Middle Ages. It ended in disaster, so I call it the

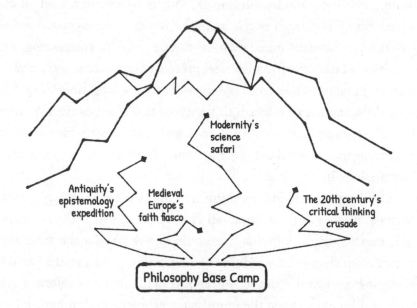

### Four Failed Attempts to Summit "Mount Wisdom"
(Diagram omits psychology's recent "Bias binge.")

"medieval faith fiasco." The third—a historical adolescent—tries to leverage the concept of *science*. It grew up in the early modern period and sallied forth during the scientific revolution; consequently, I call it "modernity's science safari." The fourth centers on the notion of *critical thinking*. It's barely a century old, so I call it the "twentieth century's critical thinking crusade."

Each of these initiatives was well intentioned. Three of the four helped to limit the influence of bad ideas. (The other—the faith fiasco—was an experiment that backfired: it inadvertently bred superstition and folly and brought on the Dark Ages. I'll say more about that in chapter 11.) For now, I want to examine why the other three failed to realize their promise. From a wisdom-cultivation standpoint, each fell far short of its potential. Let's see if we can understand why.

## Antiquity's Epistemology Expedition

Thousands of years ago, philosophers noticed that reasoning with others is a useful way to detect and remove bad ideas. As the Scottish philosopher David Hume would later put it, "The truth springs from arguments among friends." So they offered this modest suggestion: reason together, and test ideas for reasonableness. Hang on to the ideas that prove reasonable, and let go of those that prove unreasonable. This, they argued, is the best way to pursue wisdom—and the right way to prevent bad ideas from spreading. As we'll see, they were right about this—in ways we'd all do well to heed.

The philosophers of ancient Greece and Rome soon realized, though, that everything depends on how you define *reasonable*. Get the definition right, and you have an excellent mechanism for filtering out bad ideas; get it wrong, and you can do more harm than good. The plan was to track down the true meaning of *reasonable*, share it with the world, and in this way provide everyone with a handy way to distinguish between worthy and unworthy opinions. Philosophers hoped that, by doing this, they could make wisdom more common and folly less common. They launched this quest with high hopes, dug into the problem—and found that they'd set themselves a fiendishly difficult task.

We philosophers have since learned a lot about what "reasonable" *doesn't* mean. This is important information, for (as we'll see) most of us rely on conceptions that compromise mental immunity. Philosophy, though, has yet to produce a consensus alternative. As a result, humanity's reasoning practices rattle and wheeze like dying tractors. Here's the truth: these practices are functioning at a fraction of their true capacity to resolve and enlighten. In chapter 12, I'll sketch a better understanding of reason's requirements and show that, properly tended, our reason-giving practices can sing like well-tuned race cars.

## Modernity's Science Safari

A second approach is mere centuries old. It starts with this observation: scientists are doing something very right. When it comes to finding out how the world works, and building consensus around reliable findings, the natural sciences are in a class by themselves. They have an astonishing track record of dissolving bad ideas and precipitating good ones. So why not take the scientific method and apply it in other domains? Why not use it to figure out what's right and what's wrong? Or resolve public policy disputes? Why not use it to dissolve the dogmas that sow religious division, and liquidate dangerous political ideologies?

This approach has been with us since the scientific revolution. It was a primary driver of the Enlightenment—the flourishing of reason and science that brought us modern technologies, human rights, and basic democratic liberties. In recent years, it has again come into vogue. In 2001, America's National Science Foundation launched an initiative to promote STEM learning: education rooted in science, technology, engineering, and mathematics. Initially motivated by concerns about America's economic competitiveness, the effort soon carried another hope: that a solid education in the STEM disciplines would teach young people how to think in responsible, evidence-based ways about other things. Can a solid grounding in STEM make us less vulnerable to climate denial, political propaganda, and religious extremism? With 9/11 also occurring in 2001, the concept struck a chord. Since then, large technology companies, well heeled foundations, government agencies, and education administrators have all rallied around the prescription "More STEM learning!" And money—lots of it—has flowed into efforts to remake American education.

Two decades in, it's clear that our massive investment in STEM learning hasn't "stemmed" the tide of ideological thinking. Why? Apparently, people balk at the idea that the scientific method applies outside the STEM disciplines. We compartmentalize—think in evidentially grounded ways about some things, but not others. As we'll see, a powerful orthodoxy prevents us from applying STEM thinking in anything like a systematic way. This orthodoxy tells us that science isn't competent to settle value questions. As the saying goes: science can tell us what *is*, but not what *should be*.

A little background: advocates for science needed this distinction to carve out a space free from religious interference. At his heresy trial for promoting a sun-centered model of the solar system, Galileo is said to have muttered, "The Bible shows the way to go to heaven, not the way the heavens go." Ever since, Western civilization has been organized around a division of cognitive labor: science will tend to the facts, and religion will tend to our values. It was a necessary compromise—a sort of noncompete agreement that allowed science and religion to coexist.

But four hundred years later, we clearly need to rethink it. Why? Because the domains where ideologies flourish—ethics, politics, and theology—remain relatively untouched by the scientific attitude.[4] It's now clear that we need to think in more evidentially grounded ways about right and wrong. Rational accountability matters in value discourse too. The simple fact is this: we don't reason clearly and productively enough about what matters. But this is a problem we can address. Suitably generalized, the "scientific method" can be used to resolve the questions that divide us into ideological camps. In fact, it can connect us to stable sources of meaning and accelerate moral progress.[5]

## The Twentieth Century's Critical Thinking Crusade

A third initiative centers on the concept of *critical thinking*. A hundred years ago, the philosopher John Dewey introduced the phrase to name a quasi-scientific frame of mind. His insight was sound: responsible thinkers test ideas and try not to rely on the ones that don't survive scrutiny. As we now like to put it: we can teach people how to "think critically," and thereby reduce their susceptibility to bad ideas.

This approach, too, has fallen short of expectations. Despite being the focal point of higher education for one hundred years, our species remains distressingly prone to irrational thinking. There's some evidence that higher education imparts a limited immunity to some forms of ideological contagion,[6] but on all accounts, the effect is weaker than hoped. One study found that "many colleges fail to improve critical thinking skills."[7] Another found that, while a large majority of professors *claim* to impart critical thinking skills, relatively few can say what they mean by critical thinking or explain how their teaching imparts it.[8] In 2016, 43 percent of American college graduates voted for the disastrously unqualified and unprincipled Donald Trump.[9] This massive failure of America's critical thinking factory should be a wake-up call for us all.

I no longer find the concept of critical thinking particularly useful. It's mostly a vague, feel-good term that means "the way we educated people like to think." It's really a conceptual black box, one that hides important differences. It's not a solution, but a placeholder for one. Yes, the term *critical* hints at the need to reduce our susceptibility to bad ideas, but the concept of critical thinking does little more than gesture clumsily at the traits that make that possible.

Immunity to bad ideas depends on far more than the critical thinking skills we like to talk about in higher education. Indeed, our focus on *skills* has led us to overlook the better part of the mind's defenses. (It's more important to shape the deep *sensibilities* that marshal these skills for one or another purpose, and mold the resulting *habits of mind*.) Meanwhile, we need to acknowledge this truth: the critical thinking paradigm has not served us particularly well.

Reason, science, and critical thinking: these concepts give shape to some of our best efforts to prevent outbreaks of bad ideas. Each effort is well intentioned and worthy of admiration. None, though, can claim true success. Now we can see why: each approach has limitations rooted in its defining concept. The conceptual toolbox we've inherited isn't channeling our efforts in the right way. As a result, we're not doing enough—or enough of the right things—to promote responsible cognition. In this sense, philosophy's reason project—and its science and critical thinking–based variants—are failing us.

## Psychology's Bias Binge

In recent years, psychologists have developed an explanation of this long history of failure. Basically, they've shown that cognitive biases are pervasive and sometimes innate. For example, we're all prone to *confirmation bias*—the tendency to notice evidence *for* a belief and not notice or downplay evidence *against* it. We're prone to *belief persistence*—our beliefs tend to linger, even after the evidence for them is discredited. And our reasoning tends to be *motivated*—skewed by self-interest and hard to distinguish from rationalizing. Assemble facts like these and it begins to look like objectivity just isn't in the cards.

Learning about our cognitive biases can be humbling, and humble thinkers tend to part with bad ideas more easily. This fact gives the bias research some therapeutic properties. Unfortunately, the approach has unhealthy side effects. Backed by decades of research, influential scholars now argue that objectivity and reason are false ideals. Some write off the whole concept of fair-mindedness or give up trying to achieve it. A few insist that we're all equally ideological (a false equivalence) or assert that persuasion is just another way to exercise dominance.[10] All these conclusions are false, and all feed the prevailing cynicism about reason. All of them diminish our reliance on reason-giving dialogue. And they mess with mental immune systems.

I get it: biases exist. They make perfect objectivity unattainable and genuine dialogue difficult. They can close minds and harden hearts. All this is true. But this, too, is true: we can't let the perfect be the enemy of the good. A worldview free of all distortions is probably beyond us, but there's always room to think in *comparatively* clear and fair-minded ways. Yes, everyone has biases, but it doesn't follow that we're all equally hostage to them. Nor are we all equally ideological. Some cling to their beliefs with great tenacity, and others prove remarkably persuadable.

A lot of thinking today is infected with something logicians call "false equivalence." Seeking to be scrupulously fair-minded, we call out failures on "both sides," declare a pox on both houses, then wash our hands of the whole mess. This is a popular way to avoid taking responsibility—and a real inhibitor of critical thinking. As I like to put it, it's a "mental immune disruptor."

We need to combat our proneness to false equivalence with insights like this: *some minds are comparatively susceptible to ideological fixation, and others are comparatively immune.* Then, we need to ask questions: What accounts for the immunity that some have? And how do we develop it? We need to know, because small improvements along this dimension have big implications for our world.

## Mind-Parasites

In the mid-1990s, I was teaching college students critical thinking in frigid upstate New York. I was cold, lonely, and unhappy with my work. I'd chosen one of the best textbooks around and was doing my best to make the subject interesting, but my students seemed . . . listless. I couldn't blame them: like most critical thinking textbooks, mine catalogued the hundreds of ways thinking can go wrong, and the long lists of fallacies seemed to be sapping their enthusiasm for the subject. (Curious, isn't it, how lists can make one listless?) Worse, the textbook made thinking look like a minefield: without meaning to, I was probably diminishing their enthusiasm for thinking!

Then I hit on a wrinkle. Truth be told, it fell into my lap. The journal *Ethics* asked me to review a book titled *Challenges to the Enlightenment*.[11] I took the assignment and encountered an essay by Richard Dawkins titled "Viruses of the Mind." Dawkins was by then a rising star among public intellectuals, famous for his work in evolutionary biology. Years before, he'd unveiled his concept of a *meme*—the idea that behaviors can replicate by imitation and spread like genes do. In "Viruses of the Mind," Dawkins expanded on the idea, suggesting that many regrettable cultural phenomena can be modeled as epidemics.

Dawkins then fashioned his idea into an anti-religious axe. (His poster child for the infected mind was a trusting child sent to a Catholic nun for religious instruction.) I wanted something different: not a secular weapon but an equal-opportunity tool. Why not fashion this idea into something we can *all* use on *all* kinds of bad ideas—be they religious or secular, conservative or liberal, yours or mine?

To be fair, Dawkins didn't just skewer religion in his essay. He also proposed a new field of inquiry. He called it "information epidemiology," and it is part of the fledgling science of cultural evolution. This science brings the concepts of biology to bear on mental and cultural phenomena, and promises to revolutionize our understanding of all kinds of things: fads and fashions, movements and marketing, politics and propaganda.

The concept of memes has been with us for nearly half a century. That's a long time to come to terms with the phenomenon of destructive memes and the "infodemics" they cause. Why, then, do we not have a practical way to control their spread? What are we missing?

## Mental Immune Systems

In an easily overlooked passage, Dawkins compared children to "immune deficient patients . . . wide open to mental infections that adults might brush off without effort." To me, this hinted at a second richly provocative idea: minds have immune systems—operations that protect them, to one or another degree, from bad ideas. It implied that these systems can be underdeveloped, or even damaged. I wanted to see this idea spelled out in detail. Shouldn't *cognitive immunology* take its place alongside *information epidemiology*?

Uncertain, I decided to run the idea past the students in my critical thinking course. On a snowy winter afternoon, I welcomed them to class and helped them settle in. Then I posed this question: "Can a mind become infected?" They looked puzzled. "You mean a brain?" one of them asked. "No," I said, "I mean a *mind*." "Infected by what?" asked another. "Bad ideas," I said. I encouraged them to examine the notion, so they discussed it. About ten minutes later, their verdict was in: to them, it made sense. (Nowadays, of course, it would take a similar group about ten seconds to reach this conclusion: raised in a world where bad ideas routinely "go viral," young people now find the concept of mind viruses obvious.) "All right then," I replied, "are we talking about *other people's* minds or *yours*?" Nervous laughter, followed by a sobering silence. I let the silence linger, then broke it softly: "So which of your ideas are legit, and which are mere mind infections?"

A little later, one student asked a lovely question: "How do you cure a mind infection?" "By getting rid of the bad idea!" volunteered another. A third wondered if it's possible to inoculate minds. "Wait a minute," said a fourth: "Is that what this critical thinking stuff is all about: inoculating our minds?" "BINGO!" I said, smiling broadly: "Being a critical thinker is about having a strong mental immune system. In this class, we're building our immunity to bad ideas."

For the rest of the semester, those students were "all in" on learning critical thinking. We ditched the textbook and learned how the body's immune system works. We learned that T-cells and other lymphocytes hunt down biological parasites. Minds, we concluded, need a similar defense. We realized that reasons and questions are like antibodies: used properly, they hunt down bad ideas and neutralize them. I taught them a fun way to test ideas—a little something I call the "reason-giving game." In this game, "players" get to ask questions and give reasons. The rules clarify the commitments they undertake in the process. If everyone plays by the rules, a constructive dialogue unfolds and spits out a verdict—something both players can validate as (mutually) reasonable.[12] Then I turned my students loose on the topics they cared about. They threw themselves into the work and became markedly more inquisitive. Class discussions acquired a wonderful vitality, and performance on exams improved. I'd stumbled on a flat-out *better* way to teach critical thinking.

## Cognitive Immunology

The following semester, I shared Dawkins' ideas with faculty colleagues. "Mere metaphor," said one. "Misleading," said another. "Scientific reductionism run amok," said a third. For them, I think, the concept of mind-parasites hit too close to home. For me, though, the ideas were genuinely explanatory. Don't moral panics, conspiracy theories, and science denial bear all the hallmarks of cognitive epidemics? Aren't extremist ideologies essentially outbreaks of unreason? And in cases like these, aren't cognitive immune systems failing more or less by definition?

Ultimately, I saw that the "mere metaphor" objection doesn't hold water. Nobody else was talking about mental immune systems, so I was free to define the phrase as I liked. And it wasn't hard to define it in a way that made "Minds have immune systems" true. If we define a mental immune system as the mind's wherewithal for screening out bad ideas, the existence claim becomes straightforward—a matter of scientific fact. (A similar argument can be made about bad ideas: define the concept properly, and their existence becomes not a matter of opinion but a question to be resolved by scientific investigation.)

Metaphors have a funny way of morphing into literal usages. Dawkins defined the concept of a meme by analogy with the concept of a gene, but as people got comfortable with the idea, they stopped using scare quotes around the word *meme*. They began taking meme-talk seriously, and the word entered the lexicon of science. Now, people think of memes as real things.

By the way, any pattern that persists long enough to be named can be responsibly thought of as real. This means that the insubstantiality of memes—a property shared with all kinds of information—is not a disqualifier. The same would be true of mental immune systems. In this way, our ontology—the catalogue of things considered real—expands.

Similar developments brought genes themselves into being. At first, genes were merely postulated—unknown entities that somehow encode for heritable traits. Decades later, we discovered the helical structure of DNA and associated genes with segments of it. The same goes for emotional epidemics, atoms, electrical "current," and thousands of other entities: metaphors helped bring them into being. Of course, atoms, genes, and emotional epidemics existed long before anyone thought to name them; the fact remains that they became real *to science* when scientists began taking a new metaphor seriously.

Friedrich Nietzsche described languages as "mobile armies of metaphors." That language of immunology is one such army, and it's about to colonize our understanding of critical thinking.

As I got used to the idea of mental immune systems, I started to see things I'd missed. Things like these: Critical thinking is best understood as a conspicuous aspect of *mental immune function*. The excuses people give for thinking in sloppy and irresponsible ways? They qualify as mental immune *disruptors*. Habits of thought that allow bad ideas to proliferate? What are they but mental immune *disorders*? You know how hypercritical people can suffer from "analysis paralysis"? That turns out to be an *autoimmune disorder of the mind*. (When an immune system attacks the body, that's called "autoimmunity." There's a perfectly analogous mental phenomenon.) Why are terrorists so often cut from religious cloth? Perhaps faith-based believing can *compromise* a mind's immune system. Deranged ideologues, with their minds full of unthinkably toxic ideas—people like Robert Bowers? What are they but poster children for *mental immune system failure*?

The concept isn't all doom and gloom: we can master aspects of critical thinking and thereby strengthen the mind's immune system. We can learn to ask good questions and *boost* our immunity to bad ideas. As we'll see, certain forms of instruction can *inoculate* minds against mind viruses. Systematic efforts to promote cognitive immune health will someday prevent epidemics of unreason.

In short, I found that dozens of critical thinking–related facts and questions could be framed in the language of cognitive immunology. And the reframes weren't just amusing variants: they shed real light on the phenomena. They were directing my attention in a more fruitful way. The language of immunology was like a lens, bringing clarity to a domain my philosophical forebears had struggled to bring into focus. I began to see how dialogue goes off the rails. How ideologies subvert rationality norms. How cognitive "immune disruptors" disorder minds. I saw root causes and began to see solutions.

## What If?

What if we employed the conceptual resources of *virology* to better understand mind-parasites Don't some ideas short-circuit critical thinking the way some viruses short-circuit the body's immune system? Can the tools of *epidemiology* help us grasp how ideologies spread? Can the insights of *immunology* help us model mental immune function? What if we took the idea of *cultural immune systems* seriously, and figured out why they so often fail? Why not take a systematic approach to strengthening mental immune systems? Why not catalogue the most disruptive tendencies of thought and find ways to keep them in check?

What if we enlisted the nobler passions in the fight against ideology (as no less a luminary than Plato recommended)? What if we worked *with*, rather than *against*, the human need to *belong*? Could we satisfy this need with communities of *inquiry*, rather than communities of *belief*? Belonging to a community of scientists seems to strengthen resistance to ideological thinking; could belonging to a community of inquiry afford the rest of us similar benefits?

What if we afforded members of our culture personal identity options that serve as a bulwark against ideological infection? Identities like scientist, skeptic, rationalist, and freethinker all put our penchant for "identity-protective cognition"—defensive thinking, basically—to work, but in a way that counteracts our weakness for self-serving beliefs. (This is smart design, and it's reminiscent of the way the US Constitution uses the separation of powers to pit naked ambition against itself.)

What if we acknowledged the human need for transcendence and spiritual connection and sought to address this need in intellectually honest ways?

Our newly globalized civilization badly needs a science of mental immune health. It won't emerge, though, until we give it a solid conceptual foundation.

# CHAPTER 2

# The Cognitive Immunology Toolbox

### Naming the problem

In a world deluged by irrelevant information, clarity is power. —*Yuval Noah Harari*

On rare occasions, I will ask one too many questions. When this happens at home, my wife sets me straight. She fixes me with a dogged gaze, gives her head a shake, and mutters, "Flaming clarifier." Once in a great while, I am chastened.

Heidi has a point: we philosophers often push for clarity, and sometimes we overdo it. We can demand clarity where there's little to be had. Or we suspend judgment, seek definitive resolution, and wait too long to act. The Greek sage Aristotle understood these failings and advised philosophers not to expect "more precision than the subject-matter allows." Wise words, and they've achieved a rare status: thousands of years after he scribbled them, thinkers still heed them. (*That's* the kind of influence we philosophers crave!) It was Heidi's cheeky designation, though, that really changed me. Her words had an efficacy that Aristotle's lacked.

It's possible to expect too much clarity, but it's also possible to expect too little. Just yesterday, I met a genial fellow in an ice-cream shop. He was wearing a T-shirt that appeared to announce a core tenet of his philosophy. It featured bold brown lettering that read GET SHIT DONE. This struck me as terrible advice, so I caught his eye and gave him a rueful look. Then I asked: "Do you really think that's a good idea?" He looked puzzled and asked what I meant. I gestured at his shirt and clarified: "Encouraging people to do random shit: You really think that's a good idea?" He glanced down, laughed, and shook his head. "Probably not," he admitted. We chatted amiably, and I allowed that the T-shirt's lack of specificity was relatively harmless. He liked my larger point, though: some shit isn't worth doing. By the time we got our ice-cream cones, he seemed inclined to retire the T-shirt. Score one for us clarifiers.

We humans proudly label ourselves *"Homo sapiens,"* but no close observer of human behavior thinks we deserve that designation. We fail to think things through, and, time and again, it gets us into trouble. Why is "Look before you leap" a saying? Because we're prone to leap *before* we look. So I stand my ground: I wield questions in the fight against folly, and don't apologize for being a card-carrying member of the clarifier clan.

Now, Heidi is a marvelous specimen of the implementer set: she's simply terrific at getting stuff done. So when she pokes fun at my need for clarity, I counter by bemoaning the missteps of "flaming implementers." Permit me to clarify: a *flaming clarifier* is anyone too busy clarifying to get shit done; a *flaming implementer* is anyone too busy getting shit done to wonder whether the shit they're doing is really *worth* doing. So Heidi and I laugh together at our failings. Decades of self-deprecating humor have changed us both, I think: we each appreciate what the other brings to the table, and generally meet somewhere in the middle. It's a middle that's only moderately de-muddled, but hey: Aristotle would approve. (He taught balance in all things.)

## First Things First

When I give talks about mental immune systems, I get two very different reactions. Some people—I think of them as the flaming implementers—seize on the idea and begin applying it. They see its potential to diagnose the root causes of, say, science denial and want to run with it. Or they get excited about its potential to transform critical thinking instruction and begin suggesting novel teaching methods. Folks like this really impress me: they're quick to grasp the idea's practical significance and eager to put it to work. For them, questions like "How do we strengthen mental immune systems?" crowd to the fore and demand immediate attention.

Good for them. I mean to take up such questions. But more cautious, quizzical folks—the flaming clarifiers among us—respond differently. Their foreheads sprout skeptical furrows. They wonder whether minds really have immune systems, or ask me to define my terms. Some challenge my assumptions. These, too, are admirable responses.

Alas, I can't address everyone's questions at once. If you're an implementer, then bear with me: I need to answer a few clarifying questions first. Why them first? Well, until they're answered, we can't be sure that your implementer's questions are the right ones to ask. Let's make sure that mental immune systems really do exist—*then* we can figure out how to strengthen them. This turns out to be the right approach, because a little clarity turns the idea into a truly transformational tool.

Actually, it's more of a tool *kit*. For there are several ideas here, and each of them has important uses. In this chapter, I want to fashion a set of conceptual tools. I'll do this by defining key terms and showing that the resulting concepts make sense. More than that: I think these concepts *refer*. They direct attention to an overlooked natural system. They let us see mental immune systems for what they really are: entities that have a major impact on our well-being.

With the concepts of cognitive immunology in hand, we can coax better performance from mental immune systems and break the grip that divisive ideologies have on human minds. We can make reason and dialogue normal again, and get back to flourishing.

But first things first.


## Bad Ideas

I use the term *bad idea* to mean what most people mean. Let's make it official: *a bad idea is one that is false, misleading, harmful, or otherwise problematic*. More precisely, an idea can possess any of several "good-making" or "bad-making" qualities. Being true is a good thing. Being false is bad. Being well evidenced counts *for* an idea, and being poorly evidenced counts *against* it. Ideas can also be helpful or harmful, especially when we rely on them. Believing is an especially influential form of reliance, so generally speaking, when we assess an idea, we should try to anticipate the effects of believing (or accepting) it. The likely benefits of believing count, and so do the likely harms. Consequences for *self* matter, and so do the consequences for *others*. None of these claims should be controversial.

Notice that an idea can be good along one dimension but bad along another: true but dispiriting, say ("Global warming is real"), or useful but almost surely false ("The Creator of the universe won't let anything bad happen to me"). Or advantageous for some but harmful to others ("I belong to a superior race of humans"). The bad ideas worth discussing are successful mind-parasites they have significant defects but manage to spread anyway. For example, the idea that *we matter more than they do* has a long and destructive history. So does the idea that *violence is the answer*. By contrast, the idea that *all human beings have rights* has done a great deal to protect human freedoms.

It's not unreasonable to want a more precise definition. Later, I'll have more to say on the subject. For now, just note a few things. First: aside from limits of time and attention, nothing prevents us from taking an honest look at *all* of an idea's properties—the good making, the bad making, and the neutral. Second, nothing prevents us from summing up the results of such inquiry in an overall assessment of an idea's worth—a goodness or badness rating, if you will. Third, there are ways to do this that give due weight to relevant considerations. All of this is true. But so is this: in such matters, we mustn't expect more precision than circumstances allow.

Some will ask: "Who's to say whether an idea is good or bad?" The answer is simple: *we* are. It's up to *us* to assess them. It's up to us to shed the bad ones too. When we fail to assess ideas, the bad ones proliferate and end up causing harm. So don't let the "Who's to say?" question deter you: it masquerades as a substantive philosophical question, but it's actually a responsibility-avoidance strategy.

Take a minute to fully process the point: "Who's to say?" is *not* a profound question. In fact, it's the opposite of profound: it slyly suggests that *none of us has standing to say what's good or what's bad*. In this way, it cuts value inquiry short. It prevents conversations and thoughts from delving deeper. It excuses mental laziness. It inhibits critical thinking and produces superficial minds. In this sense, it's a *cognitive immune disruptor*: something that interferes with the testing and removal of bad ideas.

Some worry that goodness and badness are "subjective," or in the eye of the beholder. This is nonsense. The good-making and bad-making properties of an idea are facts, to be determined by honest inquiry as other facts are. For instance, the harmful effects of incitements to violence may be hard to measure, but they're very real. There's always a fact of the matter as to how beneficial or harmful an idea is, even if it proves hard to gauge. The same is true of the other good-making and bad-making properties of ideas: we don't need to rely on intuition or subjective opinion: we can examine the facts and see what's so. (Spoiler alert: "Values are subjective" is another cognitive immune disruptor.)

A second key definition: an *ideology* is an interlocking system of

bad ideas. Or by extension, a system of bad beliefs. Some researchers study *systems of misbelief*—infectious mental structures that "subvert the interests of their hosts."[1] I have something similar in mind,
only "self-interest-subverting" isn't the only relevant kind of badness.
Falsehood and stubborn resistance to rational revision are also bad
qualities, as is a tendency to subvert the interests of others. Note that
this definition makes *ideology* a pejorative term—or, as I prefer to
think of it, a diagnostic one.

Some use the term *ideology* as a neutral descriptor for any system of beliefs or values. This represents a missed opportunity. Why?
Because we don't need another synonym for *worldview* and *belief
system*—our bases there are covered. Nor should we indulge the view
that all belief systems are created equal. They aren't. What we need is
a way to talk about genuinely problematic systems of belief.

Let's get real: some worldviews are toxic and need to be called
out. The ideology of white supremacists is antithetical to human
flourishing. The "greed is good" ideology of Wall Street creates huge
inequities (and countless iniquities.) Creationism has no explanatory
or predictive value. Neofascism is morally revolting. Meanwhile, evolution provides a better understanding of our origins, and Gandhian
nonviolence can work to combat oppression. Unlike people, worldviews are not created equal. (As I use the term, the last two don't
count as ideologies—not until they can be shown to be problematic.)

An important vein of research shows how "sacred values" create
moral rigidity and cognitive dysfunction.[2] This research informs my
conception of ideology, so I should say a bit about it. The key point
is that sacred values needn't be religious: secular and political coali-
tions also tend to sacralize things, rendering certain behaviors taboo.
For example, left-wing culture warriors sometimes try to "cancel" a
person deemed politically incorrect. As scholars use the phrase, this
too amounts to value sacralization. It works like this: a group deems
something to be of surpassing importance, and taboos begin to form.

Tiny deviations from relatively arbitrary norms get treated as unforgivable transgressions. The group becomes hypersensitive to signals of disloyalty, accusations of heresy and apostasy proliferate, and punishments grow disproportionate. This is how orthodoxies form and, often, how thinking comes unhinged. Belief systems that cement coalitional loyalty are usually ideologies.

The ideologies worth discussing are influential. Often, they're infectious. And rigid. Many exploit our need to belong and become identity defining. If you've ever said to yourself "I'm a Republican," "I'm a Communist," or "I'm a Christian," an ideology—or something like an ideology—has begun to shape your identity. When ideologies take root, they tend to become resistant to rational revision. The most influential interfere with the mind's ability to assess them fairly: they shut down critical thinking or exempt core tenets from critical scrutiny. Some ideologies have shut down an entire culture's (or subculture's) reasoning practices. Think of the stifling orthodoxy that prevailed through Europe's Dark Ages: for over a thousand years, ideologues suppressed inquiry and dissent. Or Stalin's regime of terror, which slaughtered millions and corrupted even the Russian sciences. Ideologies in this sense are a true scourge, and we need a word to designate them. *Ideology* is the best available.[3]

## Mental Immunity

A *mental immune system* is a mind's wherewithal for filtering and shedding bad ideas. Think of it as the infrastructure that allows one to think critically. Critical thinking *skills* are a conspicuous feature of these systems, but inclinations and motivations and dispositions and sensibilities and habits of mind are also key infrastructure. Even character traits like curiosity and humility are foundational to mental immune health. For without these traits, we don't examine and update our beliefs. It also follows that the *contents* of your mind can influence mental immune function. Believing you have all the answers, for example, interferes with the humility needed to unlearn bad ideas.

Note that, on my proposed definition, mental immune systems are real. Minds *do in fact have* infrastructure for shedding bad ideas, so they exist. We don't fully understand how curiosity and the disposition to ask questions are implemented in the brain, but that's not a reason not to name mental immune systems. If it were a cogent objection, we'd have to discard pretty much all talk of mental states. Put differently, mental immune systems are functionally defined, and that functioning is observed to happen. We may not understand *how* they exist (materially), but it's a safe bet *that* they exist (in some form).

Take a moment to absorb the deep philosophical lesson here: a thing needn't be a discrete chunk of matter to exist. Lots of interesting phenomena—languages and norms, numbers and beliefs, fads and trends, epidemics and immunity—exist in more abstract or distributed ways. Also, many of science's most important discoveries were initially hypothetical; somebody posited an unseen something to explain something we *could* see, initiating a scientific scavenger hunt. I've mentioned that biologists posited genes decades before they discovered DNA. This is not an isolated case: the Higgs boson, the planet Neptune, and many chemical elements were conjured into existence with words and reasons, and only later "found" to exist. The mind's immune system is destined to follow suit.

The real obstacle to recognizing the existence of mental immune systems is linguistic inertia: the stubborn reluctance to use words in creative and revealing ways. And that, of course, is a lousy reason to stand pat.

*Mental immune function* is what mental immune systems do: ask questions, test ideas, harbor reservations, and revise opinions, for example. One purpose of a mental immune system is to screen out bad ideas. Another is to let in good ones. Like a bouncer stationed at the gates to a festival, it checks credentials and tries to admit only the duly ticketed. It tries to identify troublemakers and deny them entrance. One way to do this (but not the only way) is to admit only the *warranted* ideas. The process is imperfect, though: some good ideas are turned away, and some bad ideas gain entry. So a healthy mental immune system also has agents circulating *inside* the festival. These agents—questions, reasons, doubts—bump up against festivalgoers and try to identify the bad actors that got past the gatekeeper. And then bounce them.[4]

Another analogy, this one my own: if the mind is a garden, its immune system is like its gardener. The latter's job is to weed the garden of bad ideas, seed it with good ones, and arrange plantings into beautiful and useful patterns. The best gardeners take on weeds of *all* kinds: not just volunteer seedlings and annoying invasives but deep-rooted thickets of misconception. Look into the matter, and you'll come to a transformative realization: most of us inherit gardens teeming with cognitive weeds, and pass on similar gardens to our children. (Our political and religious ideologies, for example.) The best among us manage to pull a few weeds or plant a colorful shrub or two. Here's the bad news: worldviews are invariably full of problematic elements. The good news? Nearly every conversation we have offers opportunities to spruce up a mindscape.

Mental immune systems work more or less well. Mental *immunity* is a matter of degree. It's the inverse of *susceptibility*: those with more immunity are less susceptible, and those with less immunity are more. You can be strongly immune to certain kinds of bad ideas and only weakly immune to others. For example, you can be highly resistant to the blandishments of alien abduction theorists but vulnerable to the appeals of demagogues. Or immune to the entreaties of Mormons but a sucker for Scientologists. You can do an excellent job of screening out new interlopers but a poor job of bouncing the ideational troublemakers you've grown up with. Mental immunity is complicated.

## Immune Dysfunction

Certain kinds of mental immune dysfunction deserve to be called "disorders." An underactive mental immune system can let in all kinds of nonsense. Conspiracy thinking, for example, is a well-recognized disorder characterized by pat dismissals of contrary evidence. The phenomenon is spoofed in the story of Fred the Flat Earther:

Fred dies and goes to heaven. Saint Peter meets him at the gates and explains that new residents get to meet God personally. In fact, God is feeling rather chatty, so Fred can ask God anything he likes. "Make your question a good one, though," explains Saint Peter: "I've got to keep the receiving line moving." Fred thinks it over, and when his turn comes, he's ready. He steps forward proudly and says, "God, I've devoted my life to promoting the idea that the Earth is flat, so I really have to know: Is it flat or round?" "I'm afraid you were wrong, Fred," says God. "The world is very round." Fred's face registers shock, then realization: "This conspiracy goes higher than I thought!"

Over time, a minor cognitive failing—a weakness for wishful thinking, say—can progress into outright derangement. The need to believe in God, for example, can metastasize into the desire to slaughter infidels. Nurse your sense that your opinions are treated unfairly, and it can curdle into toxic partisanship. (Witness the backlash against "political correctness.") Ignore inconvenient truths and your worldview can drift away from reality. (The rise of climate science denial comes to mind.) Fail to resolve the inconsistencies in your outlook, and you sow the seeds of moral confusion. (Think of the Trump administration's penchant for dismissing criticism and its utter inability to provide moral leadership.) These are all cognitive immune disorders, and clearly, they can culminate in catastrophic mental immune failure.

Meanwhile, an *overactive* mental immune system can attack good ideas. For example, philosophers play with extreme forms of skepticism: doubts about the reality of everything outside of the mind, for example. Traffic in such doubts, and you can lose all conviction. Climate skeptics marshal comparably inflated doubts: they forestall needed action and expose us all to serious risks. Inflated doubts about morality can leave you an ethical fence-sitter, a cynic, or a nihilist. Later, we'll diagnose several disorders of this type.

We'll also investigate the *causes* of mental immune disorder. I mean to expose some powerful mental immune *disruptors*. These are things that interfere with healthy mental immune function. It turns out there are many: some of them are ideas; others are attitudes, norms, biases, conversational gambits, and cultural conditions. An inflated ego can interfere with mental immune health, as can a culture war. I've mentioned the rhetorical question "Who's to say?" in this connection. We'll see later that it tends to derail efforts to develop a more nuanced understanding of rights and responsibilities. In this way, it provides cover for suboptimal ideas.

Fortunately, there are ways to enhance mental immune function. A mental immune *booster* is anything that helps to build immunity to bad ideas, improve our openness to good ones, or enhance our ability to tell the difference. For example, you can teach someone that correlation is an unreliable indicator of causation, thereby freeing him or her from a tendency to jump to certain conclusions. Teaching people to recognize their biases can have a similar inoculating effect.

By *mental inoculant* I mean something that induces the mind to manufacture antibodies. Take the realization that it's easy to overgeneralize. Internalize this truth and you're more apt to ask questions. You're also more likely to look for exceptions to seductive rules. The thing to see, of course, is that critical questions and counterexamples are like antibodies: healthy minds produce them to fight off bad ideas. Like the body, the mind can be said to have an *adaptive immune system*.

Anything deliberately designed to stimulate the mind's adaptive immune system can be termed a *mind vaccine*. (Stay tuned for examples.)

## Cultural Immune Systems

The utility of these concepts grows if we extend them to networked minds. Cultures and subcultures have immune systems too. After all, they do things to prevent bad ideas from spreading. *A culture's immune system is its infrastructure for limiting the influence of bad ideas.* Critical discourse, journalistic fact-checking, scientific hypothesis-testing, laws protecting the right to dissent: these are all elements of cultural immune systems.

When a scientist asks to see the evidence, she's expressing (and enforcing) a key scientific norm. When a professor pens "Really? Why?" in the margin of a student paper, he's trying to promote reflection and accountable talk. When a voter tells a politician to "Cut the crap!" she might be expressing frustration at the lack of sincerity in political discourse. All these maneuvers attempt to inhibit the manufacture and spread of nonsense, and all can be thought of as part of a culture's—or subculture's—immune system.

When a culture mobilizes its fact-checkers to blunt the effects of a disinformation campaign, that can be thought of as a *cultural immune response*. When it teaches critical thinking, it boosts *collective immunity*. When a media literacy course makes a group less vulnerable to propaganda, it confers an important kind of *herd immunity*. We can speak, then, of *culture-level cognitive immune health*, and every day we encounter reasons why we need to begin tending it carefully. Especially these days.

When a subculture browbeats dissenters into silence, it damages its own immune system. When it promotes blind faith, it compromises aggregate immunity. When it teaches young people to accept things on the say-so of self-styled authorities, it increases its susceptibility to demagoguery. When it allows its citizens to become ideologically polarized, and political discourse breaks down, it can be said to have a *cultural immune disorder*. The concept of *cultural immune disruptor* points to the root causes of our present predicament.

Mental and cultural immune systems share some interesting properties, and I need to draw attention to some of them. For this, an umbrella term proves useful. A *cognitive immune system*, then, can be individual or collective, mental or cultural. I'll refer to the study of cognitive immune systems as *cognitive immunology*. I'll call some applications of that science *cognitive immunotherapies*.

## Lens

In the seventeenth century, a Dutch scientist named Antonie van Leeuwenhoek opened a window into the world of the very small. He fashioned a microscope, examined things like pond scum, blood, and semen, and discovered a dimension teeming with microbial life. His discoveries paved the way for much of modern medicine.

To me, the concepts of cognitive immunology form a similar lens. They open a window on an overlooked world and allow us to see surprising things. Turn this lens on common conversational norms, and you begin to see the root causes of our hyper-partisan politics. Turn it on prevailing assumptions, and you'll see cognitive immune disruptors in action. Point it at our reasoning practices, and you'll begin to understand why true critical thinking is so rare. You'll grasp why we're starved for meaning, and how propaganda works. And you'll begin to see remedies.

Cognitive immunology will take us far beyond the reigning "critical thinking" paradigm. It offers better explanations, better diagnoses, and better prescriptions. If I'm right, it also harbors a deep solution to humanity's ideology problem. For now, it's enough to understand the field's budding scientific credentials.

Should anyone press you for it, the "nutshell" philosophical argument is this: just as we can derive scientific conclusions from facts combined with the *medical* axiom "Health is good," we can derive scientific conclusions from the facts combined with the *ethical* axiom "Well-being is good." The latter set can be every bit as scientific as the former. Brute linguistic inertia is the only thing keeping us from recognizing rigorous ethical reasoning as scientific. But unthinking adherence to traditional ways of speaking isn't an argument. In fact, it's high time we stretched our concept of science in just this way.[5]

Here, it makes sense to shift our attention from theory to practice. For the real proof is in the "putting": What can we *do* with the tools of cognitive immunology? Do they shed light on root causes? Do they help to explain otherwise inexplicable phenomena? Implementers, you've waited long enough. Let's put the concepts to work!

# CHAPTER 3

# The Widening Gyre

*Why mental immune systems collapse*

What I hated even more than the conflict was the lurid
spectacle of a world of unreason. —*Ellen Glasgow*

In the early morning of September 11, 2001, four teams of religious
radicals boarded passenger jets in the northeast United States. After
takeoff, each team stormed its plane's cockpit and wrested control
from its flight crew. At 8:46 a.m., one of the four crashed its plane
into an iconic New York City skyscraper. At work in a converted
warehouse on Pittsburgh's South Side, I watched several colleagues
race past my desk. I followed them and found dozens of coworkers
gathered around a small TV. On-screen, smoke was rising from one
of two twin towers. A reporter wondered aloud whether the crash
was an accident. Suddenly, a second jet flashed into the picture and
disappeared into the adjoining tower. It was no accident; our country
was under attack. We watched as the buildings crumbled, knowing
that hundreds were trapped inside. One question loomed over everything: *How could this possibly happen?*

## Hijacked Minds

The bones of an answer emerged in the ensuing days. The whole thing had been meticulously planned. Nineteen disaffected men had acquired basic aviation skills, purchased plane tickets, and smuggled weapons on board. Then they overpowered the flight crews and turned their transports into guided missiles. The pilots among them became the missiles' guidance systems, and piloted themselves—and all aboard—to oblivion. This left the question of motive: What could anyone hope to gain from such senseless carnage? The whole point, apparently, was to kill infidels—to please God and win a martyr's reward. No one knows whether Allah was pleased, but it's a safe bet the attackers never received their rewards: after all, their brains were torn apart in the crash, and the conscious minds dependent on those brains ceased to be. We do know this: because a few allowed themselves to become addled by ideology, thousands lost their lives.

The attackers' moral disorientation contrasts with their logistical success: none of them had a functioning moral compass, but still, they found their targets. Apparently, a common measure of reason—logistical savvy—can coexist alongside profound moral confusion. How does *that* work? To me, the answer is obvious: the minds in question were hijacked. Before the hijackers could commandeer the planes, bad ideas had to commandeer their minds. They managed to weaponize civilian airliners, but only because ideologies had weaponized *them*. Mind parasites had turned fellow humans into cultural pathogens. Everyone involved was used.

I'd been thinking about mental immune systems, so I had another question: Why were the attackers' minds not immune to such terrible ideas? Why wasn't the simple "Do no harm" test weeding out the murderous intent? Apparently, mental immune systems had been breached. They'd broken down. Nine-eleven wasn't just a wake-up call; it was a massive failure of at least nineteen mental immune systems.

## The Falconer's Call

In the years that followed, airport security screenings reminded us of our vulnerability. Conspiracy theories multiplied. Gun sales soared. Domestic terrorism took off. Privacy protections eroded. Economic inequality rose. America launched a fraudulent war, destroyed thousands of lives, and wasted trillions of dollars. Evangelical Christians chipped away at the church/state separation wall and began pushing an aggressively theocratic agenda.[1] (Even today, powerful evangelicals actively seek to bring about Armageddon in the Middle East; apparently, they believe mass carnage there will persuade Jesus to return.[2] Another mind virus? You be the judge.) Strident voices ramped up the "culture war," and even noncombatants grew polarized. Well-funded propaganda campaigns spread doubts about evolution, global warming, and scientific expertise. Opportunistic politicians derided experts as "elites," and willful ignorance spread. American politics got crazier by the day.

Day after day, reading the newspaper reminded me of W. B. Yeats' famous poem "The Second Coming":

> *Turning and turning in a widening gyre*
> *The falcon cannot hear the falconer;*
> *Things fall apart; the center cannot hold;*
> *Mere anarchy is loosed upon the world,*
> *The blood-dimmed tide is loosed, and everywhere*
> *The ceremony of innocence is drowned;*
> *The best lack all conviction, while the worst*
> *Are full of passionate intensity.*

The poem gave full expression to my fears: full of passionate intensity, ideologues had loosed anarchy. Decent people wanted to hold things together, but too many lacked conviction, and too few knew how to direct what conviction they had. Something had loosed a terrible tide, and the ceremony of innocence was drowning.

My mind turned, with compulsive regularity, to the big *why*-question. Why is all this happening? Do the many forms of contemporary craziness have a common cause? Yeats' poem certainly suggests as much: the gyre widens because "the falcon cannot hear the falconer." We become deaf to some centering call, and *that's* why things spiral out of control. Was that the deep story here? To find out, I listened carefully. I found that I could make out the falconer's call. It was the call of *reason*.

Time to connect the dots. The "blood-dimmed tide" was loosed because mechanisms meant to control the spread of bad ideas (think floodgates) weren't functioning properly. In other words, mental and cultural immune systems were breaking down. These systems include gatekeepers tasked with admitting only good ideas. To this end, they examine ideas' credentials—reasons *for* and reasons *against*, basically—and try to turn away the bad ones. Meanwhile, the mind employs a similar screening process to identify the bad ideas already on board. It's supposed to work like this: when doubts arise about a belief, check its reasons; if they don't check out, escort it to the gate and send it packing. (For most of us, it's relatively easy to turn away new ideas we *don't* favor and relatively hard to banish familiar ones we *do*; over time, we grow attached to our beliefs—even the bad ones.)

In the early 2000s, I was struggling to achieve clarity about all this. What is it, exactly, that is subverting mental immune systems? What's stressing them and causing them to fail? That's when a child opened my eyes to the root cause—with a joke at my expense.

## "Be Reasonable!"

I've mentioned my younger son's encounter with divinity. When he was four, Kai got to high-five a guy he took to be God. Around the same time, his older brother, Reece, perfected a decidedly irreverent way to poke fun at his old man. Then about six, Reece would playact a comical exchange, spoof me, and crack himself up. He experimented and found that he could skewer my sacred cow—*and* get grown-ups to laugh. At me. This delighted him, so he performed the little ritual again and again.

Here's how it went. I'd be parenting the little guy and would explain that he *couldn't* do X because of this, or *had to* do Y because of that. Reece would scowl and do what I took to be his best dad imitation. He'd summon a stern expression—the most forbidding his cherubic face could muster—wag his index finger, and command himself to "BE REASONABLE!" Then a mischievous gleam would enter his eye. He'd stick out his lower lip, half suppress a smile, and shout a defiant "NO!" I'd bust out laughing, and he'd grin from ear to ear. We both loved it, and for years it was an inside joke between us.

Reece had grasped that I put a lot of stock in reasons. He'd also figured out that my reasons had limited power to control him. He was putting me on notice. He was saying: "Those reasons of yours? I can turn off their power to control me. *Your* rational leverage hinges on something *I* can suspend at will!" His "NO!" was a shot across the bow, a declaration of independence.

But it was more than that. Reece wasn't reacting to me per se. Nor did it matter that they were *my* reasons. I now think that he was pushing back against *reason itself.* I'd helped normalize the expectation that he behave reasonably, but it wasn't me he was needling. It was the norm I was channeling. Neither my countenance nor my demeanor is particularly forbidding, so I now think the stern taskmaster ("BE REASONABLE!") was reason itself. Reece realized that you can choose to ignore this taskmaster. In fact, *anyone* can ignore the force of *any* reason at *any* time. He was making a philosophical point: reasons have this curious weakness; without your voluntary acquiescence, they have *zero* power over you.

Clever kid. And wise beyond his years. But he never meant it as a serious challenge. His amusement was a clear sign that he got the joke: it would be deeply perverse to defy reason in this way. Now I hope this point seems obvious to you; if not, consider it in this light: dismiss the reasons not to smoke cigarettes, persist in smoking, and eventually you'll pay a price. And so it goes for every reason: wherever a reason communicates a relevant consideration, we ignore it at our peril. So in the end, Reece's skit was a playful observation about the limits of reason.

This got me thinking: Could this be the deep reason dialogue so often breaks down? Think about it: reasons seldom work to resolve deep differences of opinion. They almost never resolve religious differences, and seldom alter party affiliation. Why can't we just sit down and reason our way to a shared understanding of what matters? Why not reason our way to wise public policies? Reece's pugnacious "NO!" gave me a fresh perspective on why reasons so often fail: perhaps *willful unreason* was somehow at the root of it all.

Absent a willingness to accede to them, reasons are impotent. In the face of unwillingness to change one's mind, they *can't* do their jobs. If reason is the philosopher's Achilles, stubborn refusal is its fabled heel. If science is a citadel, pugnacious denial is its weakest point. If critical thinking is higher education's Superman, tenacious believing is its kryptonite. I'd set out to understand how reasons work

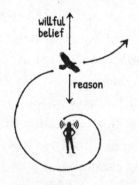

# The Widening Gyre
### How thinking goes haywire

and eventually came around to the thing I should have noticed first: at the very heart of the life of reason lies an act of *submission*, a willingness to follow good reasons where they lead. Negate that submission via an act of will, and thinking begins to go haywire.

To do its job, the mind's immune system—its security team—must care about reasons. Its "bouncers" must be willing to turn away interlopers, no matter how attractive or beguiling. Defy reason, and you confuse them. You weaken your mind's immune system, and invite mind infections. Bad ideas accumulate and begin reshaping your thoughts. They can even corrupt your character.

## What Would Change Your Mind?

In February 2014, two contestants entered a packed, nine-hundred-seat auditorium at the Creation Museum in Petersburg, Kentucky. They were there to debate the scientific merits of the biblical account of Creation. Anticipation had been building for weeks, and an estimated audience of 3 million tuned in online. Ken Ham, the pugnacious "young-earth" creationist who'd built the museum, would later orchestrate the building of a $70 million "reconstruction" of Noah's Ark. He took the stage before an appreciative crowd and, with great seriousness, defended the literal truth of the origins story that appears in the book of Genesis. His opponent that evening was an impossibly angular science educator: the TV personality Bill "the Science Guy" Nye. Nye tried to show that the Genesis story was scientifically untenable—that it amounted to little more than fable. Needless to say, neither man succeeded in persuading his counterpart.

It's worth pondering why the exchange failed to produce a meeting of the minds. To start with, the two men inhabited different worlds: one the subculture of evangelical Christianity, the other that of science. These two subcultures have different standards of reasonable belief, so the exchange was bound to be difficult. To assume that cross-cultural dialogue is bound to be fruitless, though, is to sell it short. For just as we can discuss the merits of creationism, we can examine competing standards of rationality and find out whether they make sense. It's important that our standards for evaluating ideas not be arbitrary or dysfunctional, so epistemologists strive to test such standards. Can we really resolve such questions? Absolutely—provided we bring humility, curiosity, and a collaborative spirit to the task.

After opening statements, the debate's moderator posed what turned out to be the evening's essential question. "Gentlemen," he asked, "what would it take to change your mind?" In context, he probably meant "change your mind about evolution," but his framing of the question was suggestively general. Nye responded easily, distilling his answer to one word: "evidence." He then mentioned several findings that would force significant changes to evolutionary theory—even discredit it entirely—if only such evidence existed. It was a perfect expression of the scientific attitude: Give me good evidence, and I'll change my mind.

Ham's reply was equally illuminating. "I'm a Christian," he said. "No one is ever going to convince me that the word of God is not true." Asked to reveal the extent of his open-mindedness, he replied with a defiant affirmation of faith. Apparently, his commitment to the Bible's being true was a deal-breaking obstacle to learning much of what biology can teach us. Even today, it keeps him ignorant of a beautiful science. And many in the audience appeared to *admire* that defiance.

Now contrast the two replies. Nye was signaling mental flexibility—a willingness to learn. He was saying: I'm willing to adapt to challenging new information, provided it proves reliable. Such willingness—particularly the willingness to let go of bad ideas—is a prime indicator of mental immune health. Ham, on the other hand, was signaling *in*flexibility—a stubborn unwillingness to rethink cherished beliefs. His *will to believe* had made him tenaciously irrational—and unable to reason judiciously about the origins of life. As I like to put it: his mind's immune system had been compromised.

Nye's answer was an expression of what psychologists call the "growth mindset"—the attitude that one can and should learn even from inconvenient truths.[3] Carol Dweck has shown that the growth mindset contributes to well-being in surprising ways.[4] It promotes resilience, success in school, and better relationships. People with a growth mindset are better adjusted because, well, they adjust to the world around them. Summing up her empirical findings, Dweck puts it this way: the growth mindset "allows a person to live a less stressful and more successful life." Meanwhile, Ham's words were the perfect expression of what psychologists call the "fixed" mindset—an attitude known to create all kinds of psychological and social problems. The fixed mindset is not morally equivalent to its opposite: it's a species of mental immune disorder.

Many experts think the growth mindset is an important lever: teaching it is probably key to improving our collective lot. There's still much to learn, though, about how to cultivate the growth mindset. What do we do, for example, when a mental immune disorder impedes *moral* growth?

## Unreason and Moral Disorientation

Ken Ham's attitude yielded a worldview out of touch with reality. On the question of life's origins, he can't distinguish fact from fiction. This much seems clear, but I had two related questions: Can the same attitude leave one out of touch with *morality*? Can willful unreason also compromise your ability to tell right from wrong?

I looked into it. Here's what I found: beliefs sold as moralizing are often *de*moralizing. People will themselves to believe them and, in the process, corrupt their mind's immune system. Ken Ham proves to be an interesting case. In his writing, he actively advocates for corporal punishment—the spanking and beating of children. Why? Because in Proverbs 13:24, the Bible tells us not to spare the rod, lest we spoil the child. Also, Ham believes gay marriage should be made illegal. His reasoning? Leviticus 18 and 20 tell us that it's an abomination for a man to lie with another man. By his own admission, nothing was going to persuade him otherwise.

Based on such reasoning, Ken Ham's influential organization (Answers in Genesis) lobbies for a ban on same-sex marriage. It also encourages Christian parents to beat their children. In a 2013 article on the organization's website, Ham cited chapter and verse to clarify what this means: "You shall beat [your child] with a rod, and deliver his soul from hell." In fact, he says, this holy method of instruction is "God-given."[5]

I think it's important to begin our moral reasoning at the other end. Why not start with the self-evident wrongness of beating children? Or the ample evidence that corporal punishment leaves lasting scars?[6] On the gay marriage issue, why not begin with the manifest unfairness of denying consenting adults a basic freedom? Or start with the benefits of loving commitment and find ways to promote it in nontraditional forms? If the Bible endorses slavery—a *true* moral abomination—surely it merits something less than slavish obedience on these other topics.

Tread this path, and the inferences get reversed. Reflect carefully on this reversal, and you'll realize something important: certain attitudes about faith and evidence tend to be morally disorienting. They make it difficult to think in responsible, grounded ways about right and wrong. What I call "bad faith" has a real tendency to block moral growth. (Later, I'll argue that "good faith" is very different.)

Why do hundreds of millions of well-meaning Catholics oppose the family planning services that could solve our planet's overpopulation problem? Are they evil? Perhaps not, but church doctrine seems to have created deep moral confusion on the subject. Why do millions of American conservatives persist in supporting a party that actively prevents action on climate change? Are *they* evil? Perhaps not, but if failure to act results in climate catastrophe, history will not remember them kindly.

Or consider the case of America's Christian evangelicals, who voted overwhelmingly for the manifestly immoral Donald Trump in the 2016 presidential election. Why can't we call their moral confusion what it is? Mightn't faithful obedience to evangelical "thought leaders" like Ken Ham—who endorsed Trump in droves—induce moral disorientation? (Note that Christians show little reluctance to credit such a hypothesis when the religion in question is Islam, and the "thought leader" is Osama bin Laden.) The truth here will make many uncomfortable, but we can't in honesty shy away from it: religious habits of mind can corrupt a person's understanding of right and wrong.

Religions, of course, have no monopoly on moral confusion. Secular ideologies can also disorient and derange. Nazism, Stalinism, and the ideology of white supremacists are clear examples. Generally speaking, political ideologies tend to arouse tribal passions, close minds, and block moral development. Left-leaning Bolshevism deranged many Russians in the 1910s, and hard-right fascism deranged many Germans in the 1930s. (I want to postpone the question of whether moral confusion is more endemic on the left or the right; better to work out a clear understanding of reason's requirements, dialogue together, and see where we end up.)

Become deaf to reason's call, and your moral compass is likely to go haywire. Acquire the deafness, and lose your way.

## Willful Belief

You needn't be off the deep end to be affected by an ideology: for every deranged ideologue, there are thousands of not-yet-radicalized believers ready to spread confused ideas—about politically incorrect speech, about the proper organization of economies, about the evils of secularism, about the godliest candidate for public office, etc. You can find moral disorientation within churches and without, inside and outside the academy, on the left and on the right, at the fringes and in the center. Blatant moral derangement is just the tip of a *huge* iceberg.

It's always tempting to attribute all the moral disorientation to "them," and none of it to "us." This is a mistake. The psychologist Dan Kahan has suggested that "identity-protective thinking" is ubiquitous.[7] Here's his idea: when information threatens your identity, it's very hard to think in fair-minded ways. Or ask questions that could destabilize your sense that you matter. Dwell on this fact, and you'll soon see that willful belief is rampant, and none of us are immune.

For my part, I am no model of rational rectitude. I'm prone to the temporary madness that infects "Steeler Nation"—the fan base of my city's football team. Every autumn, I revel in the tribal solidarity it affords. When big games approach, I'm buffeted by silly superstitions. Should I wear my lucky T-shirt? Cross your fingers, man: it's third and long! My carnivorous habits form a meatier example. I've studied the arguments for becoming a vegetarian and know them to be overwhelmingly strong. Yet time and again, my forays into vegetarianism founder on weakness of will and considerations of family harmony. I'm a flawed advocate of the life reason.

I have no wish to point fingers. I'm trying to diagnose a phenomenon that underlies many deformations of thought—some of them my own. Here's my hypothesis: the epidemics of unreason currently sweeping the globe are rooted in the apparently innocent phenomenon of *willful belief*. Simply put, *willful belief corrupts cognitive immune systems*.

Presumably, it works like this: as willful belief becomes habitual, you lose your responsiveness to reasons and evidence. Your mind's bouncers stop caring about the right things. As we'll see, willful belief degrades the mechanical linkage between critical thinking and belief revision. It's like riding the clutch in a manual transmission car: over time, you can damage it so that it no longer conveys torque to the wheels. *That's* how we damage cognitive immune systems: by de-coupling thinking and belief revision.

Incidentally, defiance of reason needn't be blatant. Quiet failures to update your beliefs can also damage the mechanism. So can well-intentioned loyalty to beliefs branded as moralizing. (Many religions sell God-belief as necessary for morality, but as countries grow richer and better educated, they rethink this myth.[8]) In fact, good intentions can pave the way for moral confusion via just this mechanism: willful belief in one domain "spills over," creating mental immune weakness in other domains.

For a long time, the evidence for this hypothesis remained mostly correlational. For example, religiosity correlates with science denial and fact-resistant politics. Op-Ed columnists like Thomas Friedman, Paul Krugman, Max Boot, and Thomas Edsall, though, have begun connecting the dots.[9] In May 2020, Friedman conjectured that all these phenomena are rooted in cognitive immune disorders.[10] In June 2020, Krugman decried a "plague of willful ignorance."[11]

Then in July 2020—as this book was going into production—a team of Canadian psychologists published the results of a study that ought to settle the matter. They found that if you lose the "meta belief" that beliefs should change with the evidence, then your susceptibility to conspiracy thinking, science denial, and moral rigidity increases.[12] Put differently, attitudes conducive to willful believing are strongly predictive of religiosity, science denial, fact-resistant politics, and conspiracy thinking. This is very direct evidence that these phenomena have a common cause—and that willful believing is that common cause. Later (in chapter 9) I'll develop this hypothesis into a detailed model of how these systems degrade, and show that it explains a good deal.

In the meantime, evidence continues to pile up: willful believing compromises mental immunity.

At its core, the life of reason requires *submission*: a willingness to follow good reasons where they lead. Such submission is curiously faith-*like*, for it involves a relinquishing, an obedience, a humble acquiescence. Put differently, an attitude comparable to religious faith lies at the very heart of the life of reason. Of course, there are also key differences: unlike submission to the tenets of a faith, *rational* submission insists on being open-minded, attuned to evidence, and committed to updating one's beliefs.

Willful believing can become habitual, but so too can rational submission. We can discourage the former and cultivate the latter. This is the key to instilling the growth mindset. It's also a powerful way to inoculate minds against ideological contagion.

But how does any of this differ from the view that prevails in the community of professional educators: that we need more and better critical thinking instruction?

## Critical Thinking on Steroids

My father gave the commencement address at my elementary school graduation. I remember squirming in my chair, craving anonymity as he held forth on the latest thinking about dinosaurs. Scientists, dad said, had uncovered some surprising truths about the big lizards. In fact, he was now having to *unlearn* things his teachers had taught him! This was his message for us: *Be prepared to unlearn things teachers have taught you.* It was interesting to watch the teachers onstage as he set forth this principle. One of them frowned unhappily. Two or three shifted uncomfortably. Another shot the school principal a look that seemed to say "Who invited *this* guy?" Later, classmates ribbed me about Dad's "dinosaur speech." But its lesson stayed with me.

Cognitive immunology has a similar lesson for us. Yes, it's important to install knowledge, but it's also important to *uninstall* misinformation and misconceptions. More narrowly, it's great to *upload* critical thinking skills, but you also have to *off-load* immune-disruptive ideas. A school system can impart every analytical skill in the book, but if students graduate thinking they're entitled to their political ideology's articles of faith, we've failed to create responsible citizens. The presence of skills isn't enough; the absence of confounding factors also matters. The cognitive immunology approach points to the importance of *subtractive* learning—the removal of unsustainable and disruptive ideas.

Having critical thinking skills is no guarantee that you'll apply them. Or apply them with any consistency. We need to surround critical thinking skills with appropriate dispositions, habits, and traits of character—things like curiosity, diligence, and fair-mindedness. Otherwise, critical thinking skills get applied unevenly. Or selectively. Skills alone do not a healthy immune system make.

There are *many* facets of mental immune health—many more than are dreamt of within the critical thinking skills paradigm. In fact, there's a huge loophole in the critical thinking–equipped mind—one that ideologies often exploit. Psychologists have a term for it; they call it "motivated reasoning." A motivated reasoner will think critically about views they dislike but spare their own views comparable examination. Outfit a motivated reasoner with critical thinking skills, and you don't get a fair-minded person; you get a skilled propagandist. Ideologues are just highly motivated reasoners—lobbyists for some preconceived agenda. Critical thinking skills by themselves do nothing to ensure fair-mindedness. Or for that matter, open-mindedness.

A genuinely healthy mind is open to persuasion. It distinguishes between reasoning and rationalizing. It holds itself to the same standards it applies to others. I once watched a professor sketch a dazzling argument. Basically, she showed that a common assumption about norms can't possibly be right. It was a brilliant refutation, and everyone present was duly impressed. Then, a fellow student pointed out that you could apply the same argument to *her own published* view about norms. And when you do, don't you get the same result? The professor stopped dead in her tracks. Her brow furrowed. She held up an index finger, asking for a minute to think. The room quieted.

How would she react? Would she get defensive? Finally, the professor smiled and congratulated the student for an excellent insight. "I guess I need to rethink my position," she said. I've forgotten the substance of her argument, but I won't forget her humility and fair-mindedness. For me, that was the day's deep lesson.

Somehow, we've managed to build a culture that dispenses powerful critical thinking skills with abandon but neglects the virtue of fair-mindedness: a culture awash in cleverness but thirsty for wisdom.

So how do we change that?

# CHAPTER 4

# Six Immune-Disruptive Ideas

### . . . and their antidotes

Never underestimate the power of bad ideas. They
must be refuted again and again. —*Llewellyn Rockwell*

Bad ideas are always sneaking past mental defenses. Falsehoods
pass for true. Fallacies gain our trust. Malignant misconceptions
pose as benign and become part of the way we think. And once on
board, these stowaways tend to attract others of their kind. For example: believe that God will save us, and you're less likely to support
efforts to address climate change. Accept that science is a global conspiracy, and all kinds of falsehoods will take root in your mind. It's
as if the mind's gatekeepers vetted each new idea with the question
"Will this fit in with those already on board?" Then grant it admission if the answer is yes.

It's not hard to see how a mind regulated in this fashion could
come unglued. When existing beliefs become the measure of truth,
thinking can spiral away from reality. Also, the approach can cause

worldviews to diverge from one another, setting people at odds. Some bad ideas are problematic in yet another way: they actively disrupt mental immune systems. Just as HIV can compromise bodily immunity, these ideas compromise mental immunity. In fact, certain ideas have rendered entire cultures immune deficient. In this chapter, I want to illuminate the phenomenon of immune deficiency, then expose several especially immune-disruptive ideas. To that end, a story . . .

## Acquired Immune Deficiency

In 1981, the US Centers for Disease Control (CDC) formed a task force to study what it called "the 4H disease," a strange condition that seemed to target only homosexuals, heroin users, hemophiliacs, and Haitians. Researchers knew they had an epidemic on their hands, but little else. They soon learned that the disease can fatally compromise a person's immune system. By 1982, the disease had a name: acquired immune deficiency syndrome, or AIDS. Naming it, though, just left the task force with more questions: What causes AIDS? How big a threat does it pose to public health? And most important: How do we contain the epidemic?

The challenges were many, but the public health community took them on. Within a year, the task force learned that AIDS spreads by exposure to HIV—the human immunodeficiency virus. HIV attacks the immune system, rendering its victims "immune deficient." When an AIDS patient dies, the direct cause is usually some other condition; the root cause, though, is HIV. And it turns out we're all susceptible.

The task force found that HIV is transmitted by unprotected sex, dirty needles, and blood transfusions. This explained three of the four H's: why homosexuals, heroin users, and hemophiliacs were over-represented among the afflicted. Genuine understanding had replaced guesswork, and the CDC was able to launch an evidence-based effort to contain the epidemic. The recommended policy interventions, though—among them free condoms and needle-exchange programs for heroin users—were unpopular with the American religious right. As a result, the public health response was inadequate. AIDS became a global pandemic. By 2014, the disease had killed an estimated 35 *million* people—almost as many as the First World War.[1] Another 35 million still have HIV. Even so, the public health community deserves credit for limiting the scope of the damage. Their efforts have saved countless lives. Meanwhile, new treatments have improved the prospects of those diagnosed as "HIV-positive."

This story illustrates how deadly bad ideas can be. It also contains important lessons about immune systems. It was AIDS that propelled the concept of an *immune disorder* into the public eye. News coverage taught many of us that an immune system can become "deficient"— that is, underactive, and unable to fight off certain diseases. We also learned that an immune system can be *over*active and prone to attack the body's own tissues. Scientists call disorders of this sort "autoimmunity."

Since then, immunology has revolutionized our understanding of biological health. We now know that health requires an immune system in the "Goldilocks" zone: neither overactive nor underactive. We know that cancer can blind the immune system to its presence. We know that gluten can trigger an autoimmune reaction. Immunologists have shed light on arthritis, lupus, diabetes, psoriasis, hyperthyroidism, and a hundred other conditions. Immune function affects our joints, muscles, nerves, brains, lungs, skin, and blood—pretty much every aspect of bodily well-being. In some ways, immunology is now a central organizing paradigm of modern medicine: successfully modulate immune response, and often, the body will heal itself.

Many nonscientists now understand the importance of avoiding biological *immune disruptors*. Things like the pesticide DDT. Or the chemical BPA, which is found in some plastics. Millions now use the concept to steer clear of substances that create health issues. Meanwhile, the concept of an *immune booster* nudges people *toward* things that enhance immune health. Vitamin D, green tea, and exercise are all known to have immune-boosting properties.

In twenty years of teaching, I've encountered dozens of *cognitive immune disruptors*—ideas that diminish the mind's ability to ward off bad ideas. Apparent pillars of common sense, I've seen them obstruct critical thinking again and again. They license evasion. They excuse unaccountable talk. They subvert dialogue, block moral inquiry, and provide cover for dysfunctional beliefs. They help bad ideas proliferate and harden into ideologies. In this chapter, I want to call out six that can render a mind immune deficient. I hope to raise awareness of the trap they create so we can all steer clear of it.

Fair warning: some of these ideas have probably sunk roots in *your* mind. This doesn't mean they actively warp your thinking, but they very well could. By uprooting them, you can strengthen your immunity to bad ideas. Help remove them from the meme pool, and you'll enhance our collective immunity to ideological contagion.

## Six Ideas

Why is our Internet-connected global culture so alarmingly prone to outbreaks of unreason? I think six ideas must be counted among the culprits:

1. Beliefs are private, and no one else's concern.
2. We have a right to believe what we like.
3. Values are subjective—relative, that is, to a fundamentally arbitrary set of preferences.
4. We have no standing to criticize other people's value judgments.
5. Basic value commitments are not subject to rational assessment.
6. Questioning a person's core commitments is fundamentally intolerant, mean-spirited, offensive, or unkind.

Each of these ideas can be made to seem true. Each is widely accepted. Each is used to rationalize irresponsible cognition. And each one rests on a confusion. Fortunately, simple distinctions can clear up much of the confusion. Ideally, this deactivates the idea and prevents it from suppressing mental immune response. Let's take them in turn.

## First Immune-Disruptive Idea (IDI-1)

Consider the idea that a person's beliefs are private, and no one else's concern. Notice that it's only half true. Only one person has direct access to any belief; in this sense, beliefs really are private. But it doesn't follow that they're no one else's concern. Many of our beliefs—perhaps most of them—have an indirect impact on the well-being of others; in this sense, they're a matter of broader public interest. For example, beliefs about parenting can have big effects on children. Beliefs about vaccines can affect public health. Beliefs about political parties affect voting behavior, which in turn affects the common good.

The problem is that we tend to confuse two senses of "private." One lends the idea plausibility—enough to help it become a mental stowaway. The other transforms it into a handy rationale for irresponsible believing. Pay attention to serious conversations: you won't have to wait long to see this confusion at work. Once, I called attention to an implication of a student's belief, and he said, "Question my words if you want, but my beliefs are *my* business." Another student was more polite: "My beliefs work for me; please don't ask me to rethink them." "How will you grow," I responded, "if you won't examine your beliefs?" Now I can express the point in immunological terms: the idea that beliefs are private inhibits the identification and removal of bad ideas; it weakens mental immune systems.

In a highly networked world—a world where anyone with an Internet connection can broadcast ideas to thousands of others—"private" beliefs become a matter of public interest. Even mundane cases of irresponsible belief can ramify in ways that impact the well-being of others. The belief that vaccines cause autism, for example, has consigned thousands of children to avoidable illness. Stubborn strains of climate denial have slowed our transition to renewable energy sources; as a result, our planet is warming and generating devastating hurricanes. Hurricanes, of course, don't discriminate between responsible parties and bystanders.

The harm caused by one person's irresponsible believing, of course, is often small. But the cumulative effects of much irresponsible believing can be huge. One solution is to adopt a more public-spirited conception of belief. As the nineteenth-century polymath W. K. Clifford put it: "Belief . . . is ours not for ourselves but for humanity." By embracing this sentiment and distinguishing the two senses of "private," we can neutralize this first immune-disruptive idea.

## Second Immune-Disruptive Idea (IDI-2)

Many insist on their "right" to believe what they like. Or as some put it: "Everyone is entitled to their opinion." This idea too exploits ambiguity, for in many parts of the world, people enjoy a *legal* right to believe what they will. Even the *Universal Declaration of Human Rights* affirms that citizens must be afforded "freedom of conscience." But here's the thing to see: a legal and a moral right are different things. As a matter of law, white supremacists are entitled to their opinions; the US Constitution protects their right to voice them. Were we to outlaw such beliefs, we might empower a thought police.

But none of this implies that we're *morally* entitled to such opinions. Here's the truth: we need moral norms to regulate many things the law has no business regulating. Morally, I have no right to indulge in white supremacist fantasies. Neither do you. The same goes for homophobic head trips and misogynistic delusions. The idea that people of a certain sort are vermin? It's wrong no matter what the law says. And it's perfectly appropriate to condemn such toxic nonsense. More generally, responsible people don't blindly help themselves to the cognitive liberties our culture so noisily proclaims; they make themselves responsive to rational considerations. "Everyone is entitled to their opinion," though, remains a pervasive meme, and a convenient excuse for evidence-defying (and decency-defying) attitudes. It's the centerpiece of a morally corrupt—and immune-compromising—ethos.

The truth is that we have responsibilities pertaining to belief formation and maintenance, and to use "rights" talk to suggest otherwise is, well, irresponsible. Again, we can acknowledge this without advocating for an Orwellian thought police. For there are many noncoercive, nongovernmental ways to hold someone accountable for their beliefs. We can do so with honest inquiry and gentle instruction, for example. Mild disapproval, forthright criticism, and public satire also have their place. Note that none of these is remotely Orwellian. "Rights" talk has a role to play in preventing *coercive* interference with the freedom of conscience, but it shouldn't be used to prevent the application of *persuasive* pressure on belief.

## Third Immune-Disruptive Idea (IDI-3)

Consider the claim "Values are subjective." These three words capture a simple insight: right and wrong don't seem to be out there in the world, at least not the way rocks and trees are out there. Instead, the goodness or badness of things seems to be "in here"—mere figments of our minds. Moreover, different minds value different things. For centuries, people have used words like "Values are subjective" to make these points. The claim is difficult to deny, so it enjoys widespread acceptance. Unfortunately, it also trades on an ambiguity and makes values appear arbitrary. It's not uncommon, for example, for people to say things like this: "You value the rule of law, but I value freedom; in the end, I guess, it's all subjective."

It's true that values are *mind dependent*: nothing would be good or bad, better or worse, right or wrong if minds hadn't evolved. (If you're not satisfied that this is true, try this thought experiment: imagine a universe without any creatures in it: just rocks and space dust, say. Then, ask whether any rearrangement of its elements could possibly make such a universe the least bit better or worse. Finally, draw the obvious conclusion: impact on sentient critters—that is, creatures with minds—is what makes things good or bad.)

Here's the key point: none of this implies that values are *arbitrary* or *mere matters of subjective preference*. For example, our preference for kindness over cruelty isn't arbitrary: kindness is objectively more conducive to shared well-being. Mutual cruelty is a genuinely lousy way to enhance our prospects. We value love over hatred, helping over harming, justice over injustice, honesty over dishonesty, and respect over disrespect for equally objective reasons.

If you confuse the two senses of *subjective*, though—as many of us do—the search for moral understanding appears pointless. For why should we inquire into what's *really* right when there's no such thing? Why not settle for *what seems right to me*? Why investigate the complex considerations that bear on the morality of abortion when it's so much easier to think: "Killing babies is just wrong; that's my truth, and I'm sticking to it"? (The sentiment "I think a woman's right to choose should be absolute; end of discussion" also blocks moral reflection.) On both the left *and* on the right, settling for subjective truths prevents us from developing deeper understanding.

Importantly, the "values are subjective" idea also hamstrings resolution-oriented dialogue: if you have your subjective truth and I have mine, why bother discussing who's right? When ideas like this spread, moral and political discourse become unproductive and eventually grow toxic. The resulting nexus of attitudes—philosophers call it "relativism"—has compromised value discourse for thousands of years. Plato identified relativism as a major source of folly twenty-four hundred years ago.[2] Ever since, philosophers have sought better ways to prevent its spread. The diagnosis developed here—that relativism is a cognitive immune disruptor—opens up a promising new front in this long-running battle.

*Of course* values depend on the existence of minds: that doesn't make them relative to a set of arbitrary preferences. The medical sciences build on a decidedly nonarbitrary value premise: health is better than sickness. Secular ethics builds on an equally nonarbitrary premise: shared well-being is better than shared suffering. Moreover, there are objective grounds for preferring means that really work: means that *do* work are objectively more effective than those that don't. Let's not pretend, then, that all values are equally valid: they're not. The most important values are *not* "merely subjective."

The idea that values are fundamentally subjective is profoundly dysfunctional. It implies, falsely, that value inquiry is pointless. It fosters a facile and foolish dismissiveness of philosophy. It delegitimates important questions. It kills curiosity and breeds a fixed mindset. It's a huge obstacle on the path to a better world, and needs to be torn up by the roots.

We remove it by teasing apart the two senses of *subjective*—mind dependent (which values are), and rationally arbitrary (which values usually aren't). With the distinction in hand, we can substantially improve cognitive performance. The same can be said of the other distinctions I've made, between two kinds of privacy and two kinds of rights: each can boost mental immunity.

## Fourth Immune-Disruptive Idea (IDI-4)

A fourth immune-disruptive idea states that we lack standing to question other people's value judgments. This idea is seldom made explicit, but it's the active ingredient in the rhetorical question "Who's to say?" Here's how it works: invite folks to reflect on values they've internalized uncritically, and they're apt to experience discomfort. For example, you might point out that I'm complicit in a racially oppressive system, making me defensive. (Nobody likes to discover that they're not on the side of the angels.) The question "Who's to say?" then shows up as a conversational security blanket.

People use this question all the time to deflect questions about their values. It arises with disturbing frequency in amateur philosophy discussions. Sometimes, the words ooze a plaintive humility. This can cause sympathetic people to drop the subject. No one wants to come across as dictating values to another, so the investigation comes to an end, and the discomfort goes away.

But so does the opportunity to learn and grow. Sadly, "Who's to say?" has become a culturally conditioned reflex. It implies that you need special standing to make certain kinds of moral judgments: perfect impartiality, say, or godlike omniscience. But this is false: you don't need any such thing. All you need is curiosity, or some way of shedding a little light on the subject.

Reflect on the matter, and the question "Who's to say?" should appear in a very different light. Pay attention to how people use the question, and you'll see people diverting themselves (and each other) from the discomfiting task of judging worth. "Do huge campaign contributions corrupt our political system? Who's to say?" for example: it just kicks the can down the road. At bottom, the question is a responsibility-avoidance strategy.

In this way, we inadvertently arrest our own cognitive and moral development. We can evade hard questions for a time; eventually, though, we pay a price for the evasive cognition we allow. The ideological turmoil we're experiencing today? It's rooted in decades of neglect, a neglect fostered by the disarmingly humble sentiment "Who am *I* to judge?" The question passes the buck to future generations.

Here's the truth: anyone who has noticed *anything* of possible relevance to the rightness or wrongness of something has standing to raise questions about it. Were we to raise the next generation to understand this, it would be a great boon to moral progress. Not only *may* we challenge conventional moral wisdom, we *must*. There's simply no nonnegligent alternative.

## Fifth Immune-Disruptive Idea (IDI-5)

Another problematic idea says that basic value commitments are not subject to rational assessment. The key word is *basic*, and again, a subtle confusion is at work. Here's the background: thousands of years ago, philosophers noticed that arguments must employ unargued premises. They drew the apparent conclusion: everyone treats some things as "basic" (or not in need of arguing). When this idea worms its way into a mind, though, its host will often use it to protect cherished convictions from critical questioning. For example, some philosophers argue that we're entitled to treat God's existence as basic—and thereby immune to requests for evidence.[3] The rationale is disarmingly simple: "Everyone has to exempt *something* from critical questioning, otherwise such questioning corrodes all; I claim this exemption for my belief that X." This excuse is employed by both religious and secular ideologues, and philosophers have struggled to articulate a cogent reply. For centuries, it has provided shelter for dogmatic convictions.

As we'll see, this very argument helped to subvert the cognitive immune systems of antiquity. In fact, it may have brought on Europe's Dark Ages. Apologists for religious dogmas are exploiting it again today in ways that compromise mental and cultural immune health. If you rely on assumptions that seem like they need to be accepted without question, you too have been touched by this idea.

We can disarm the idea by pointing out that it confuses two things: the need to employ unargued premises, and the supposed right to exempt particular ideas from critical questioning. Mathematicians will state their axioms and get on with the task of deriving theorems. We allow this. Experimentalists will make working assumptions and see what their experiments generate. Often, this is responsible scientific conduct. Each of us treats some things as basic and tries to move forward.

Responsible believers understand, though, that basicness does not confer exemption from rational assessment. You can take something for granted in one investigative context and subject it to critical examination in another. The history of mathematics furnishes a lovely example: for a very long time, mathematicians took Euclid's fifth postulate for granted. (This postulate states, essentially, that parallel lines will never meet.) This supposition allowed them to "do" Euclidean geometry. Then, some fifteen centuries after Euclid, they finally got around to questioning the postulate—and discovered other useful systems of geometry. (Scientists have since discovered that space is curved—and best described with non-Euclidean geometries.)

The fact that a belief is a starting point for *my* reasoning doesn't oblige *you* to show it unquestioning deference. Nor does the fervency of my foundational convictions require you to grant or allow them. The conceptual confusion surrounding the concept of basic belief is fascinating. Later, I'll show that it effectively derailed the rationalist project. For now, it's enough to notice that some people exploit the confusion to excuse dogmatic believing.

## Sixth Immune-Disruptive Idea (IDI-6)

Finally, let's examine the idea that it's fundamentally intolerant, transgressive, offensive, mean-spirited, or unkind to question a person's core commitments. At best, deeply empathetic people wield this idea in a misguided effort to spare others the discomfort of having to rethink core assumptions. At worst, culture warriors steeped in identity politics use it to impugn the character of those who challenge identity-defining beliefs. Question the wisdom of building separate bathrooms for transgendered Americans, for example, and you can find yourself accused of harboring hate.[4]

Such accusations shift attention from the substance of the critique to the character of the critic; they function, in other words, like an ad hominem attack—a tactic logicians have long recognized as fallacious. (*Ad hominem* is Latin for "against the person.") Good argumentation doesn't indict the character of its participants; it focuses on the validity of the idea at issue.

When secular activist Ayaan Hirsi Ali characterized some tenets of Islam as oppressive of women, many could see only an "attack" on a venerable faith tradition. The Southern Poverty Law Center, long a pillar of progressive activism, mistook these criticisms for hate speech and condemned Hirsi Ali. Never mind that her claims were true and compassionate: they were reflexively dismissed as intolerant. Examine the online discourse that erupts around hot-button cultural issues, and you'll see this dynamic play out again and again. You'll see culture warriors on both the left and the right casting aspersions and ginning up outrage. Sadly, outrage prevents people from reasoning clearly and fairly. Clearly, the idea is subverting rational discourse— and with it, our resistance to morally disorienting ideologies.

A challenge to a core, identity-defining belief can be upsetting. It can destabilize your sense of worth. But that doesn't make the challenge unkind. For it is unwise to build an identity on shaky value foundations. When someone points out that you're in danger of making such a mistake, they're arguably doing you a kindness. Yes, there's an element of "tough love" in it, but that doesn't mean it's not a blessing in disguise. It's worth suffering some discomfort to acquire understanding—conviction that's genuinely stable in the face of questioning. Later, I'll explain how you can achieve and maintain the relevant mindset.

At any rate, critical value inquiry needn't be aggressive, transgressive, intolerant, mean-spirited, or unkind. It can be deeply collaborative and compassionate. Professors facilitate such conversations every day. Ethicists have been doing it for thousands of years. And recently, "street epistemologists" have taken this process into, well, the streets. (YouTube features hundreds of videos of street epistemologists in action; the best ones illustrate how powerful gentle, nonaccusatory questioning can be.) The point is that you can't characterize such questioning as an "attack" without doing the cause of critical inquiry a disservice. Yet this is exactly what so many outraged culture warriors are doing.

To sum up, we have six widely accepted ideas, each based on a confusion. Each is what philosopher Daniel Dennett calls a "deepity"—something that looks true and wise until you clarify it, at which point it's revealed to be false, foolish, trivial, or two-edged. As a philosophy professor, I know that people reach for these ideas to make uncomfortable questions go away. They interfere with healthy cognitive function. Their ready availability makes it hard to think deeply about the things that matter most. They quite literally deprive us of meaning.

They also reinforce one another. Together, they imply that the pursuit of meaning is a profoundly individual undertaking. On the picture they paint, we shouldn't interfere with one another's searches for meaning and purpose, not even with questions. But this picture blocks our path to what we *truly* need: a responsible, shared under-

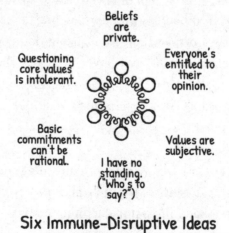

Beliefs are private.

Questioning core values is intolerant.

Everyone's entitled to their opinion.

Basic commitments can't be rational.

Values are subjective.

I have no standing. ("Who's to say?")

## Six Immune-Disruptive Ideas
...that together give our culture an acquired immune deficiency

standing of what matters. It interferes with value inquiry. It compromises our ability to think together and leaves us vulnerable to ideological infection. You might say it's given us an "acquired cultural immune deficiency."

## A Playbook for Defenders of Dodgy Ideas

Understanding that certain ideas inhibit critical thinking is one thing. Ending their baleful influence on public discourse is another. What must we do to fully "deactivate" these ideas—that is, prevent them from interfering with healthy cognitive function?

Many assume that it's enough to demonstrate a bad idea's falsity. Sadly, it doesn't always work that way. For one thing, we humans are more attuned to the apparent *utility* of ideas. If an idea feels useful, many will cling to it, even after it's exposed as baseless. Also, we've seen that ambiguity can prevent mere falsification from doing the job: one interpretation of the words can provide cover for a second, more problematic interpretation. It turns out many bad ideas escape accountability in this way: they exploit their semblance to sensible ones. For example, the concept of faith acquires positive connotations from its kinship with the notions of hope, trust, and loyalty. Then some use it to excuse irresponsible believing. In this way, closed-mindedness gets rebranded as a virtue.

Science buffs will recognize this phenomenon as akin to biological mimicry. You know that caterpillar that looks like a twig? It evolved to mimic tree branches and hide from hungry birds. Many species exploit a similar strategy. In fact, deadly microbes are known to mimic friendly ones and fool the body's immune system. Some of the world's most destructive ideas do something similar: they mimic benign ones and bypass mental defenses.

Informal logicians create catalogues of common errors in reasoning. They label the errors "fallacies" and try to heighten our awareness of logic pitfalls. I want to do something similar with immune-disruptive ideas. Only I want to go beyond naming them. I want to give them cheeky labels and raise awareness of the dysfunction they cause. I want to change the way you *feel* about them. They say you can't fight emotion with logic alone; I believe that. Sometimes, you have to fight fire with fire.

Imagine a malicious intelligence intent on compromising our culture's resistance to bad ideas. What kind of advice might such a being peddle? Well, he (I'll assume it's male) might come up with something like the following. I call it the "Postmodern Playbook for Defenders of Dodgy Ideas":

*The Privacy Contrivance*—Want to turn aside troubling questions? Start by reminding your questioner that *your* beliefs are not *their* concern. Start by remarking that your current beliefs work for you; then imply that that settles the matter. If the questioner persists, insist that belief is a private matter and ask them to leave you alone.

*The Right to Believe Ruse*—If someone is impolite enough to imply that one of your beliefs is irresponsible, simply remind them that, when it comes to belief, we have no responsibilities. If that doesn't work, insist that your "right to believe" trumps whatever minor responsibilities we might have in the way of belief maintenance. If necessary, remind them that liberty of conscience is a fundamental right.

*The Thought Police Ploy*—If someone tries to dissuade you of something, just ask: "Who appointed *you* the thought police?" Stress the word *you*, preferably with a hint of exasperation. Alternatively, indicate that you find their political correctness Orwellian. The trick is to imply that criticism amounts, somehow, to authoritarian control. (This often works to silence critics.)

*The Who's to Say? Gambit*—Any time someone suggests that you might hold yourself to a higher standard, shrug helplessly and say, "Who's to say what's right or wrong?" This classic reply functions at multiple levels. First, its apparent humility will make you look open-minded. Second, it suggests that your critic's standard has not been established to anyone's satisfaction. And here's the best part: it challenges your interlocutor's *standing* to question you.

*The Sacred Belief Stratagem*—Everyone knows that sacred things must be treated with awe and deference. You can use this to protect beliefs that mean a lot to you: just treat your beliefs as sacred and any questioning of them as profane. A reverent tone, for example, can help a questioner understand that the belief occupies a hallowed place in your universe. If he doesn't get the hint, though, patiently explain that the belief is considered sacred in your faith. Then thank him for not desecrating what you consider holy.

*The Faith Card*—Everyone knows this, too: articles of faith must be handled with special care. This makes playing the "faith card" an especially powerful move. To do this, explain that the belief in question is an article of faith for you—that it's central to your emotional and spiritual well-being. This implies that it would be cruel and insensitive to persist in examining the belief. This works best if you pretend that you need the belief to remain hopeful, trusting, or morally centered. Often, this will make the challenger feel crappy.

*The Faith Feint*—A more sophisticated version of the faith card involves pointing out that "everyone takes things on faith." Of course, you must hope that the questioner won't notice the difference between relying on a premise (which all of us do) and refusing to countenance challenges to a belief (which only the dogmatic do).

*The Precious Delusion Dodge*—People need their illusions. They adopt beliefs that bolster their sense that they matter, and build their identities around them. Most people know this and shy away from anything that might destabilize a cherished delusion. You can use this to your advantage. The trick here is to let the questioner know that your belief is deeply meaningful to you. Ideally, they'll conclude that they need to cut it out, or your whole sense of purpose in life will come crashing down. If need be, indicate that you "can't go there" without becoming nihilistic and depressed.

*The Offense Defense (aka the "Attack Defense")*—The best defense is a good offense. So act offended by challenges to your thinking. When you can, treat them as an affront. Play the victim. This works especially well if you can paint the challenge as an "attack." If you deploy this tactic, pretend not to see any difference between a probing question and aggressive verbal abuse.

What I've done here is amplify influential strains of our contemporary ethos, and stretch them to the point of absurdity. Note that I'm not *endorsing* this playbook. To the contrary: I'm using irony to make its tactics look silly. Certain tendencies of thought are covertly harmful; I'm using caricature to expose them. I've even depicted them as vaguely underhanded, the better to evoke distaste.

Look, it can make sense to poke fun at shared human foibles. If the humor is good-natured, it can induce a healthy humility. It's almost always a bad idea, though, to make *people* look silly. Ridicule has no place in conversations aimed at building shared understanding. Disdain and one-upmanship are toxic. Where we destroy charity and trust, dialogue loses its power to transform. Yes, this playbook contains an edgy kind of humor. You may even find that it stings a bit—just as a booster shot can sting. But it's not for tearing people down.

From time to time, I encounter playbook tactics in live conversation. When I do, I try to meet them with friendly, thought-provoking questions. So here's the real playbook—tips you can use to strengthen the mental immune systems in your orbit:

| Immune-disruptive idea | Ambiguous term, or... | How to help others shed the idea |
|---|---|---|
| Beliefs are private. | private | Ask: "What do you mean by 'private'? Surely you don't mean 'no one else's concern?' Don't our beliefs impact others?" |
| We have a right to our beliefs. | right | Ask: "Do you mean a legal right or a moral right?" or "Should we do everything we have a right to? Surely not!" |
| Values are subjective. | subjective | Ask: "What do you mean 'subjective'? Surely you don't mean 'fundamentally arbitrary' or 'anything goes'?" |
| "Who's to say?" | (no standing to question) | Say: "We're to say! It's up to us to shed bad ideas! If not us, who? If not now, when?" |
| You can't question basic value commitments. | basic | Say: "But of course we can! We can't just exempt basic beliefs from scrutiny: not without subverting reason!" |
| Questioning core commitments is unkind. | (misguided niceness) | Say: "Not at all! To find stable sources of meaning, we have to inquire together!" |

"My beliefs work for me, so let's not go there." Immunity-strengthening reply: *"But what about your beliefs' effects on the well-being of others? Aren't they important too?"*

"I've got a right to my beliefs." Immunity-strengthening reply: *"Don't rights come with responsibilities?"* or *"Don't our responsibilities sometimes override our rights?"*

"Stop trying to police my thoughts!" Immunity-strengthening reply: *"I don't want to police your thoughts; I'm just appealing to your better judgment. Can we examine the idea together?"*

"Who's to say what's right or wrong?" Immunity-strengthening reply: *"Surely it's up to us to say! If we don't take responsibility, who will?"*

"This idea occupies a hallowed place in my world, so I'll thank you to leave it alone." Immunity-strengthening reply: *"Are you suggesting that we exempt all sacred beliefs from scrutiny? What if everyone did that?"*

"My opposition to gay marriage is a matter of faith." Immunity-strengthening reply: *"How do we keep the concept of faith from becoming a license to believe whatever one wants? If articles of faith automatically get a pass, how do we prevent unaccountable believing?"*

"Everyone takes things on faith, so who are you to point fingers?" Immunity-strengthening reply: *"Isn't there a difference between relying on a premise for certain purposes and clinging tenaciously to an article of faith?"*

"Let's not go there; Joe's whole sense of purpose in life could collapse." Immunity-strengthening reply: *"If Joe's sense of purpose is that unstable, he probably needs to work through some things. Perhaps he'd appreciate a chance to examine his assumptions."*

"I'm offended. Your questions are nothing more than an attack on my worldview." Immunity-strengthening reply: *"I'm not interested in attacking anyone; I just want to examine this idea and find out if it's true and genuinely helpful. Will you join me in conducting an honest assessment?"*

## Accountable Talk[5]

In subcultures that normalize responsibility dodges, irresponsible beliefs often flourish unchecked. For example, some religious communities play the faith card and breed magical thinking about human health.[6] Academics infected with "postmodern" notions of intellectual accountability produce reams of nonsense.[7] Some liberals embrace an inflated concept of tolerance and dismiss trenchant criticism as cultural imperialism. Some conservatives denounce efforts to promote accountable talk as "political correctness" run amok. When maneuvers like these become normal, cultural immunity declines.

Other subcultures, though, uphold high standards. Scientific communities are an obvious example, as are some philosophical traditions. Nor should we overlook medicine, engineering, and the social sciences. None of these is perfect, but in all of them, we can speak in a meaningful way about progress. Other examples: Humanists inhibit our native tribalism by insisting that all humans matter, and matter equally. The Jain and Quaker religions do a remarkably good job of inhibiting violence. The point is that certain mental disciplines successfully strengthen people's resistance to bad ideas. Those who practice these disciplines exhibit heightened mental immune response—greater resistance to ideology-induced moral disorientation.

If we consistently call out the accountability-avoidant habits of mind described in this chapter, that alone will substantially boost our resistance to bad ideas. But what else can we do?

# CHAPTER 5

# Fighting Monsters

### *. . . without becoming one yourself*

> Whoever fights monsters should see to it
> that, in the process, he doesn't become
> one himself. —*Friedrich Nietzsche*

The contents of your mind—your beliefs—matter. But so does your attitude. In this chapter, I want to examine several attitudes that compromise mental immune systems: "attitudinal immune-disruptors," if you will. I'll also describe an attitude that strengthens mental immune systems: what you might call an "attitudinal immune-booster." Understand the differences, adopt the right one, and your resistance to mind-parasites will grow.

Actually, the word *attitude* captures only the inward aspect of the relevant phenomenon. For each of the attitudes I'll discuss also has an outward-facing aspect: what we might call a "posture" or "mode of comportment." In this way, I'll also be contrasting ways of conducting your cognitive affairs. Understand the differences, practice one of them, and you can help inoculate our culture against ideological contagion.

You'll benefit directly too. Many imagine that the quality of a person's thinking is largely a matter of intelligence. That's nonsense.

The way you use your intelligence is much more significant. Learn the "way of inquiry" described in the coming pages, and you'll do more with the brainpower you have. In fact, you can take your thinking to an entirely new level.

## The Way of Belief

In November 2015, four extremists donned explosive vests. Three of them headed to a soccer stadium near Paris, France; the other took a seat at a small Parisian café. One tried to enter the stadium and was turned away by a security guard. He detonated his vest anyway, causing panicked bystanders to spill into the streets. The other three followed suit, blasting themselves to bits and injuring bystanders. Five gun-wielding accomplices then opened fire at locations across the city. Before the attack ended, nine attackers had killed 130 and injured 413.

The ideology behind the attacks was partially clarified when the Islamic State claimed responsibility. Its statement explained the thinking behind the attack: apparently, Parisian culture's offensive mix of "prostitution and obscenity" was to blame. Later, witnesses described the pitiless attack as accompanied by exultant cries of "God is great!" Clearly, neither Parisian nor secular culture has a corner on the obscenity market.

As a horrified world sought answers, reporters struggled to construct a coherent narrative. American politicians squabbled over whether the term *Islamic extremist* was a helpful or harmful category. French politicians debated wildly different policy responses, from tough immigration restrictions to stronger displays of liberal values. Analysts explained that virulent ideologies were spreading across the Internet and spawning "home-grown" terrorism. Finally, all this prompted NBC's Savannah Guthrie to pose the truly essential question. With genuine wonder in her voice, she asked her cohost: "How do you combat an ideology? How do you defeat an *idea*?"

How *do* you defeat an ideology? When faced with this question, many of us leap to the obvious answer: since ideologies are infectious, we need to prevent exposure. It seems we need to quarantine bad ideas: build barriers, in other words, between ideologies and the minds they might infect. And so, many seek to build walls between people and dangerous ideas. But ideas prove maddeningly difficult to quarantine. This makes the wall builders anxious, so historically they've policed their walls. And as their anxiety mounts, they turn to increasingly coercive enforcement measures.

History tells a long, sad story about ideological barrier enforcement. For example, authoritarians will label dissenting views "traitorous," then exile, imprison, or torture dissidents. Theocrats have been known to label competing ideas "sacrilegious," then excommunicate, stone, or burn those who voice them. Words like *traitor, heretic, infidel, blasphemer,* and *witch* have all been used to dehumanize those who traffic too freely with heterodox ideas. Concepts and techniques like these were staples of ancient political and religious regimes, and millions have been sacrificed at their altars. Such measures do more than constrain behavior: they also create barriers in people's minds. At the birth of the common era, Christianity pioneered another sort of mental barrier: it made doubting the Holy Spirit an "unforgivable sin"—one punishable by eternal torment (Mark 3:29, Matthew 12:32).

Remember my account of the debate between Bill "the Science Guy" Nye and creationist Ken Ham? How the moderator invited both men to answer the question "What would change your mind?" You'll recall that Nye displayed a certain openness by saying that he tries to change his mind every time he encounters real evidence. I find this a perfect expression of the scientific attitude—the willingness to go where the evidence leads. When his turn came, Ken Ham replied: "I'm a Christian; nothing is going to convince me that the word of God is not true." This defiant avowal bespoke a different attitude: an identity-based unwillingness to follow the evidence. Ken Ham had shackled himself to the word of God and erected an internal mental barrier. I want to give the attitude and posture at work here a name. Let's call it "the way of belief," because it starts with resolute commitment to certain beliefs, then pushes back against anything that might disturb them.

In changing and uncertain times, the way of belief seems to offer an anchor. Many experience it as a touchstone or way of grounding oneself. No doubt some see it as a defense against bad ideas. When the beliefs in question assure you that you're one of the good guys, they prove especially tenacious.

Ham's expression of the way of belief was notably pugnacious, but the attitude takes milder forms. Like when we quietly brush off uncomfortable questions. Or stonewall needed belief revision with the thought "I have a right to my opinion." Or bypass a learning opportunity with the question "Who's to say?" If you've ever done something like this—and who among us hasn't?—you've participated in the way of belief. You've got something in common with Ken Ham.

I don't mean to single out religious modes of thought. In Mao Zedong's cultural revolution, a secular ideology closed millions of minds, and the Chinese people were subjected to a murderous campaign of secular "thought reform." The brutal suppression of "thought crimes" depicted by George Orwell in the fictional *1984* had a real-world counterpart in Stalin's secular Russia. More recently, conservatives have criticized university speech codes and campus "safe zones" as Orwellian. Colleges, they say, have become hostile to conservative viewpoints. There is truth in this complaint. The predominance of liberal expectations creates blind spots. Also, there's an element of coercion in the belief-regulation norms conservatives deride as "political correctness." Conservatives experience these norms as oppressive; they feel pressured to remain silent about things they care about.

History teaches that coercive belief regulation doesn't end well.

Too often, it results in closed societies that stifle the exchange of ideas. But what's the alternative?

## The Socratic Method

If coercive ideology-prevention measures aren't the way to go, then perhaps we should look at *persuasive* measures. Why not combat problematic ideas with *reasons?* Surely dissuasion is the civilized and humane solution to the ideology-mitigation problem. This brings us back to the Socratic method.

Recall that Socrates would invite people to share their opinions about important subjects, then ask them to clarify their views. He'd use questions to elicit—that is, draw out—the person's underlying commitments and patiently draw attention to their implications. Usually, this would expose inconsistencies and highlight the need for belief revision.

There's much to admire in this approach. For starters, it was a hugely civilizing advance over older, more coercive approaches to regulating belief. As a philosopher and anti-ideology activist, my admiration for it is almost unbounded.

Almost. For it's now clear that the Socratic method is suboptimal. The problem is that it easily becomes combative. Indeed, Socrates himself was often combative. He used the method to produce "gotcha" moments that enraged his interlocutors. In his legal defense, he adopted the superior attitude of a debunker and all but called himself God's gift to Athens. This thoroughly alienated his jury. Plato's most carefully crafted dialogues, such as *Meno* and *Republic*, feature a gentle and artfully moderated Socratic method. Even there, though, the method is portrayed as arousing resentment and anger. Today, we know that attempts to correct an ideological conviction can deepen moral or political rigidity. Psychologists call this phenomenon the "backfire effect."[1]

At any rate, the variant of the Socratic method that tends to trigger obstinate tenacity merits a name. I call it "the way of the culture warrior."

## The Way of the Culture Warrior

A culture warrior understands that ideas can be dangerous and works to combat the ones he or she deems evil. The aim is to defeat those ideas and make the world safe for beliefs that are good and true. Culture warriors typically locate the evil ideas in others and the good ones in members of their own tribe. We see this all the time in politics, and where competing religious sects contend for dominance. It even surfaces in scholarly debates between rival schools of thought: between advocates of competing economic theories, for example. It's easy to grow attached to an idea—the idea, say, that a free market is fundamentally just—and begin bending the facts to fit. Zealous culture warriors treat words as weapons of war: they use reasons to attack the ideas they take to be evil and defend the ideas they take to be good. They treat them, in other words, like sword and shield.

The Socratic method was once new on the cultural scene, and many Athenians viewed it as a threat to the moral and civil order. Even today, many view secular debunkers in this light. For the most part, though, we now understand that reason-giving is a comparatively humane and acceptable way to wield influence. (It sucks to be shown up by a condescending debunker, but it's better than being burned at the stake.) Socratic wisdom, in other words, has begun to pervade our culture. We've come a fair ways in twenty-four hundred years.

When a reason-wielding culture warrior causes offense, it's worth remembering that belief-regulation methods can be much, much worse. Inquisitions and thought police are just the most obvious examples. Another involves fear of eternal torment. A young woman once contacted me by phone. She needed a philosopher's advice, she said, then told a heart-rending tale. She was raised to believe in hell but realized some years later that it was pure fiction. Still, she said, she couldn't entertain the possibility of God's nonexistence without experiencing a kind of existential panic. Her professors were encouraging her to think for herself, but childhood exposure to the idea, she explained, had left her emotionally crippled and unable to enjoy critical thinking. I listened sympathetically and praised her courage. I provided what assurance I could. I failed: this deeply inquisitive woman had to drop out of college to preserve her sanity. Thinking about her fills me with sadness. I now see the idea of hell as an instrument of emotional abuse.

Apologetics—the branch of theology devoted to proving Christianity to be true—represents a strange hybrid of religious devotion and the way of the culture warrior. Apologists pose as inquirers and champions of reason, but their real aim is to grind reasons into rhetorical axes and wield them for the faith. I'll use the phrase *way of the culture warrior*, then, to designate both secular and religious, liberal and conservative, abusive and disabusive approaches to combatting ideas thought to be dangerous. This lets us ask a more targeted

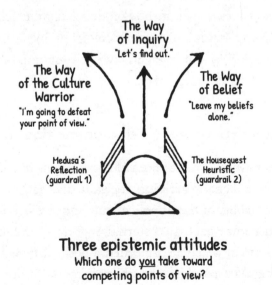

The Way
of Inquiry
"Let's find out."

The Way
of the Culture
Warrior
"I'm going to defeat
your point of view."

The Way
of Belief
"Leave my beliefs
alone."

Medusa's
Reflection
(guardrail 1)

The Housequest
Heuristic
(guardrail 2)

## Three epistemic attitudes
Which one do you take toward
competing points of view?

version of Guthrie's question: Is the way of the culture warrior the right way to combat bad ideas?

Probably not. For religious culture warriors offend secular sensibilities, and secular culture warriors offend religious sensibilities. Right-wing culture warriors make people on the left defensive, and left-wing culture warriors make people on the right defensive. Culture warriors escalate conversations into debates and debates into open hostility. They inflame partisan passions, embarrass "opponents," and alienate friends. They damage relationships, create misunderstanding, and sow division.

Pointing fingers at the ideological elements of another's beliefs is like admonishing them to calm down: it tends to backfire. It arouses anger, resentment, and irrational tenacity. Then, when beliefs don't change in response to our arguments, we get frustrated. We yield to impatience and say things we regret. We alienate our fellow travelers and lose their trust. Meanwhile, the crusader's mentality can blind us to the ideological elements of our own thinking.

Culture wars create ideological quagmires. In fact, the way of the culture warrior turns value discourse (especially political and religious discourse) into a minefield. It's easy to see why well-meaning people refuse to set foot upon it. It shouldn't *be* a minefield. Or even a battlefield. We can't just ignore our ideology problem, though, and hope it will go away: lack of engagement is no solution.

So again, what's the alternative?

## An Accidental Experiment in Ideology Mitigation

For about twenty years, I ran a series of experiments in ideology mitigation. I met almost daily with ideologically diverse groups, and we worked through some of the most difficult and divisive issues there are. We talked about what makes some things good and other things bad. We discussed how people come to know the difference between right and wrong. We asked how morality is rooted in the world and inquired into the nature of fairness. We inspected the relationship between morality and religion and explored the merits of accepting things on faith. We asked whether minds are just the workings of brains, and whether souls survive death.

These are the questions around which ideologies form. They're also the questions that my discipline—philosophy—works hard to think about in clear, fair-minded, and responsible ways. Philosophers don't often think of their inquiries as experiments in ideology mitigation, but viewed in a certain light, they turn out to be just that.

I learned what I could from the great philosophers and picked the brains of my mentors. Mostly I just tried things in my classes and paid attention to what worked. I discarded the tactics that didn't seem to help build shared understanding and kept experimenting with the ones that did. It was elementary trial and error, requiring no great intelligence or wisdom. But over time, it led to something singular: an antidote to ideological thinking.

Here's the story. In 1993, I landed a tenure-track professorship. After five years of graduate study, I was finally a professional philosopher. Eager to impart the wisdom I thought I'd acquired, I threw myself into teaching. I was anxious, though, to appear smarter and more competent than I felt, so I devoted many hours to preparing each lesson. I analyzed every word of the assigned readings, pored over secondary readings, and labored to understand historical context. I worked out answers to every student question I could foresee. I drafted and redrafted my lesson plans, obsessing over tiny details.

How to put this? I stank. I was anxious and lacked confidence. Discussions were tentative and lackluster. Students were bored and unresponsive. Increasingly insecure, I prepared even more obsessively. My lectures grew more polished and detailed. But still, there was no spark, no sign of deep engagement with what I knew to be fascinating issues. A voice in my head kept asking: "What's wrong with these students?"

The real question, of course, was "What's wrong with me?" The semester dragged on, and winter break finally arrived. So did my course evaluations. They confirmed what I'd begun to suspect: as a teacher, I was a miserable failure. I'd spent a decade preparing for this career only to find that I was unsuited for it.

A second semester loomed, and I needed to try something different. I settled on candid humility: I stopped pretending to be an expert and began saying things like, "I don't know: What do you think?" And then, because I wanted to know—because I needed to know—I listened. I mean *really* listened. I started to notice things I'd been missing. Student comments weren't always well expressed, but if I listened with enough care, I could almost always appreciate the core insight. I made a habit of helping students develop and express their points clearly. I listened with sympathy to ideas of Christian, Jewish, and Confucian origin. I heard answers that would qualify as existentialist, pragmatist, and nihilist. I encountered living echoes of stoicism, rationalism, and social contract theory. Rather than pronounce verdicts, though, I'd simply invite the group to examine the alternatives. "So," I'd ask, "which of these answers makes the most sense?" We'd share our perspectives, and they'd be all over the map.

Then I'd ask a question that created a sense of common purpose: "What conclusions can we reach together? What can we not merely *say*, but instead *show* to be true—to the mutual satisfaction of everyone in this room?" In other words, we formed a small community of inquiry and began seeking *responsible shared understanding*.

In a way, I was crowdsourcing my search for answers. I'd climbed off my "expert" pedestal and adopted the role of facilitator. In this role, I simply urged students to seek common ground. I asked them to express their convictions clearly and back them with reasons. I posed questions and encouraged them to raise their own. I counseled them to express their reservations: "If something doesn't feel right, say something: you're probably picking up on something that will help us all." I praised experimentation and risk-taking, and applauded the courage of those who took unpopular positions. I insisted that everyone listen intently and take opposing ideas seriously. We tested one another's claims, maintained mutual respect, and simply saw where it led.

Within two weeks, I knew I was on to something. Student engagement surged, and discussions grew lively. My own interest increased, and I began to enjoy myself. My anxiety dissipated, and I began to learn rapidly. Teaching became a guilty pleasure: here I was, getting paid to educate students, and I'd tricked them into educating me! "People get paid for this?" I wondered. "What a racket!"

My spring semester ended, and the dreaded course evaluations arrived. I braced for disappointment and opened the envelope. The assessment on top began like this: *"This course has made me reevaluate myself, my beliefs, and my world. It has shaken me deeply, and I can't wait for my next philosophy class!"* That student's experience, it turns out, was no outlier. It was representative. I was floored. What had happened? I knew I wasn't educating them—not in the traditional sense; I wasn't dispensing a wisdom that I possessed. Nor was "them educating me" the whole truth. Only one conclusion made sense: we'd stumbled on a *process* that was educating all of us. This process bore more than a passing resemblance to the Socratic method, but over time, I began to see and explore differences. For example, the Socratic method is widely understood to be a *teaching* method that requires an expert guide; my own approach was more of a collaborative *learning* exercise. I started calling my approach "collaborative inquiry," and year after year, I refined it.

I clung to the new approach like a life preserver and let the tides of collaborative inquiry take me where they would. Day after day, I put my philosophical convictions on the line, and for years, they changed almost daily. This, I was surprised to find, was okay. In fact, it was more than okay. I realized that challenges to my beliefs aren't threats; they're opportunities. I came to welcome them and made a point of greeting them with enthusiasm. In some strange way, my openness had left me not rootless, but more grounded.

For years, I enjoyed a front-row seat to an extraordinary phenomenon: collaborative, reason-giving dialogue *working* to unite ideologically diverse groups. Somehow, inquiring together—and really listening to one another—was opening minds, provoking reflection, and altering deep sensibilities. I watched people rethink their views, overcome their differences, and sometimes, build robust consensus. Multiple, diverse intelligences were tapping into wisdom that I alone couldn't command. I now understand what Napoleon Bonaparte meant when he said: "There is someone wiser than any of us, and that is all of us."

Aggregating wisdom can be tricky. It works only if you bring the right attitude. And employ the right process. Otherwise, you get the philosophical equivalent of the pointless business meeting. (I've facilitated a few of those too.) Paradoxically, it also requires a certain willingness to trust the process—a certain "faith" in reason. Having experienced the power of collaborative inquiry—not just once, but hundreds of times—I now have this faith in spades. Only it isn't faith exactly, for I have evidence that it works.

Collaborative inquiry—what I now call "the way of inquiry"—isn't just for classroom use. It's a general-purpose approach to building common understanding. And it works to open minds, dissolve ideological attitudes, and resolve political conflicts. It's our way out of the ideology quagmire.

## The Way of Inquiry

Ken Ham's answer to the decisive debate question was emblematic of the way of belief. Bill Nye's answer was an expression of the way of inquiry. These are fundamentally different ways of conducting one's cognitive affairs. One is pugnacious and unbending; the other is collaborative and flexible. Each has strident external expressions, and each has a telltale internal monologue. The internal monologue of an inquirer goes something like this:

"I've got a lot to learn. And unlearn. Over time, we all take on problematic assumptions—beliefs that can harm both us and others. This being so, I have a responsibility to examine my beliefs and modify them in light of what I learn. The questions and challenges of others are a great help in this: they afford me the opportunity to reflect, to learn, and to grow. Whenever possible, I shall welcome them."

It is said that effective people reframe challenges as opportunities. Well, practitioners of the way of Inquiry reframe verbal challenges as *growth* opportunities. They understand that we have a duty to examine our beliefs and don't resent the need to perform that duty. They understand that, in order to grow, we must sometimes shed the very beliefs that once protected us, just as mollusks must shed the shells they outgrow. Instead, inquirers welcome challenges—indeed, all challenging and surprising information—as opportunities to learn.

And unlearn. Most of us think of learning as *additive*: a matter of inputting information and acquiring new knowledge. But some learning is *subtractive*: we gain new information, or reflect on things we already believe, and discover that we don't really know what we thought we knew. This can be humbling, especially if one is insecure, ego-driven, or hostage to an additive concept of learning. The wise, though, come to appreciate such lessons. They embrace the need to whittle away mistaken preconceptions and cheerfully renounce problematic beliefs. They deliberately adjust confidence levels that turn out to be misplaced and gratefully abandon counterproductive ideas.

W. B. Yeats wrote that "education is not the filling of a pail, but the lighting of a fire." He was right: the mind is no mere knowledge receptacle. Nor is the process of building an enlightened worldview merely cumulative. Skilled learners actively create mental models, then chisel away at them, much as a sculptor might chisel a block of marble. Reigning educational paradigms, though, almost wholly neglect active, subtractive learning—until finally, at the college level, a thin veneer of "critical thinking" is layered atop years of rote and additive learning. But this is too little, and much too late.

An educational paradigm genuinely suited to imparting wisdom will incorporate subtractive leaning from the get-go. It will stress that it takes time and effort to craft a worldview worth sharing, and it will strive to awaken an artist's passion for that craft. In the future, learning should center on something that ignites that passion. Something like the way of inquiry.

Back to our ideology problem. Can we act against ideological thinking without becoming ideologues? Can we fight this monster without becoming monstrous ourselves? We can. The trick is to reject both the stubbornly defensive posture of the believer and the aggressively militant stance of the culture warrior. For both postures engage our native tribalism, and compromise mental immune health. Each is *pre-ideological*, in much the way that precancerous cells are precancerous. Culture wars create a kind of vicious cycle, where culture warriors and ardent believers drive each other into ideological bunkers. The political polarization and incivility we're witnessing today are a direct result of this dynamic.

The alternative is the way of inquiry. True inquirers treat dialogue not as a battlefield but as a hallowed space for minds to meet in understanding. Put differently, real thinkers don't wage dialectical battle—they engage others in collaborative inquiry. Their attitude is: let's be curious, work together, and find out what's true. If we discover that *you're* right, I agree to back down; but if we discover that *I'm* right, you agree to back down. That's how dialogue and inquiry are supposed to work. That's how *thinking* is supposed to work. Reflect on this, and you'll come to realize that *cognitive immune health requires a collaborative spirit*.

It can be hard, though, to maintain the proper attitude. Especially when a culture war breaks out. Get a little defensive, and you can lose your way. Stray a little in the direction of being *offensive*, and you can also lose your way.

But what if the path had guardrails? Imagine one to the right of the path, carefully designed to prevent lapses into the way of belief.

Imagine another on the left, carefully designed to prevent lapses into the way of the culture warrior. What might such guardrails look like?

## The Houseguest Heuristic

Ardent believers tend to treat favored beliefs like heirloom furniture, or even partners for life. They develop a sense of loyalty to them and regard those who challenge them as unwelcome houseguests—as disturbers of domestic tranquility. Inquirers, though, flip this around. From their perspective, our fellow humans are the lifelong partners: fellow travelers during our stay on this small planet, and beings we must learn to tolerate, understand, even cherish. They view *beliefs* as the houseguests: friends, perhaps, but always in danger of overstaying their welcome.

With a little practice, you can learn to regard beliefs as houseguests. This goes a surprisingly long way toward solving the problem. Now, sometimes it makes sense to treat a belief as an *honored* houseguest. Belief in human rights, for example, merits a large measure of deference. So does the Golden Rule—treat others as you'd like to be treated. Sometimes, a belief will remain a friend for life. Even so, it pays to regard beliefs as visitors who might wear out their welcome at any time. They are not you.

The metaphor works by opening a gap between your beliefs and your sense of self. It's like mindfulness meditation: you create a gap between your thoughts and your sense of self, and the gap frees you from the tyranny of involuntary mental habits. By habitually regarding beliefs as temporary houseguests, we create a gap that frees us from the tyranny of involuntary belief.

Ideologues practice the way of belief: they strongly identify with their beliefs, making them integral to their sense of self. They then experience challenges as personal attacks. To them, questions to core beliefs *feel* offensive. Genuine inquirers, though, are careful to avoid this trap. They regard their beliefs as transients—as ideas that have taken up temporary residence in the mind. If we keep learning, many such beliefs will move on; if we grow too attached to the ones we have, we stop learning.

The importance of this mental adjustment is hard to overstate. I've mentioned the work of psychologist Carol Dweck. She studied the effects of what she calls "fixed" and "growth" mindsets and found that shifting from a fixed to a growth mindset is profoundly beneficial.[2] She might as well have been talking, though, about the way of belief and the way of inquiry. In effect, Dweck's research confirms what philosophers have long known to be true: those who embrace the way of inquiry are ushered into a realm of extraordinary possibility. Genuine, transformative dialogue becomes possible, and with it a powerful sense of connection to others. Continual growth becomes possible too.

Meanwhile, those who refuse to shift their perspective obstruct their own capacity for self-transformation. They damage their mind's immune system and compromise their capacity for constructive dispute resolution.

But you can't expect others to undergo this transformation unless you're willing to do the same. It's a matter of fairness, or reciprocity: If you want others to be persuadable, you must make yourself persuadable. If others are going to expose their beliefs to scrutiny and revision, then you must put your own on the line. What we have here is no less than a corollary of the Golden Rule: treat your own beliefs as you would have others treat theirs. But the way of belief hypocritically defies this most basic kind of reciprocity. It flouts the Golden Rule. Meanwhile, the way of inquiry embodies it. Go figure.

In the end, it was my willingness to learn from others that allowed others to learn from me. I let go of the pretense that I had all the answers, and my attitude and posture changed. Sensing this change, others opened up, and the answers came—not to me, but to us. This is the essence of the way of inquiry. It's also essential for mental immune health, and the solution to our ideology problem.

## Medusa's Reflection

The way of inquiry and the way of the culture warrior differ in important respects. Culture warriors want to persuade but don't always make themselves persuadable. Often, they seek to drive a wedge between other people and their beliefs—all the while refusing to allow others a real chance to dislodge their own. Religious apologetics is a clear example of this type of hypocrisy.

In truth, though, we're all capable of it. Even Socrates—arguably the patron saint of the way of inquiry—succumbed to it in the end. At his trial, he adopted the pugnacious stance of the culture warrior and thoroughly alienated his jury. Days later, he confessed to his friend Crito that he had grown deaf to the entreaties of others. Crito was there pleading with him to escape into exile—an entreaty Socrates couldn't hear—so arguably, it was not Socrates' fidelity to reason but his temporary lapse into obstinate unreason that in the end cost him his life!

It's easy to mistake the way of the culture warrior with the way of inquiry. The two paths sometimes overlap, and forks in the trail are not always well marked. When dealing with dangerously destructive ideologies, it's easy to slip into a martial, or warlike, frame of mind. In this very book, I've said that we need to "combat" ideological thinking. Like ideologies themselves, the way of the culture warrior is seductive. Here, too, we need a guardrail.

A story from Greek mythology avails. According to legend, Medusa was a ravishingly beautiful yet monstrous maiden. She had live snakes for hair and a killer superpower: gaze upon her, and you would turn to stone. Many sought to seduce or kill her, but all were transformed into impotent statues. But Athena, the goddess of wisdom, knew that reflection drained Medusa's visage of its terrible power. So she equipped Perseus with a mirrored shield and instructed him in its use. This allowed Perseus to aim his blows without looking directly at Medusa. He avoided her petrifying gaze, slew her, and became a hero. In this story, we find a beautifully constructed allegory for how to combat ideologies: we must fight them with *reflection*.

Imagine what it would be like to do battle as Perseus did. You'd have to hold your mirrored shield not *between* you and Medusa, but *away* from her. You'd have to abandon the warrior's standard shield-forward defensive posture. You'd have to turn your back on a monster and fight every instinct you have. You'd have to face the same direction Medusa is facing and might actually see things from her perspective! You'd have to direct your gaze into the shield, and in it, you'd see a monstrous image—with *you* in the foreground. Everything would be reversed, so your gut-level instincts would be unreliable. Significantly, every attempt to gain a clear view of the evil you are combatting would reveal . . . your own image, looming larger than the evil itself!

Perhaps there are lessons here for those who would combat ideologies. Ideologies are like Medusa: both seductive and terrible. Some embrace them and their beliefs harden, effectively turning to stone. Like Athena, wisdom counsels that you can't fight ideologies directly. Instead, you must forsake the usual defensive posture and employ reflection. You must turn around and see the world from the vantage point of the ideologue. Yes, you can turn a critical eye on an ideology, but only by examining a reflected image that subjects you to scrutiny as well.

To practice the way of inquiry, you need to challenge questionable ideas. But you've got to resist the temptation to attack those who host those ideas. The German philosopher Friedrich Nietzsche may have said it best: "Whoever fights monsters should see to it that, in the process, he doesn't become one himself."

When a difference in perspective arises, start by adopting the right attitude. Resist the urge to see the other guy as the problem and yourself as the solution. View the situation as a learning opportunity. Perhaps you will learn, perhaps the other guy will learn, but either way, an opportunity has arisen to build shared understanding. The question is no longer "What *can I* believe?" but "What *should we* believe?" It's not about winning over (that is, defeating) the other guy, it's about winning the other guy over. Or letting her win you over. It's about determining the truth and building shared understanding.

There's right attitude, and there's right practice. Regarding the latter, when a difference arises, the parties involved should initially *suspend judgment* so they can investigate the matter with some measure of impartiality. Then, they should conduct a joint inquiry. During this phase, each party is entitled to draw attention to considerations he or she finds relevant. We do *that* with reasons. In collaborative inquiry, reasons aren't used as weapons; they're pointers used to direct attention to relevant considerations. (Now, *that's* how you beat rhetorical swords into plowshares!) Each consideration is weighed and given its due. Finally, all the relevant considerations are aggregated— in a way I'll discuss later—and a determination is made. With the information assembled, the claim at issue is jointly judged either reasonable or unreasonable. If found to be reasonable, the claim is redeemed and becomes available for shared use. If found to be unreasonable, the claim is withdrawn and no longer available for, say, premising. Either way, the two parties can proceed with expanded common understanding. That's how you build shared understanding.

Reason-giving dialogue, in other words, has a definite structure. We can model this structure—that is, represent it simply—as a kind of game. In the 1990s, I designed such a game to teach the way of inquiry. My students seemed to enjoy playing it, so I wrote up the rules and dubbed it the "reason-giving game." Since then, thousands of students have played it, and hundreds of thousands have played an online game based on it.[3]

The way of belief is a *cognitive immune disruptor.* It promises to purify minds of bad ideas but ends up compromising our ability to identify bad ideas. The same goes for the way of the culture warrior: it blinds us to the flaws in our worldviews and prevents us from thinking well. Both strategies backfire. The way of inquiry, however, is a *cognitive immune booster*. It's a mind inoculant: an antidote to ideological thinking, and a way to improve cognitive performance. I urge you to adopt it as your own.

The way of inquiry is also the way to heal America's ideological divide. Cynics will scoff at the suggestion, but their cynicism shouldn't be mistaken for realism. Cynicism about reason's power to reconcile us is what Rutger Bregman calls a "nocebo"—a self-fulfilling negative expectation.[4] Far better to believe in the power of reason-giving dialogue and let positive expectation drive a virtuous spiral.

I'm not saying the resulting conversations will be easy. But the more fully we submit to better reasons, the easier they become. Take it from me, a guy who's facilitated thousands of difficult conversations: they *can* become a joyful, collaborative pursuit of shared understanding. In fact, they *will*—but only if we embrace the way of inquiry.

In these opening chapters, I've tried to foreground cognitive immunology's usefulness. To establish it as a real science, though, we must delve more deeply into foundational issues. The first concerns the nature of bad ideas. *What makes good ideas good, and bad ideas bad?* Or in immunology-speak: *What makes a mind parasite a mind parasite?* I take up this question next.

# PART II

# Mind-Parasites and Public Health

Public opinion, I am sorry to say,
will bear a great deal of nonsense.
There is scarcely an absurdity so gross,
whether in religion, politics, science,
or manners, which it will not bear.

—Ralph Waldo Emerson

# CHAPTER 6

# The Ethics of Faith

## *What is responsible belief?*

To follow by faith alone is to follow
blindly. —*Benjamin Franklin*

In this chapter, I want to put my claims about the way of inquiry to perhaps the sternest test of all: the task of bridging the divide between secular and religious worldviews. Turns out it's possible to reconcile even nonbelievers and people of faith. The trick is to inquire, openly and honestly, into the nature of responsible believing. By traveling this path together, we end up forging common ground. We also answer a foundational question, namely: "What makes good ideas good, and bad ideas bad?" In this way, we can enhance our ability to distinguish mind-parasites (or bad ideas) from mind symbionts (or good ideas).

Allow me, then, to rewind 150 years, to a pivotal moment in the history of ideas: a moment when two intellectual titans clashed over the ethics of belief, and the immune health of a civilization hung in the balance.

## A Fateful Clash of Ideas

William Kingdon Clifford was a young man in a hurry. In 1860, at a mere fifteen years of age, he enrolled in King's College London. Just ten years later, he boldly conjectured that matter and gravity are manifestations of curved space-time. In this, the precocious mathematician anticipated the central tenets of general relativity theory, one of the most celebrated scientific accomplishments of all time. Remarkably, Clifford did this at the still-boyish age of twenty-five, an astonishing forty-five years before Albert Einstein published his definitive paper on the subject.

Of course, Clifford hadn't worked out the details. He wasn't equipped for that. Besides, he was too busy. He simply shared his conviction that matter is a wrinkle in space-time, then set off to observe the alignment of wrinkles we call a solar eclipse. En route, his ship wrecked on a rocky wrinkle off the coast of Sicily. He was fortunate to survive. Never one to waste a good story, Clifford would later convert this experience into an important contribution to philosophy—a major wrinkle in the fabric of ideas.

Passionately devoted to solving conceptual puzzles, Clifford routinely worked late into the night. Overworked and sleep-deprived, he suffered a mental breakdown. Three years later, and just eleven days before Einstein was born, he died in relative obscurity. He was just thirty-four years old.

Clifford accomplished a great deal in his short life, and not only in mathematics and physics. A year before his death, he ventured into philosophy and gave some thought to "the fatal superstitions that clog our race." He directed his considerable intellect, in other words, toward a solution to our ideology problem. His essay on the subject would be published as "The Ethics of Belief"—now considered a philosophical classic. In it, he tells a story of shipwreck, and highlights a neglected branch of moral theory. He sketches an elegant mechanism for reining in dangerous ideologies and left us to work out the details.

Clifford's central contention was this: believing things upon insufficient evidence is not just unreasonable, it is unethical. Put differently, ethics extends beyond the realm of action and into the realm of thought. Consequently, those who accept things on faith don't just compromise their realism; they also compromise their character. Clifford even borrowed the language of religious evangelicals to make his point:

> Belief [is] that sacred faculty which prompts the decisions of our will, and knits into harmonious working all the compacted energies of our being. . . . [It] is ours, not for ourselves, but for humanity. It is rightly used on truths which have . . . stood in the fierce light of free and fearless questioning. Then it helps to bind men together, and to strengthen and direct their common action. It is desecrated when given to unproved and unquestioned statements, for the solace and private pleasure of the believer. . . . [Responsible people] guard the purity of [their] belief with a very fanaticism of jealous care, lest at any time it should rest on an unworthy object, and catch a stain which can never be wiped away.

"Sacred." "Desecrated." "Purity." "Fanaticism of jealous care." This is not the language of disinterested assessment; it's the language of someone passionate about mental hygiene. Clifford even compares the spread of bad ideas to a "pestilence," and says that those who suppress doubts commit "one long sin against mankind."

Clifford's views on the subject had diverged sharply from mainstream opinion. He understood that his stance "seems harsh when applied to those simple souls who have never known better; who have been brought up from the cradle with a horror of doubt, and taught that their eternal welfare depends on what they believe." He appears, though, to have underestimated the obstacle this would create for the uptake of his ideas, for he never addressed the concern directly.

This is unfortunate, for his scruples are not inherently intolerant. Yes, they can be used to underwrite harsh judgments (just imagine harsh condemnation of a naively trusting child), but they can also be applied with moderation, sympathy, and humanity. Immoderate application of the sufficient evidence standard can be distasteful, but that doesn't make the standard wrong. Confusion on this point has persisted for several generations, preventing a fair assessment of a remarkably beneficial idea.

Let's clear up that confusion now. In any domain, high standards can be applied without moderation; that's no reason not to adopt those standards and apply them *with* moderation. Thus, we can encourage responsible believing without condemning irresponsible believing. (*Inadvertently* irresponsible believing, of course, merits especially gentle treatment: not condemnation but instruction.) More generally, we can embrace high ethical standards when it comes to belief but promote adherence with instruction, encouragement, and praise. These simple concessions to human feeling might have lessened emotional resistance to Clifford's proposal.

But Clifford was impatient to improve humanity's lot, and had but a year to live. So he adopted a moralistic stance, and his commitment to "free and fearless questioning" took on the aspect of a crusade. Simply put, his manner became that of a culture warrior, and his moralistic fervor turned people off. And his insight—the one with real potential to mitigate our ideological tendencies—was largely lost on intervening generations.

In fact, it was lost on William James, the eminent Harvard philosopher, who studied Clifford's argument and authored the classic rebuttal. James combined brilliant insights and blistering *ad hominem* attacks. He honored Clifford by taking his "ethics of belief" idea seriously but also ridiculed him as a tantrum-throwing *enfant terrible*—French for "spoiled child." In the process, James forged an influential defense of faith: what he called "our right to adopt a believing attitude in religious matters." Simply put, James employed the language of *rights* to blunt the force of Clifford's emphasis on *responsibilities*.

Philosophers disagree about who won the debate, but in several ways, James won a decisive victory. His defense of faith became surprisingly influential, and Clifford's ethic of belief underwent little in the way of scholarly development. Meanwhile, in the court of public opinion, James's more permissive views proved more popular. He ended up concluding that we have a right to believe "any hypothesis [that] tempts our will," and that general thesis—that *everyone is entitled to their opinion*—became the centerpiece of a hugely consequential cultural consensus. It became an article of both religious and secular faith.

More precisely, Clifford's "sufficient evidence" standard came to prevail in science, technology, engineering and mathematics—the so-called STEM fields—and James's "right to believe" thesis came to prevail in PET—the realms of politics, ethics, and theology. I'm tempted to say that Clifford won over the techies, and James won over the fuzzies, but the truth is more bizarre: Clifford's thesis became the governing principle of humanity's *left* brain, and James's thesis essentially colonized the *right*. (In popular psychology, the left hemisphere of the brain has been linked to analytical STEM tasks, and the right hemisphere appears to be implicated in more holistic and creative tasks. The research on this is disputed, however, and many tasks activate both hemispheres. My claim, in other words, is more heuristic than neuroscientific.)

Clifford meant for his sufficient evidence standard to apply across the board. In fact, he stated his claim with outlandish generality: "It is wrong always, everywhere, and for anyone, to believe anything upon insufficient evidence." Evidently, Clifford thought this ethic should be applied both to statements of fact and statements of value—to both descriptions and prescriptions. (Philosophers call statements about what *is* "descriptive," and statements about what *should be* "normative" or "prescriptive." It's generally thought that scientists should stick to the facts and leave value judgments to ethicists and theologians.)

By pushing back, though, James won a kind of exemption for the domains in which value judgments loom large. This outcome has been extraordinarily consequential: engineering and the sciences have blossomed, producing wonders no denizen of the nineteenth century could have foreseen. Politics, ethics, and theology, on the other hand—the domains where evidential standards haven't taken hold—have languished. They remain mired in ideological division and boast little in the way of positive progress.

When it comes to the domains where values figure prominently, many now claim a blanket right to believe what they like. Sadly, few acknowledge that, in these domains too, we have responsibilities having to do with belief. James' thesis, in other words, has become a kind of meta-ideology: an all-purpose excuse for indulging in wishful thinking. As we'll see, this seriously weakens cultural immune systems, hampering our collective ability to fight off ideological infection.

One hundred forty years after Clifford published "The Ethics of Belief," faith remains a potent cultural force. Ideologies flourish unabated, and, in the interim, ideology-fueled conflicts have consumed something on the order of 140 *million* human lives.[1] Year after year, we fail to draw the right lessons from the Clifford-James debate, and year after year, we lose about a million of our brothers and sisters to the problem Clifford meant to solve.

Perhaps it's time we revisited the Clifford-James exchange. Perhaps this time, we can gain clarity about the nature of responsible belief. And develop much-needed mental immunity.

## The Shipowner Parable

Is it morally permissible to accept things on faith? The question is divisive, and W. K. Clifford and William James held passionately opposed views on the subject. Yet still they managed to have a constructive, illuminating debate. Religious culture warriors claim James as their champion and tend to dismiss Clifford. Secular culture warriors claim Clifford as their champion and tend to dismiss James.

But there's a third way: we can practice the way of inquiry. That is, we can suspend judgment, appreciate good arguments on both sides, and seek common understanding. So let's examine the arguments, and give each its due. It turns out we can learn from both men—and in the process, build a bridge between religious and secular worldviews. We can also resolve a question of deep importance to cognitive immunology, specifically: Does religious faith strengthen or weaken mental immune systems?

Clifford opened his case with a parable. The owner of a passenger ship is troubled by indications that his vessel is less than seaworthy. He understands that it's not terribly well built and knows that it has suffered wear and tear. Then a boatwright in his employ brings some expensive structural issues to his attention. These doubts, though, make him unhappy. So he suppresses them. He reminds himself that the ship has weathered many storms. He "dismiss(es) from his mind all ungenerous suspicions about the honesty of builders and contractors." He "puts his trust in Providence." In these and similar ways, he puts his mind at ease. Then, with the best intentions, he sends the ship to sea. When it sinks, hundreds of passengers are consigned to the ocean floor. He collects the insurance money and suffers no remorse.

Clifford invites us to reflect on this story. I ask my students—religious and secular alike—to discuss the case, and extract lessons we can all agree on. They invariably begin by agreeing that the shipowner is morally at fault. Okay, I say, but what exactly did he do wrong? Well, he was negligent, and put his passengers' lives at risk. What was the root cause of the failing? Well, he nurtured a comforting but irresponsible belief. What should he have done differently? Clearly, he shouldn't have suppressed his doubts. It seems he had an obligation, instead, to adjust his level of confidence to the available evidence.

These are all conclusions that Clifford means for us to draw, and I have yet to meet the person unwilling to draw them. (In more than twenty years of teaching, I've discussed the case with maybe a thousand students.) I've learned, though, that it's possible to reach these conclusions and fail to fully appreciate their import. So I urge my students to reflect more deeply. Let me get this straight, I ask: The shipowner's moral failing was rooted in irresponsible believing? That's right, they say. Doesn't this show us that there *is such a thing as* irresponsible believing? Of course, they say: So what?

So belief is not a realm governed solely by rights; responsibilities also come into play. Clifford has shown us that we have epistemic *duties*: obligations that reach inside our skulls and constrain what it is right or moral to believe. ("Epistemic" is a handy bit of philosophical jargon; it means "having to do with belief, knowledge, and cognition." Clifford's shipowner parable shows us that epistemic duties exist.) There are, or at least should be, shared standards of responsible believing. My students think about this and agree that the conclusion is inescapable.

The parable shows us that we need an ethics of belief: epistemic standards exist (or should exist), and we can try to make these standards explicit. Given that irresponsible and divergent believing creates a host of problems, a well-developed ethics of belief could pay substantial dividends. So why not inquire together and develop a shared understanding of our epistemic rights and responsibilities?

There's another important implication. It seems we're not entitled to believe whatever we please. The notion that we have a blanket right to believe what we like turns out to be a myth. In fact, the parable shows that even value judgments can be morally impermissible. The shipowner had no right to believe "My ship is seaworthy"; nor was he entitled to the corresponding value judgment: "It's okay to load this ship with emigrants and send it upon the deep." Both beliefs were wrong. They were untrue, they were unjustified, and they were immoral.

Sometimes, a student will say: Hang on a sec: Can't we fault the shipowner's actions, while leaving his thinking free from ethical restraint? Isn't it enough to subject *overt behavior* to critical review? After all, internal beliefs must achieve outward expression to harm others. Great question! I say: What do you guys think? The students discuss it. Invariably, they end up siding with Clifford: if we exempt thinking and believing from ethical evaluation, and regulate only overt action, it's often too little, too late. Beliefs matter, and it's important that we do our best to believe responsibly. It may be a bad idea to regulate beliefs *legally*, but we certainly need to regulate them *morally*.

Notice that these are not partisan conclusions: they're conclusions that both religious and secular students come to easily. The same is true of liberals and conservatives. Indeed, any reasonable person can work them out for him- or herself. In fact, they're conclusions we're rationally bound to draw. Clifford has shown us that irresponsible believing is a real thing: some beliefs are simply not morally permissible.

Had Clifford limited himself to these modest observations, his proposal might have encountered less resistance. Basic epistemic responsibilities might be more widely recognized, and "belief ethics" might be a respected domain of inquiry. Belief ethicists might have accomplished a good deal in 140 years: What if our collective understanding of responsible belief had progressed as rapidly as, say, our understanding of genetics?

The insights of belief ethics, it turns out, have immune-boosting power. Understand your responsibilities vis-à-vis belief formation, and your mind's immune system gets stronger. Clifford's exchange with James also has foundational significance: it illuminates the fundamental nature of the mind-parasites we call "bad ideas." Had Clifford and James together employed the way of inquiry, cognitive immunology might well be an established field, and educators would have far better tools for imparting responsible belief-formation habits. Had these things happened, the ideological conflicts of the twentieth century might have played out differently.

We'll never know, though, because Clifford took a different path. As we've seen, his manner became that of a culture warrior. His aggressively general conclusion had an intemperate, accusatory quality: "It is wrong always, everywhere, and for anyone, to believe anything upon insufficient evidence."

Off-putting? You could say that. But was Clifford wrong?

## Is Evidence the Hallmark of Responsible Belief?

Is it morally permissible to believe things on insufficient evidence? W. K. Clifford answered with a resounding *no!* With this answer, he essentially dismissed all poorly evidenced beliefs as bad. But is this right? *Are* all poorly evidenced beliefs bad? I ask my students what they think. Some think this conclusion makes sense and embrace it with enthusiasm. Others aren't so sure. Okay, I say, let's seek common ground. Let's examine Clifford's argument. Are there gaps in it?

Someone will point out that Clifford moves quickly from a particular case—that of the shipowner—to a very general conclusion. "Excellent observation!" I say. In fact, Clifford generalizes with freakish abandon. Always, everywhere, anyone, anything—and all in the same sentence? Yes, there's a gap in Clifford's argument, and it's a wide one. What does he do to bridge it? We look up the relevant passage: "[In]asmuch as no belief . . . is without its effect on the fate of mankind, we have no choice but to extend our judgment to all cases of belief whatever."

The idea seems to be this: Our beliefs have implications for the well-being of others. These implications can be large or small, harmful or beneficial. Some beliefs, like the shipowner's, harm quite directly. Other beliefs, like belief in original sin, have more subtle effects, quietly shaping the believer's attitudes, speech, and behavior. (A belief's behavioral effects can be hard to trace, but by their very nature, beliefs alter our disposition to behave in characteristic ways.[2] For example: really believe that people are out to get you, and you'll start exhibiting paranoid behavior.) Your beliefs, in other words, may not affect others directly, but they can't help but impact others indirectly. Consequently, we must do our level best to form responsible beliefs. And modify or let go of irresponsible ones.

Some students decide that this argument does a pretty good job of bridging the gap. Beliefs, they conclude, really are ethically implicated, and evidence really is the hallmark of responsible belief. Others have doubts about the sweeping generality of Clifford's conclusion, or worry about the implications for the world's faith traditions. Opinions start to diverge.

Let's break it down, I say. Has Clifford shown that all beliefs really are ethically implicated? Invariably, we achieve a robust consensus on this point: both secular and religious students are prepared to concede that belief is ethically freighted. So why is the larger point controversial?

Eventually, someone will ask the key question: How do we know that being based on evidence is the real hallmark of ethical belief? I then help him or her amplify the point. Isn't Clifford assuming that well-evidenced beliefs invariably confer benefit, and that poorly evidenced beliefs invariably cause harm? I point out that these assumptions are unlikely to be true: some faith-based beliefs are probably beneficial, and some evidence-based beliefs are probably harmful. Faces light up with some combination of insight and hope. Heads invariably nod: a belief's evidential basis is one thing, and its power to benefit or harm is another. There seems to be a real problem here.

You've raised a great question, I say. Specifically: Is the "sufficient evidence" standard the true measure of responsible belief? We'll take up this question soon. For now, note that Clifford hasn't established that all faith-based believing is immoral. However, he *has* established a more basic point: we have actual moral responsibilities with regard to belief formation and maintenance. True, the precise nature of these responsibilities—the correct standard of responsible belief—remains an open question, but we should all be able to agree that there's an important difference between responsible and irresponsible believing. It would benefit us all to have a clear understanding of the difference.

Think of your mind as a garden. You could seed it indiscriminately, but that doesn't seem wise. You could *weed* it indiscriminately, but that, too, seems unwise. Ideally, we try to seed our minds with good ideas and weed them of bad ones. All of this is done with imperfect knowledge of which is which. Yet we know this much: if you neglect your mental garden, weeds will eventually overrun it. Now think of your mind as a plot in a much larger community garden. Neglect your plot, and the weeds run riot. When they germinate, weeds will spread into neighboring plots. Clearly, you have an interest in your neighbors weeding *their* plots; don't they have an interest in you weeding yours? Good neighbors care enough to weed their mental gardens.

The point can also be put in immunological terms. Good neighbors care enough to keep their mind's immune system in good working order. They screen out mind-parasites for their own sake but also for the sake of others. Cognitive immune health is a team sport.

The great coronavirus epidemic of 2020 is teaching the world a comparable lesson. Just yesterday, I came across a Facebook meme that said: "The coronavirus is an important reminder that health isn't private. As a species, we live in herds. Everyone's health relies to some extent on everyone else's. Healthcare has to be public because health is public." The anonymous author of this meme was surely thinking of *biological* health, but the claim has got to be true of *cognitive* health as well. Shouldn't the science of public health, then, be working to prevent outbreaks of bad ideas?

## Faith's Libertarian Champion

Regardless of their religious leanings, people of goodwill should be able to agree: "faith" mustn't become a blank check to indulge in irresponsible believing. Clifford, though, didn't just indict *bad* faith: he used the shipowner parable to put faith itself on trial. He played the prosecutor and built a case that *all* faith—bad and good, religious and secular—is a morally irresponsible indulgence.

This indictment put faith in need of an able public defender. That defender surfaced in the person of William James. James was born into a wealthy, intellectually gifted New York family (the novelist Henry James was his brother). He studied at Harvard and got his medical degree in 1869. He struggled with mental illness, though, and never practiced medicine. Instead, he developed an enduring interest in human psychology. He studied and wrote about "soul-sickness"—what we today call "depression"—and became an early advocate of positive psychology.

James understood that the world's religions offer resources for battling depression, anxiety, and existential despair. He spent years studying the varieties of religious experience and wrote a classic book on the subject. He dabbled in spiritualism, educated himself in philosophy, and came to view religious ideas and practices as mental health interventions.

James knew from personal experience that willful belief can be a useful antidote to despair. This led him, in 1896, to publish a caustic and impassioned rejoinder to Clifford. He titled it "The Will to Believe," and in it, he developed "a defense of our right to adopt a believing attitude in religious matters." In a way, it was the first fully modern, scientifically literate defense of faith.

His arguments still command respect. Not only did James avoid supernatural assumptions, he built his case on real facts about human psychology. He developed a serious challenge to Clifford's evidentialism and helped to prevent the sufficient evidence standard from taking root in value-centric domains.

"The Will to Believe" also proposed an alternative ethics of belief. James contended, contra Clifford, that "we have a right to believe at our own risk any hypothesis (that) tempt(s) our will." In effect, he argued that each of us is entitled to our opinions. The message found a receptive audience, in part because it gave people permission to employ willful belief in their battle with inner demons. James helped to shape an influential cultural norm, one that says, in effect, that no one should interfere with another's right to believe.

In essence, James helped to establish a libertarian ethos vis-à-vis belief. His argument helped persuade intervening generations to treat cognitive liberties as paramount. The supposed "right to believe" became practically sacred, and behaviors with the potential to interfere with that right came to be seen as transgressive. Even simple reminders of our cognitive responsibilities get caught in this net. Even honest criticism—which can in fact "interfere" with belief—is delegitimized. In this way, critical thinking is systematically discouraged.

The analogy with economic libertarianism is robust. Those who fetishize property rights, for example (imagining that they override all else) often come to see assertions of economic responsibility as transgressive. It is this felt sense that property rights are absolute that causes many libertarians to characterize taxation, in all its forms, as illegitimate. For if property rights are absolute, and taxation forces people to relinquish their property (as it does), taxation is wrong. In the same way, if the right to believe is absolute, and criticism interferes with belief (as it does), then criticism must be regarded as wrong.

You needn't reject criticism in any explicit way to be infected by this ethos. All that's required is a cultural milieu that treats certain types of inquiry as unseemly. If you've ever shied away from expressing your reservations because "Hey, aren't others entitled to their opinions?" or because "Reasonable people can disagree," you've felt the pull of intellectual libertarianism. William James died in 1910, but over a century later, his ghost lives on.

In practice, of course, we often hedge our commitments to Jamesian intellectual libertarianism. Consider the common saying (often attributed to Daniel Patrick Moynihan): "You're entitled to your opinion, but not entitled to your own facts." The second half of this expression points to an important truth: in factual discourse, we have obligations that supersede our supposed "right" to believe or say what we like. Half aware of these exceptions, we often retrench, when pressed, to a weaker view: each of us is entitled to our basic *value* assumptions. Our views about what *is* are ethically constrained by the facts, but our assumptions about what *matters*—our articles of faith—are not. Thus, James articulated a comparatively permissive ethics of belief—one that won out, over Clifford's, in the court of public opinion. It went on to prevail for over a century.

## Is Belief Voluntary?

William James's "The Will to Believe" is of more than just historical interest. It also contains philosophical insights: enduring contributions to the ethics of belief. So, let's hear from the defense. How did James defend the so-called right to believe? He did it by raising four excellent questions:

1. Is belief even voluntary?
2. What about poorly evidenced beliefs that have the power to benefit us: Does it really make sense to ban them?
3. When we believe, we run the risk of being wrong, but doesn't refraining from belief carry risks of its own?
4. What about "self-fulfilling" beliefs—beliefs that help bring about the believed-in state of affairs?

According to James, "the whole fabric of our belief is made up of things we are absolutely impotent to disbelieve." The claim is simple but surprising: belief is involuntary. More precisely, you can't just decide to believe something you regard as implausible and thereby render it credible, even to yourself. Not sure of this? Try this experiment:

take a minute and try to believe that the sun revolves around a fixed Earth. Go on, try it. Now: How'd you do? You may have successfully *imagined* it, but did you succeed in *believing* it? Probably not. This simple thought experiment shows us something unexpected but quite generally true: belief is not under direct, voluntary control.

Of course, there are things we could do to embed geocentric cosmology more deeply in our psyches. We could assert it in a book and declare the book sacred and inerrant. We could treat the claims of geocentric astronomy with awe and reverence. We could chant them on the Sabbath and denounce challenges as heretical. We could suppress competing hypotheses and persecute heliocentrists.

Historically, of course, the Catholic Church deployed just such measures. In 1600, it tried the Italian cleric Giordano Bruno for his Copernican views and burned him at the stake. Ten years later, Pope Urban VIII took exception to Galileo's elegant demonstration that we live in a sun-centered system and had him tried for heresy. Galileo was convicted and spent the rest of his life under house arrest. The Church threatened him with torture, got him to recant, and banned his writings.

Coercive measures like these probably work to induce belief in some, but in Galileo's case, they succeeded only in inducing a disingenuous avowal. In private, he persisted in his belief that the Earth moves. (Some researchers think that a great deal of religiosity is similar to Galileo's recantation: not an honest expression of belief but a public performance meant to achieve some social outcome. The philosopher Daniel Dennett conjectures that many professed believers don't literally believe in God; what they're really doing is expressing their belief in belief.[3] On this view, religious avowals are a kind of virtue signaling.)

The important point is that we *do* influence our beliefs indirectly. We exercise conscious control, for example, over the things we say. We decide which premises we'll rely on in our thinking. We can criticize or allow the premises of others. We can direct our attention *to* the evidence, or avert it *from* the evidence. Also, we can indulge our desire to believe comforting things, or make a habit of regarding wishful thinking with skepticism. Such choices end up having a big impact on our beliefs. We make decisions and form mental habits, and the habits shape our beliefs. No one disputes these things. We may not be able to induce an arbitrary belief on the spur of the moment, but we can and do "choose" our beliefs indirectly.

If believing were *wholly* involuntary, Clifford's project would be misguided. For then, it would make no sense to preach abstinence from believing. Indeed, the concepts of "responsible" and "irresponsible" apply only to the extent that belief is voluntary. James's project, though, would be equally misguided. For if the will is "absolutely impotent" to select among competing hypotheses, why bother defending its "right to believe any hypothesis [that] tempts [it]"? Like Clifford, James defends a view which presupposes that belief is at least *somewhat* voluntary. (If belief were *wholly* involuntary, would it make any sense for God to reward believers and punish unbelievers?)

In fact, belief is partially—or rather, *indirectly*—voluntary. It follows that the ethics of belief remains a viable project. Of course, it makes sense to temper our inclination to judge people for their irresponsible beliefs. Given that believing is partially involuntary, understanding and patience are warranted. Wherever possible, we should address irresponsible believing with respectful challenges, good reasons, and gentle humor. In most cases, irresponsible believing calls for patient instruction, not condemnation.

## How to "Hack" Your Mind—with Faith

Like Clifford, James employed stories to make his case. In the stories James tells, though, faith plays the hero, not the villain. James offers examples of belief conferring real benefits. In particular, he asks us to consider the case of self-fulfilling conviction—poorly evidenced belief that brings about the believed-in state of affairs.

Of the stories James tells, my favorite involves someone having faith in a stranger's essential friendliness. In this scenario, the protagonist has no good evidence that a stranger will prove friendly but takes it on faith that she will. As a result, his demeanor is more trusting and hopeful: more conducive, that is, to friendship formation. The friendship forms, providing a kind of after-the-fact validation of the faith.

This story resonates with me because a similar experience changed my life. I like to share my story with students: In high school, I was shy and anxious. I was lonely and had few friends. Then an acquaintance pulled me aside. "Hey, Andy," she said. "Why do you always wear such a sad expression?" "I don't know," I said. "I suppose I just feel that way." "Do yourself a favor," she said: "Smile." "But I don't have any reason to smile!" I protested. "Do you need a reason?" she countered. I thought about it. "Wouldn't it be dishonest," I asked, "to display a happiness I don't feel?" "Stop being an idiot," she said: "Smile anyway."

I gave it a try. At first it felt awkward and disingenuous. But then something unexpected happened. People noticed my smile and smiled back. This warmed me, and the world felt like a friendlier place. I gained confidence, and it became easier to engage in conversation. I formed new friendships, and before long, I felt like an entirely different person. I learned later that smiling improves mental health via other pathways. For example, it releases neurochemicals that directly improve emotional well-being. I smile a lot now. I do it without apology, and I don't need a situation-specific reason to smile. It's come to feel genuine too. "Smile anyway" was the best advice I ever got.

"Smile anyway" bears more than a passing resemblance to "Just have faith." The two phrases function in much the same way. "Feeling down?—Smile anyway!" is a secular cousin to "Discouraged?—Keep the faith!" Each recommends a resolute hopefulness—a commitment of sorts to maintaining a positive attitude. There is little doubt that such commitment confers psychological and social rewards; it tends to boost confidence and instill hope. It can promote trust, create social capital, and strengthen social solidarity.

The phenomenon at work here is quite general: someone willfully adopts a certain attitude, and in so doing, transforms their experience for the better. We're talking, here, about intentionally "hacking" your own mind. Incidentally, this is arguably the founding insight of every great spiritual tradition: "mind hacks" can have a decisive effect on our well-being. When people get together and practice time-tested mind hacks as a group, the effects can be especially dramatic. This fact goes a long way toward explaining the world's religions.

For thousands of years, people have told stories about the magical properties of sacred beliefs. The Canaanites were taught that propitiating Ba'al could bring favorable weather. The Greeks knew that proper devotion to Demeter would facilitate a rich harvest. The Romans worshiped Venus hoping to kindle love. Even today, in Chinese folk religion, offerings to Shouxing are thought to confer longevity. It's not hard to imagine such beliefs affording comfort.

Today, though, beliefs about Ba'al, Demeter, and Venus are straightforward examples of irresponsible cognition. Why? It's not just that their faith traditions have lapsed: scientific advances have thoroughly discredited the causal claims at their foundation. The principles of meteorology make it quite unlikely that Ba'al will intervene to change the weather. The tenets of botany imply that Demeter won't affect the harvest. Exposure to psychology makes it hard to believe that a sacrifice to Venus will get you laid. In domain after domain, real knowledge of causal relationships turns religious wisdom into fable.

If science literacy makes divine intervention stories a tough sell, it hasn't quenched the hope that pious belief will confer magical benefits. The purported benefits of religious belief, though, get forced underground. Or more accurately: off world. It works like this: claims of worldly benefit are testable, so religions evolve to hedge their bets.[4] The rewards of piety—now conceived as salvation, eternal life, or God's favor—get displaced to an afterlife. You must die to take delivery.

It's much harder to discredit such claims. And so, they persist. Of course, the living have a hard time confirming receipt of such gifts, so crises of faith occur with predictable frequency. Science continues its advance, and stories of supernatural reward appear increasingly fabulous. Meanwhile, intellectual honesty requires us to reinterpret religious beliefs: they "pay their way," not by accurately depicting, explaining, or predicting the world, but by inducing desirable psychological effects: by providing comfort, say, or relief from existential anxiety.

In effect, James used his knowledge of human psychology to construct a more intellectually honest defense of religious faith. If we focus on the psychological and social benefits of religious belief, we can construct a thoroughly naturalistic (that is, superstition-free) understanding of how faith *works* to reward the faithful. Psychologists of religion followed James's lead, and we now know that religious belief functions at many levels. It can ease fear of death, promote trust, and bind people into tight collectives. In effect, James proposed that we capture the *functional* wisdom of the world's faith traditions and preserve it in a more honest form: a form less vulnerable to relentless scientific progress.

James reminds us that beliefs aren't just *inferentially* related to bits of evidence; they're also *causally* connected to attitudes and behaviors that affect well-being. (Think of evidence for a belief as "upstream" of it, and related logically; the consequences of a belief are "downstream," and connected causally.)

It's hard to maintain that a belief's likely effects—its downstream consequences—have no bearing on its moral standing. After all, we reject white supremacists' claims of racial superiority, not just because they lack an evidential basis, but also—and more immediately—

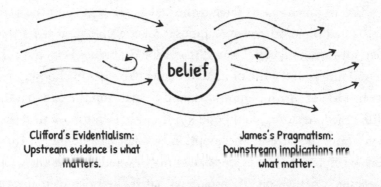

Clifford's Evidentialism:
Upstream evidence is what
matters.

James's Pragmatism:
Downstream implications are
what matter.

"Upstream" evidence and "downstream" implications of belief

because they're patently dysfunctional. We understand that believing such things is a recipe for arrogance, resentment, hatred, and racial division. We think: "No good can come from believing such things," and we reject them. Does the destructiveness of racial superiority claims count against them? What do you think?

To be clear: I'm not claiming that the downstream effects of religious belief are the same as the downstream effects of white supremacist beliefs: the two are likely to differ markedly; I'm merely observing that each *has* downstream effects—effects a conscientious person must take into account.

James, it turns out, has shown the inadequacy of Clifford's evidence-centered ethics of belief. Clifford's view is that, when evaluating a belief, we need *only* look at the "upstream" evidence. This implies that "downstream" consequences have no bearing on the rightness or wrongness of believing it. But that can't be right: the effects of believing (its foreseeable effects, at any rate) *do* merit moral consideration. They matter. It follows that evidentialism is not the whole story on responsible belief: the expected benefits of faith-based believing matter, just as the expected costs of white supremacist believing matters. Score one for James.

The argument gains force if the stakes are high, and the benefits can be had in no other way. Suppose, for example, that the adoption of an unwarranted belief would make the difference between a life of mental illness and a life of mental health. You get to choose, say, between a life of sorrow, emptiness, and despair (on the one hand), and a life of joy, meaning, and hope (on the other). Suppose that the key to winning the latter is the adoption of a faith-based belief. Imagine that the embrace of an evidentially unwarranted belief is the *only* way to escape a hellish pit of despair. What if the price of maintaining Cliffordian mental hygiene were a life of "morbid mindedness"? Under such circumstances, wouldn't you believe? Can any sympathetic person condemn such belief? I can't. This judge scores another for James.

We here encounter the third question I credit James with raising: Doesn't refraining from belief carry risks and costs of its own? It certainly does in the scenario just described. For there, nonbelief consigns the nonbeliever to a hellish pit of despair. James's point is readily generalized: if it's a bad thing to be too credulous, and thereby take on false beliefs, then it's also a bad thing to be too skeptical, and thereby miss out on true ones. It's possible, in other words, to be so fearful of taking on a false belief that one never accepts the risks inherent in the project of acquiring true ones. Or so reluctant to take on harmful beliefs that one misses out on many beneficial ones. Simply put, it's possible to be too skeptical for your own good, and thereby deny yourself the benefits—epistemic, psychological, and social—of a more trusting attitude.

We philosophers have studied this argument carefully, and the most skeptical among us acknowledge that James has a point. I would add that it's an important point, of enduring relevance to the ethics of belief. I like to put it like this: Responsible believers are not mindlessly skeptical; they strike a suitable balance between suspicion and trust. Later, we'll take up the question of what it means to strike a "suitable balance" between suspicion and trust; for now, we must credit James with landing a third telling point.

James laid the foundation for a thoroughly modern defense of faith—one with the potential to survive the relentless advance of science. In effect, he argued that we should understand religious claims not as factual statements subject to empirical testing but as pragmatic mental health interventions: mind hacks that some people need to maintain emotional equilibrium. He provided a template for a line of thought that the world's faithful deploy to this day. The common version goes like this: *"Who cares whether my religious beliefs are true? They work for me. They console me, give me a sense of meaning, and bind me to a community. And that's enough."*

The idea is to set aside the question of truth entirely and focus instead on the *utility* of believing. Isn't it enough to fill our minds with pleasing, useful, spiritually uplifting, and morality-conducive beliefs? What could possibly go wrong?

## Secular Alternatives to Bad Faith: Uplifting Attitudes Without the Dogma

Defense Exhibit 1—[Entered into evidence by solicitor William James, counsel for the defense in *Clifford v. Faith*.] A man with no good evidence that a stranger will prove friendly takes it on faith that she will. This faith gives him confidence, so he strikes up a conversation. It also makes his demeanor more hopeful and trusting: more conducive, that is, to friendship formation. The friendship forms, providing a kind of after-the-fact validation of the faith.

Defense Exhibit 2—A job candidate, with little evidence that she has what it takes to do the job, allows herself to believe that she does. The belief proves self-fulfilling: her confidence grows, and she interviews well. She gets the job, her confidence soars, and she *becomes* highly capable.

Defense Exhibit 3—Muhammad Ali (then Cassius Clay) is terrified of Sonny Liston but psyches himself up—and psyches Liston out—with confident trash talk. Repeatedly calling himself "the greatest," Ali somehow lives up to that description. Later, he is asked about his success, and says: "It's lack of faith that makes people afraid of meeting challenges, and I believed in myself."

Defense Exhibit 4—A woman is taught to believe that God will provide. As a result, she has faith that things will turn out okay. This lessens her anxieties about the future and helps her gain a kind of emotional equilibrium. Because that equilibrium is a big part of being okay, her faith is, in a way, rewarded. The idea of God does the work, but God himself gets the credit.

Stories like these are the backbone of William James's defense of faith. He calls them cases "where faith in a fact can help create that fact." I call them cases of self-fulfilling belief. His point is that our attitudes frequently "run ahead of scientific evidence." And often, that's a good thing.

What are we to make of this argument? For starters, we have to acknowledge that people need confidence, hope, trust, commitment, and resolve—five secular cousins of religious faith—and for many, religious talk works to bolster these attitudes. Second, these attitudes tend to be conducive to mental health: a confident, hopeful, trusting, and resolute mind is healthy almost by definition. Third, these attitudes are ingredients of what biologists call "prosociality"—they tend to build social capital in ways that benefit not just the self but also others. We should all be grateful, then, for the well-meaning efforts of religious people devoted to building trust, hope, and moral commitment.

James saw that Cliffordian scruples could impinge on people's "right" to willfully boost healthy attitudes. For this reason, he labeled evidentialism "insane." He had a point. For it would be unwise to prohibit all use of non-evidence-based mind hacks. Suppose that a castaway on a desert island allows herself to believe that she'll be rescued. Suppose she does this in utter defiance of the evidence, but harms no one, while quadrupling her odds of survival. How could such believing be unethical?

I'd like, at this point, to apply my training in dispute resolution to mediate the centuries-old dispute between religious and secular outlooks. What if each side has a piece of the truth? What if we don't have to choose just one of these truths and throw out the other? What if, instead, we opened up a "both . . . and" alternative to the traditional "either . . . or"?

Many religious beliefs require the believer to willfully suspend disbelief. Belief that Jesus rose from the dead, for example. The problem is that this involves the willful suspension of basic standards of cognitive accountability—standards that apply in other domains. But what if there were genuine alternatives—mind hacks that promote healthy, prosocial attitudes without requiring us to violate important norms? What if we could have the benefits of religion without pretending to know things we don't really know?

Do such alternatives exist? I believe they do. Consider Defense Exhibit 1, where "precursive" faith in a stranger's friendliness helps to bring about a friendship. James implies that the friendship "cannot come at all unless a preliminary faith exists in its coming," but is this true? Are there really no alternative paths to the hoped-for result? Here, off the top of my head, are four:

Option 1: Infer from the evidence of past experience that any given stranger is likely to prove friendly. Here the belief is not definitive ("This stranger *will* prove friendly") but probabilistic ("This stranger *is likely to* prove friendly"). It has the virtue of being evidence-based, though, and can still have the salutary effects. (Notice, by the way, that blind trust in *all* strangers is probably more trusting than is warranted, wise, or safe. This observation shows that it makes sense to temper pro-social attitudes with evidence.)

Option 2: Admit that you don't have enough evidence of the stranger's friendliness (and thereby decline, on evidentialist grounds, to *believe* it) but all the while remain *resolutely hopeful* that the stranger will prove friendly. The hope can function in place of the belief and pave the way for the friendship, but without violating evidentialist scruples.

Option 3: Just *commit* to being friendly to strangers—regardless of their likelihood of reciprocating the friendliness—on the grounds that it's the right thing to do. On this approach, you needn't pretend to know something you don't really know: you simply act friendly because that's the kind of person you wish to be. The hoped-for friendship can then form without irresponsible believing entering the picture.

Option 4: Smile anyway.

The trust involved in Option 1, the hopefulness of Option 2, the moral commitment of Option 3, and the smiling demeanor of Option 4 are all dimensions of cognitive health. Arguably, they're what faith advocates have been after all along. But none of them are inherently religious. And that's the point: the valuable aspects of religious faith can be had without willful self-deception. The intellectually questionable supernatural trappings can be left behind, because there are honest, evidentially responsible ways to achieve the same result. The same healthy attitudes that religions have long been in the business of cultivating can be induced in other ways.

Is it fair, though, to describe religious belief as "willfully self-deceptive"? Does it invariably involve "pretending" to know things you don't know? Or pretending to believe things you don't really believe? Perhaps not. Perhaps sincere religious belief is none of these things. The self-fulfilling beliefs James likens them to, however, are *all* of these things. In Exhibit 1, a man *pretends* to know that a stranger will prove friendly. In Exhibit 2, a woman *wills herself to believe* that she has what it takes to do the job. In Exhibit 3, Cassius Clay psyches himself up with extravagant claims of his own greatness. In Exhibit 4, a woman helps herself to the comforting (and quite possibly delusive) belief that God will provide.

In fact, the way James defines it, faith is *inherently* delusive. For "faith in a fact" can only "create that fact" if the belief starts off false. Think about it: James was arguing that it's okay to pretend that the not-yet-actual is already actual—provided the pretense has the potential to change the world and, in so doing, mitigate the falsehood. There's no escaping it: James was endorsing willful dishonesty—of at least limited duration. Of course, he was also laying the groundwork for a revolutionary reinterpretation of religion. James showed us that we can understand religious wisdom as *functionally* useful even when it is not *literally* true. The first step is to recognize that religious beliefs are, at bottom, expedients for inducing desirable attitudes.

A religious claim doesn't need to be true to feel deeply right. The feeling of rightness can stem instead from its power to express allegiance. Also, believers throughout history have argued for religious claims on the grounds that they're *useful*. Claims about heaven and hell, for example, are often explicitly defended on the grounds that they help keep people in line. More generally, religious claims often have a pragmatic usefulness that is mistaken for truth. The idea that "God will provide," for example, can be marvelously calming whether or not it is true. "Jesus loves me" may meet a psychological need more reality-based believing can't.

I was a Quaker for about a decade because my mother loved the

Quaker idea that "there is that of God in everyone." She lacked up-stream evidence that we are in fact God-infused but had a clear grasp of the idea's downstream consequences. By dignifying us all, the idea makes it harder to mistreat people. She liked it and signed us up.

There's a larger lesson here, and it applies to secular as well as religious beliefs. Beliefs have both logical properties *and* causal prop-erties. They can be true or false *and* they can be useful or useless. Likewise, they can be evidenced to this or that degree *and* they can be more or less harmful. Ethically speaking, *all* of these properties matter, and responsible agents take account of them all. But here's the thing: *they do so without confusing them*. Useful does not mean true; nor does well-evidenced mean harmless.

If you analyze trenchant ideological divides, you'll often find ev-idential considerations supporting one side, and usefulness consider-ations supporting the other. For example, a liberal might focus on the evidence that change is needed, and a conservative might be better attuned to the dangers posed by rash reform. One side focuses on the "upstream" case *for* change, the other focuses on the "downstream" case *against* change, and the two sides talk past each other. But there's no good reason to treat this as an *either/or* proposition; true wisdom looks at *both* sets of considerations. If we could just achieve clarity on this point—that both epistemic and pragmatic considerations matter—a great many divisive issues in the world would suddenly prove tractable.

You should be able to acknowledge the evidential basis of my liberal call to change what *isn't* working, and I should be able to ac-knowledge the pragmatic wisdom of your conservative call to con-serve what *is* working. In this way, political dialogue between liberals and conservatives could again become fruitful. The distinction be-tween epistemic and pragmatic considerations can dramatically en-hance our capacity to think well together. It's a powerful cognitive immune booster.

Imagine if all the world's children were taught to care about both epistemic and pragmatic considerations. What if we were *all* sensitive to both the "upstream" and the "downstream" properties of ideas? What kind of world might we then build?

## Why Secularization Is Probably a Good Thing

Are there *always* honest alternatives to religious belief? Will we find a secular substitute for *every* important religious teaching? Will the secular surrogates prove as awe-inspiring, as soothing, and as intoxicating as belief in God? Who knows? The only responsible way to settle the matter is to seek out these alternatives, try them, and see what happens.

The prospect of experimenting with irreligious mind hacks might strike you as risky. Couldn't such experimentation harm society? Probably not. Developed countries have been experimenting with more secular outlooks for decades, and sociologists have accumulated mountains of data on the subject. The key takeaway is this: highly religious societies tend to have *high* levels of social dysfunction (crime, murder, teen pregnancy, poverty, divorce, etc.), and less religious societies tend to have *lower* levels of dysfunction.[5] The same correlation is found among American states: more religious states tend to be more dysfunctional, and less religious states tend to be less dysfunctional.[6] These correlations don't prove that religion *causes* social dysfunction, but they suggest that it might. It's also possible that social dysfunction causes people to adopt more religious attitudes. Or a third factor, like systemic injustice, could cause both to rise. In the meantime, the evidence gives us an excellent reason to stop worrying that secularization might prove catastrophic.

Why do secular societies tend to be healthier and happier than highly religious ones? Candidate explanations abound. Perhaps articles of faith aren't as beneficial as advertised. Perhaps our societies are haunted by their hidden costs. Perhaps religiosity closes minds and increases ideological rigidity. Perhaps it interferes with the growth mindset. Perhaps disingenuous professions of faith set an example, giving others permission to be intellectually dishonest. Perhaps comforting religious thoughts pave the way for more audacious and morally problematic delusions.

Perhaps pretending to know stuff you don't know creates obstacles to real understanding. Perhaps it diminishes curiosity. Perhaps *faux* understanding prevents people from achieving (or even seeking) *real* understanding. Perhaps religious faith tends to "unhinge" reason: weakening a cultural norm that allows reasoning to function properly. (More on this possibility presently.)

Perhaps evidence-based outlooks are less vulnerable to crises of faith: more prone to bend with the evidence as it arrives, and less likely to break under the strain of accumulated denial. Perhaps a commitment to evidence-based believing promotes real knowledge of cause and effect, putting us in a better position to make a lasting difference in the world. Perhaps, for this very reason, evidence-based worldviews provide a more stable foundation for a life of meaning and purpose.

Perhaps evidentiary discipline is conducive to productive habits of mind. Perhaps it aids scientific and technological advance. Perhaps the mental discipline of evidence-based believing helps people form responsible, shared "maps" of what matters. Perhaps creating such maps is a powerful way to build more just, prosperous, and harmonious societies.

If secularization *does* tend to benefit humanity, this should not surprise us. It should free us to experiment with secular substitutes for bad faith. So go ahead: give them a try. They're unlikely to harm you personally and might benefit us collectively.

## The Hidden Costs of Religions Belief

William James made important contributions to belief ethics. Did he succeed, though, in proving that "we have a right to believe . . . any hypothesis [that] tempts our will"? Clearly not: the shipowner had no right to believe that his ship was seaworthy. What of the somewhat weaker claim that we have a "right to adopt a believing attitude in religious matters"? Again, no. The shipowner is not entitled to believe that God wants him to drown infidels. The fact that a belief is religious in no way exempts it from ethical review. If anything, the temptations of religious belief entail a special obligation of cognitive due diligence. Why? Because religious beliefs have a long history of exploiting our human weakness for emotionally satisfying but cognitively irresponsible—and ultimately divisive—beliefs. To this we can now add: they probably weaken mental immune systems.

Clifford's point, though, was not entirely lost on James. For James hedged his "right to believe" claim in a way I've not yet alluded to. Specifically, he wrote that we have a right to believe "at our own risk" any hypothesis "live enough" to tempt our will. With this, James acknowledged that it's not okay to indulge in personally beneficial mind hacks that off-load risks and costs onto others.

The point seems obvious, but it's worth dwelling on. If James is right, and the benefits of a belief merit consideration, then so, too, do its costs. To consider the one but not the other is irresponsible. Arguably, this was the shipowner's mistake: he allowed himself to feel the belief's immediate personal benefits (it eased his mind and spared him the costs of repair), but he didn't give due weight to its indirect costs (it put other people's lives at risk). Responsible believers, by contrast, consider both costs and benefits. They look at both direct and indirect effects. And they think not just of themselves but also of others. James, of course, would concede these points in a heartbeat—as will all people of goodwill.

These simple points, though, have important implications for the world's faith traditions. For it is not enough to reap the psychological and social rewards of religious faith and ignore its indirect costs. When you yourself bear the indirect costs, such inattention is shortsighted; when others bear them, it is both shortsighted and selfish.

But perhaps the key tenets of enlightened religions are over-whelmingly beneficial. This is likely to be true of at least *some* articles of faith. For example, the idea that God wants us to love our neighbors probably encourages people to help one another. Resolute adherence to the Golden Rule—"Treat others as you'd like to be treated"—probably benefits humanity. Every religious tradition has teachings that, on balance, do good.

But are religious teachings uniformly beneficial? Consider the idea that "God will provide." It appears to relieve a great deal of stress—a significant point in its favor. Does it also have a downside? Well, it might promote a lack of self-reliance. A joke takes wry notice of this side effect: A ship sinks (what is it with all these shipwrecks?) and a devout passenger manages to board a small life raft. Days later, with his food and water running out, a steamship happens by and offers rescue. Infused, though, with religious optimism, he declines. "Don't worry about me," he chirps, "I'm sure God will provide!" The steamer sails on, and the man perishes of thirst. In heaven, the man confronts God. His voice wavers with a note of betrayal: "I had utter faith in you, God: Why didn't you provide for me?" God rolls his eyes in disbelief: "Who do you think sent that steamer?"

Ethical believers do due diligence on their articles of religious faith. They look at both their "pros" and "cons." If we're going to credit the concept of an afterlife with lessening the terror of death, we must also recognize that it interferes with the realization that life is short and time is precious. It probably makes people less likely to seize the day. The idea that God has a plan may reduce anxiety, but it also reduces the likelihood that people will take initiative to mitigate climate change. Religions are very good at creating in-group trust, but they also create out-group suspicion. The idea that God created us in his image makes us feel special, but it also creates a major obstacle to an evolutionary understanding of human origins. The idea that God created the universe for our use provides people in the extraction industries with a personally enriching rationale, but it also feeds an arrogant environmental hubris. Many apparently benign religious doctrines, it seems, have hidden costs.

Responsible people are mindful of these costs. Ideally, they consider them *before* they endorse the ideas. Of course, many are raised within a religion and grow attached to its teachings long before they get a chance to think these things through. They form a religious identity, and this makes fair-minded assessment hard. (Political and secular identities, of course, can also interfere with fair-minded belief assessment.)

Is it okay to celebrate the most enlightened teachings of a faith tradition, but not renounce its morally retrograde teachings? Calling the Bible sacred may serve to promote the humane insights conveyed in the Sermon on the Mount, but it also gives credence to passages that encourage blind, murderous faith (think Abraham and Isaac). There are biblical passages that celebrate genocide (the books of Deuteronomy, Joshua, and Samuel), condone slavery (Leviticus), and exhort believers to kill nonbelievers (Deuteronomy 13:6). Responsible Christians must have the courage to do with their religion what Thomas Jefferson did with his Bible: purge it of destructive teachings.

The same goes for followers of Islam. In 2014, Islamic jihadists carried out more than three hundred beheadings, many of them on camera. The slaughter targeted humanitarian aid workers, journalists, bloggers, secularists, and people suspected of modernist sympathies. Experts believe that the beheadings were inspired by a passage of the Koran that exhorts Muslims to "smite the necks (of) those who disbelieve." Islamic moderates don't explicitly endorse this passage, but many *do* teach their children to revere the Koran. Such instruction has foreseeable implications. Of course most believers won't smite necks. But predictably, some fraction will.

Facts like these underscore the need for ethical reformation of the world's religions. We need to examine the teachings of the world's great religions, and modify them as necessary. Who must do this? Well, the criticism of outsiders is seldom welcome; it tends to fall on deaf ears. Responsibility for religious reform, then, falls on the adherents of each faith.

If the world's faithful wish to claim the moral high ground, they must understand and apply the ethics of belief. They must do what is right and courageous: identify their tradition's inhumane teachings, speak out against them, and insist that they be purged from the canon. Indiscriminate acceptance of a religion's teachings is nothing but an abdication of moral responsibility.

I issue the same challenge to those who've fallen in with political ideologies: commit to believing responsibly. Only so can you strengthen your mind's immune system. Only so can you pride yourself on being part of the solution.

# CHAPTER 7

# Thought Police Need Not Apply

## How (not) to regulate belief

The danger to society is not merely that it should believe wrong things . . . but that it should lose the habit of testing things and inquiring into them. —*William Kingdon Clifford*

What's the best way to limit the influence of bad ideas? If bad ideas are mind-parasites that sometimes harden into belief, don't we need to *regulate belief*? But how do we do *that* without creating "thought police"? In immunology-speak: How do healthy cultural immune systems regulate the contents of minds, and how do we prevent such systems from abusing their regulatory power? In this chapter, I want to recover a pioneering work of cognitive immunology and mine it for answers to questions like these. The investigation reveals that healthy cognition is broadly *scientific* in character. In fact, we can "reverse-engineer" science and cast light on the nature of mental immune health. And in the process, pave the way for something revolutionary: a genuine *science* of right and wrong.

## Regulation Without Coercion

First, a simpler question: Should we seek to regulate belief at all? Some civil libertarians will be quick to answer no, but a wiser answer is: "It depends." For there are many ways to regulate belief, and not all of them are bad. Take critical thinking, for example: most fans of it are loath to speak of "regulating" belief, despite its doing just that. So we find ourselves in this curious place, where a cultural taboo prevents us from speaking openly about strategies of critical importance to humanity's future. We can't even frame the question properly.

This must change. In the world we've managed to build, cancerous ideologies proliferate, breeding factionalism, hatred, and misery. Yet still we cling to the illusion that, when it comes to belief, nearly anything goes. Our avoidance of the belief-regulation question ultimately backfires: it breeds cognitive chaos and invites authoritarian backlash.

Overregulation is a hazard, but underregulation carries dangers of its own. And right now, our collective allergy to belief-regulation talk is preventing us from having a grown-up conversation about how best to promote responsible believing. This leaves us largely powerless in the face of ideological pandemics.

It helps to consider the full range of regulatory mechanisms. Tyrants employ intimidation to regulate dissent, and yes, that's bad. But thermostats regulate temperature to afford comfort, and that's good. Heart valves regulate the flow of blood to keep us alive. (Also good, in my humble opinion.) Traffic lights regulate the movement of vehicles to prevent accidents. And notably, our immune systems regulate the microorganisms that inhabit our bodies. So it depends: What kind of regulation are we talking about?

We need to speak candidly about cognitive pest control—about different approaches to regulating the contents of minds. What makes some approaches better than others?

Here's the truth of it: we *already* regulate belief; we just do it poorly. In the system that prevails today, parents have carte blanche to indoctrinate their children, and young people are assigned religious or political identities early. These identities close minds and breed sectarian conflict. Much learning is rote, and questioning skills are largely neglected. Critical thinking is introduced relatively late in life and is rarely linked to identity options that sustain cognitive immune health. A few of us wind up in roles that help sustain critical habits of mind—scientist, investigative journalist, movie critic—but the rest of us embrace identities that are indifferent (or downright hostile) to critical thinking: lobbyist, sales executive, Scientologist, etc. Is it any surprise that critical thinking only rarely becomes a lifelong habit?

It gets worse. Teachers tell us to "think for yourself," inadvertently implying that solitary thinking is better than collaborative thinking. We're taught that values are a personal affair, to be chosen privately or settled by tribal affiliation. We're told that meaning and purpose rest on value commitments that are essentially arbitrary. Cheesy Hollywood movies advise us to "just believe." We emphasize cognitive rights, speak rarely of cognitive responsibilities, and bellyache endlessly about other people's critical thinking lapses. I call this the critical thinking paradigm, and frankly, it's failing us badly.

Should every attempt to promote responsible believing—even gentle questioning—be demonized as Orwellian? Clearly not. The question isn't *whether* we should regulate belief; the question is *how*. Until we make this shift, we'll struggle to achieve cognitive immune health.

Again, I'm not advocating state regulation. Thought police need not apply. It doesn't follow, though, that citizens shouldn't participate in belief regulation. Nor does it follow that governments have no role to play in strengthening cognitive immune systems. The expenditure of public funds on thinking instruction is good policy. (State support of cognitive immunology research is also a good idea; in the Internet Age, it's downright necessary.)

Some will worry that we teeter here atop a slippery slope. Fortunately, its surface is not that slippery. More precisely, a few distinctions make it much *less* slippery. For example, it's one thing to *suppress* speech and another to *criticize* it: the latter is not tantamount to the former. *Legal regulation* backed by the coercive power of the state is one thing, but *social self-regulation* via collaborative inquiry is another. It's one thing to centralize epistemic authority and regulate belief from the *top down* and another to arrange for a suitable *bottom-up* winnowing process. It's one thing to *tell* people *what* they must believe and another to *show* them *why* something is true. *Coercion* is one thing; *persuasion* is another. *Indoctrination* is not *teaching*. By bringing such distinctions on board, we essentially terrace the hillside and build an environment hospitable to healthy cognitive function.

We simply must undertake this terracing project. Why? Because mental immune systems don't function well on slippery slopes. To motivate the project, let's remind ourselves what lies at the foot of the grade. In George Orwell's *1984*, a government regulates belief in truly horrific ways. Its Ministry of Truth issues a steady stream of propaganda and rigidly censors the news. It generates alternative facts and revises history to suit its purposes. Language is controlled to prevent "thought crimes," privacy is a thing of the past, and real thinking is considered seditious. The state hunts down people who think for themselves and employs torture to prevent citizens from thinking responsibly. *1984* is a work of fiction, but the belief-regulation regime it imagines had real historical precedents. (It's said that Orwell had Stalinist Russia in mind.)

Long-lived religions employ different belief-regulation mechanisms. Ask yourself what the following have in common: the promise of heavenly reward (for believers) and threat of hellish torment (for doubters); the celebration of faith-based belief; the expectation of worshipful submission; the insistence that certain things are sacred (hence off-limits to certain kinds of questioning); stories—like that of Abraham and Isaac—that glorify blind obedience; the concepts of heretic, infidel, and apostate (all of them understood to be bad, and sometimes worthy of the cruelest punishments); the concepts of blasphemy and sacrilege (understood to be sins); papal infallibility, canonization, orthodoxy, excommunication, holy wars, inquisitions . . .

There's no escaping it: religions are complex belief-regulation systems—ways of syncing up people's beliefs. They tend to be top-down or authoritarian, and they tend to stabilize beliefs that would otherwise have a hard time persisting, given basic evidentiary norms. Religious affiliation can dramatically alter mental immune function.

Independent-minded people have always chafed at religious and political thought control. And so, every age has its heretics and iconoclasts, rebels and freethinkers. A few reflexively reject any attempt to regulate belief, but wiser heads acknowledge the need to regulate it in *some* fashion. Thus, Socrates developed his Socratic method. Plato recommended reason-giving dialogue about our deepest values. Enlightenment philosophers proposed that we develop the faculty of reason. Scientists urge us to test hypotheses. Academics advise us to think critically.

All these suggestions propose that we regulate belief with reasons. All of them understand that "faith" must not become a blank check for irresponsible believing. The contrast here is irresistible: on the one side, we have faith-based systems, which tend to be top-down, organized around a centralized epistemic authority, and reinforced by a prevailing expectation of loyal obedience. On the other, we have reason-based systems, which tend to be bottom-up, decentralized, and built around the expectation that everyone think for him- or herself. This contrast can orient our search for a better way to regulate belief—and illuminate the nature of cognitive immune health.

Note that belief regulation isn't just the province of totalitarians, orthodoxies, philosophers, and control freaks. Our default cognitive inclinations regulate belief in their own fashion: inhibiting some convictions and favoring others. The same is true of prevailing norms:

they regulate our cognitive states even if we never become consciously aware of them. (Indeed, they're especially influential when we're *un-aware* of them.) Think of all the ways parents, teachers, and friends shape our beliefs: with stories and arguments, instruction and humor, approval and disapproval, encouragements and admonitions, exams and grades, irony and satire. Recently, we've added some new belief-regulation strategies to the mix: political correctness norms, liberal guilt trips, Facebook "likes," Internet trolling, cyber-shaming, etc. These are belief regulation, too, though hardly systematic.

We invariably regulate belief in some fashion—by default if not by design. When you understand that societies *must* regulate belief, and begin looking at all the mechanisms they employ to promote belief alignment, it's truly eye-opening. Societies must, and invariably do, regulate belief. They can do this well, and afford their members peaceful and prosperous lives, or they can do this poorly, in ways that diminish everyone's prospects.

Already, we've encountered several distinctions that amount to principles of cognitive immunology. First, belief regulation needn't be top-down; it can be bottom-up. Second, it needn't be coercive; it can be persuasive. Third, it needn't involve laws and thought police (or orthodoxies and inquisitors); we can instead employ shared standards and friendly reminders. Fourth, belief regulation needn't involve others imposing unreasonable restraints on us; instead, it can be about *us* imposing reasonable restraints on *ourselves*. Understanding these differences is part of mental immune health.

But what does it really mean to be "reasonable"? To answer that, it helps to review a few facts about common sense.

## Common Sense by Design

The concept of common sense enshrines a cherished pretension: that we humans are sensible critters. Our biological designation—*Homo sapiens sapiens*—doubles down on this conceit, immodestly suggesting (twice!) that full-blown wisdom is our defining characteristic. The French satirist Voltaire, though, wasn't having it. "Common sense," he wrote in 1764, "is not so common." Were he alive today, and familiar with the research on cognitive biases, he might go further. For common sense isn't just uncommon: much of it doesn't even make sense.

Human belief-formation tendencies are decidedly suboptimal. Left to themselves, they mislead. We have biases and blind spots. We harbor prejudice and misconception. Our perception is distorted, our reasoning flawed, and our judgment questionable. We're prideful, cognitively inflexible, and prone to rationalize self-serving delusions. Put human cognition under the microscope, and—well, it's not a pretty picture.

Cognitive psychologists invent experiments to demonstrate our biases. Social psychologists examine the way tribal instincts distort our perception. Gestalt psychologists and sleight-of-hand magicians expose our blind spots. Evolutionary psychologists show that our minds are makeshift contraptions, cobbled together over eons to promote survival in ancestral environments. Economists even invented a new subdiscipline (behavioral economics) to get in on the fun.

This is important research, but so far, it's had at least one baleful effect. It's managed to convince many that we're hopelessly ideological. Sadly, many have concluded that there's no point striving for clear, impartial, honest, undistorted understanding. The thinking goes something like this: Why aim for fair-mindedness when it's not in the cards? Why fight for truth when "seems true to me" is the best we can hope for? Why strive for clarity when our window on the world is inherently clouded?

Such resignation is unwarranted. It rests on a fallacy. For a tendency can be "built in" without being uncorrectable. After all, nearsightedness is built in, but we remedy it with glasses. Legal systems employ rules of evidence to counteract various kinds of partiality.

Automobiles sport side mirrors to shrink a driver's blind spots. Ways of mitigating cognitive impairments abound.

It's important, then, that we *not* leave human belief-formation tendencies to themselves. Fortunately, the defects aren't random: they skew our thinking in predictable ways.[1] This allows us to devise methods and norms that correct for known distortions. In a world like ours, responsible believing doesn't just happen: it requires deliberate effort. The habits of mind that yield responsible belief don't come naturally; with practice, though, they can become *second* nature.

Voltaire had it right: common sense ain't common. With a little effort, though, we can make it much *more* common. To that end, I want to tell the tale of an infamous philosophical abduction—the theft of a remarkable precursor to cognitive immunology.

## Who Kidnapped Pragmatism?

Charles Sanders Peirce was arguably the most important philosopher of his time. Bertrand Russell called him "the greatest American thinker ever," and "one of the most original minds of the later nineteenth century." Peirce (pronounced "purse") is also an unrecognized pioneer in cognitive immunology, the victim of an unsolved crime, and the author of an epic feat of philosophical snark.

In the 1870s, Peirce launched an influential school of thought known as "pragmatism." Thirty years later, he was widely celebrated as its founder. Then in 1905, at the height of his celebrity, he did something astonishing: he renounced it. He "kissed his child good-bye" (his words) and let his followers have it. Literally: he bequeathed pragmatism to his disciples and washed his hands of it. Then he coined a more dysphonic term and declared himself not a pragmatist but a *pragmaticist*. (Note the added "ick.") The new term, he added grumpily, should prove "ugly enough to be safe from kidnappers."

Peirce chose his new label well: over a century later, "pragmaticism" has yet to catch on. To this day, he's history's only known pragmaticist. This is unfortunate, for Peircean pragmatism had much to recommend it. (Yes, I think it important to reappropriate the original label.) In fact, it has immune-boosting properties that could transform our world. But his brainchild was kidnapped and stripped of these properties. And his fundamentally immunological insights were lost. By solving this philosophical cold case, I hope to restore the lost promise of Peircean pragmatism.

Let's start with the crime itself, and ask: *Whodunnit?* Who kidnapped pragmatism? Peirce never identified the culprits directly. Instead, he made a vague reference to "the merciless way that words get abused . . . when they fall into literary clutches," then declined to elaborate. That remark threw investigators off the scent: the case went cold, and the perpetrators were never apprehended. A lost clue and a little detective work, though, reveal the identity of the kidnappers.

Here's the clue: in 1906, Peirce wrote that he began cultivating his pragmaticist alternative because "James and Schiller made the word [pragmatism] imply 'the will to believe.'" Both William James (yes, the same guy) and Ferdinand Schiller had embraced the pragmatist label and helped to build the movement. But Peirce had grave misgivings about their use of pragmatist ideas—particularly their endorsement of willful believing. He didn't want to appear ungrateful, but needed to distance himself from the philosophy the two men were peddling. His solution involved a cryptic reference to a philosophical kidnapping and a replacement name—"Pragmaticism"—that only a parent could love.

We need only connect the dots: Peirce felt his brainchild had been abducted and abused by two close friends.

But what exactly had James and Schiller done? Well, they robbed *pragmatism* of its power to strengthen mental immune systems. The backstory makes this clear: pragmatism, Peirce wrote, follows from the notion that beliefs have consequences. That is, the meaning of our ideas resides in their implications for practice. To assess an idea properly, then, we must clarify the "practical effects" of believing it, and decide whether it's really a good idea to produce such effects. When we conduct our thinking in this fashion, Peirce claimed, we become better problem solvers. I'll take it one step further: understanding Peirce's idea can boost your immunity to bad ideas.

Pragmatism represents a departure from traditional ideas about belief evaluation. Centuries earlier, an influential picture of reason had reinforced the impression that a belief's merits are purely a function of its *grounds*—the presence or absence of "upstream" reasons. By contrast, Peirce was insisting that a belief's "downstream" consequences—both inferential and causal—are also relevant to idea appraisal. Peirce was prototyping the view I defended in the last chapter, where both upstream evidence *and* downstream consequences matter.

James loved these ideas. He dedicated his 1897 book, *The Will to Believe*, to Peirce, and spent much of the ensuing decade promoting pragmatism. Together with Schiller, he helped turn pragmatism into an influential intellectual movement. But the two men also transformed pragmatism into something Peirce despised. James, for example, defined *truth* as "whatever proves . . . expedient in our way of thinking." He even applied this notion to religious belief, concluding, "On pragmatic principles, if the hypothesis of God works . . . then it is 'true.'"

Peirce had to be dismayed by these developments. For one thing, he had a very different understanding of truth. For another, he saw that Jamesian principles could be used to rationalize beliefs that are *personally expedient* but *collectively damaging* (as Clifford's shipowner did). He grasped that these principles yield a cultural ethos that is entirely too individualistic and permissive. He shared Clifford's conviction that belief is a public trust and saw that James had bent pragmatism into a defense of willful believing. Peirce wanted no part of it.

Scholars usually present Peirce and James as kindred intellectual spirits. In truth, though, their philosophies were worlds apart. Peirce was urging us to subject beliefs to both traditional epistemic testing *and* pragmatic how-well-do-these-beliefs-serve-us testing. The idea was to do *both*, thereby making idea appraisal *more* rigorous. By contrast, James implies that we can substitute the latter for the former—a suggestion that would make idea assessment *less* rigorous. Also, Jamesian principles imply that, if a belief works for you, then it's true for you. Peirce, though, understood that you can't relativize truth in this way—not without subverting collaborative inquiry. He grasped that selfish and unaccountable believing plants the seeds of ideology and breeds irreconcilable differences. James appears not to have grasped these things.

Peirce recommends scruples profoundly at odds with the faith-based believing James sought to defend. Cognitive immunology allows us to pinpoint the difference: Peirce wanted to *strengthen* mental and cultural immune systems, and James and Schiller were *weakening* them.

In the public eye, pragmatism had become firmly linked with the Jamesian "will to believe." So what did Peirce do? He kissed his child goodbye and quietly filed for philosophical divorce. Peirce, though, was on the right track all along. His snarky kidnapping allegation invites us to reclaim the lost promise of his pragmatism.

## A Curious Juxtaposition

The question "What should we believe?" had been around for thousands of years. Then, just a century and a half ago, C. S. Peirce replaced it with a better question, namely: "By what *method* should we fix our beliefs?" With this, Peirce invites us to think together about what it means to regulate belief in a responsible fashion. His classic essay on the subject can orient our search for an answer. He called it "The Fixation of Belief."

In it, Peirce has us consider four "methods" of belief fixation. He calls them the "method of tenacity," the "method of authority," the "a priori method," and the "scientific method." Which, he asks, is the best approach? It's a strange assortment of options. The method of tenacity involves clinging stubbornly to the beliefs you have. The method of authority involves obedient acceptance of prescribed doctrines. The a priori method is about conversing awhile, then letting folks believe what they like. The scientific method involves testing hypotheses against reality and discarding those that fail.

The crux of Peirce's argument is that the first three methods all have serious drawbacks. They fail to meet basic design requirements. Each leads to cognitive and social dysfunction. We're left to infer that the scientific method is the way to go.

Right off the bat, we need to acknowledge a glaring problem with the argument. On the surface, it's what logicians call an "elimination" argument: rule out all but one, and you're left with the one that remains. The problem is that such arguments work only if you start with a complete set of options. And Peirce's set is anything but complete. He doesn't consider variants of the basic four, hybrid methods, or any of several everyday alternatives. His list is idiosyncratic and far from exhaustive—a lousy foundation, in other words, for an elimination argument. Moreover, Peirce dismisses two of the four by erecting crude caricatures and knocking them down. Logicians call this the "straw man" fallacy and stress that fair-minded people don't argue in this fashion.

In other words, the surface logic of Peirce's argument is a mess. A superb logician, Peirce had to understand this. Logicians of his caliber don't overlook such flaws. So what's really going on in "The Fixation of Belief"? Why would a certifiable genius build his signature contribution to epistemology around two glaring fallacies?

The answer is that "Fixation" is better understood as an exercise in applied cognitive immunology. It's an attempt to mitigate some decidedly dysfunctional tendencies of mind. Here's how it works: Peirce takes a known tendency of human thought and amplifies it to the point of absurdity. He declares the result a "method" and asks us to imagine taking that method seriously. In each case, the thought experiment yields a comical or tragic outcome. It's brilliant philosophical satire: a memorable send-up of key mental vulnerabilities. In each case, the exercise leaves us with a heightened awareness of a cognitive vice, and a desire to embody the corresponding virtue. It's a beautiful example of *cognitive immunotherapy*.

"The Fixation of Belief" is more parable than proof. It's a cartoon version of cultural history, and packed with insights about how to improve mental immune health. It deepens our understanding of responsible belief, sheds light on our ideology-riven time, and clarifies why science works. For all these reasons, it merits a closer look.

## Genealogy of Science

Peirce starts with the fact that we tend to find doubt irritating. The simplest way to remove the irritant, he says, is to pick an answer we like, reinforce it again and again, and dismiss any information that might disturb it. This simple method, Peirce claims, "is really pursued by many men." Today, psychologists would call this "method" a mash-up of four cognitive biases: *confirmation bias*, *motivated reasoning*, *belief persistence*, and *the sunk cost fallacy*.

This is Peirce's *method of tenacity*. It's an extreme version of what I have called "the way of belief"—the tendency to find beliefs that work for you, then stick with them. To caricature the tendency, Peirce portrays the initial adoption as rationally arbitrary, and the subsequent allegiance as absurdly inflexible. He thereby satirizes arbitrary and closed-minded believing. The extremity of Peirce's portrayal, though, makes it hard for real people to see themselves in it. This limits the concept's diagnostic power. And frankly, "method" is something of a misnomer. Stubborn tenacity vis-à-vis belief is a real thing, but it's more reflexive tendency than reflective procedure. For these reasons, "the way of belief" is a more apt designation.

After acknowledging the method's advantages—it flatters our vanity and confers at least temporary "peace of mind"—Peirce invites us to notice the drawbacks. Imagine an ostrich burying its head in the sand to cope with the anxiety caused by an approaching predator. The strategy might ease its mind, but the victory and the ostrich are likely to be short-lived. We're left to draw the obvious conclusion: you can ignore evidence for a time, but eventually reality will catch up with you.

Cognitive tenacity, Peirce observes, is also bound to create problems for a social animal. To live together, we need to partially reconcile our outlooks, and this requires a degree of cognitive flexibility. Any minimally social being will discover that closed-mindedness breeds unnecessary conflict. The method of tenacity, in other words, fails to generate enough common understanding. Its arbitrary nature, its inflexibility, and its failure to play nice with others all sow dysfunction. The same is true of the milder *way of belief*: it can buy you short-term peace of mind, but you invariably pay a price in shared understanding foregone.

Peirce imagines trying to fix the tenacity method's most glaring defect. The question, he writes, becomes "how to fix belief, not in the individual . . . but in the community." He saw that, long ago, natural selection had ginned up a partial solution: we evolved a certain deference to authority. That's why we find ourselves with a pronounced tendency to conform and obey, not just in our behavior but also in our thinking. Presumably, this tendency helped to knit our ancestors into tight collectives. But it, too, has hidden costs.

For example, religious and political institutions arise that exploit our penchant for obedience. They "keep correct doctrines before the attention of the people, reiterate them perpetually (and suppress) contrary doctrines." They demand our loyalty and celebrate faith, thereby amplifying the native tendency. Institutions work to "keep people ignorant, lest they learn of some reason" to think heretical thoughts. Often, they terrify dissenters into silence. With their backing, false and dysfunctional doctrines can gain a stable cultural niche. And sometimes persist for millennia.

Peirce calls this the "method of authority," but again, we need a better term for the underlying phenomenon. For there's nothing methodical in it; it's more unconscious tendency than conscious process. Also, from the standpoint of the believer, it's about loyalty, not authority. For these reasons, I prefer to call it "the way of loyalty." Peirce's method of authority is ultimately a cartoon depiction of the human tendency to submit and obey. With this, he anticipated a central insight of modern social psychology: our belief systems are warped by tribal allegiance.

If the mascot of the tenacity method is the head-burying ostrich, the mascot of the authority method is the obedient sheep. Sheep follow shepherds and are led to slaughter. According to Peirce, most people want nothing more than to be led in this fashion.

Loyalty-based systems of belief can persist for ages, but eventually, reflection destabilizes them. We encounter other loyalty-based systems and wonder whether it's a mere accident that we believe as we do. We begin to wonder whether our cognitive allegiances are arbitrary, and any better than the alternatives. A "wider sort of social feeling" stirs, and people grasp that obedience to arbitrary doctrines is a recipe for tribal conflict. Attitudes become more ecumenical and planetary. People realize that "willful adherence to a belief, and the arbitrary forcing of it upon others, must . . . both be given up."

Take a moment to process this last claim. In it, Peirce rejects "arbitrary" belief. He also rejects "forcing [beliefs] upon others." So coercion is also out. This much is now widely accepted. But Peirce also says that we must "give up . . . willful adherence to . . . belief." He seems to think we must outgrow such willfulness, much as we outgrow the willful obstinacy of adolescence. Unfortunately, this insight has yet to gain currency. A century and a half later, our species remains mired in its cognitive adolescence: willful belief remains rampant, and cognitive immune systems operate at a fraction of their potential.

What's the alternative, though, to willful believing? Presumably, belief based on a certain kind of submission. But submission to what? What nonarbitrary something *deserves* such submission? Peirce's answer, in a word, is *reality*. I'll examine this answer in a minute. In the meantime, notice that Peirce's insight about willful belief was utterly lost on William James. James didn't just co-opt Peirce's philosophical brand, he twisted the underlying philosophy into a defense of the very thing—willful believing—that Peirce felt we needed to "give up"! James didn't just kidnap Peirce's brainchild, he turned it against him.

Back to Peirce's parable: the terrible cruelties of the method of authority eventually creates a backlash. People awaken to the fact that "a new method of settling opinions must be adopted" and instinctively reach for a more permissive ethic. This very thing occurred in the eighteenth century: one hundred years of religious persecution left Europeans disgusted with top-down, authority-based believing, and Enlightenment philosophers were able to advocate successfully for bottom-up, reason-based believing. Peirce channels the spirit that animated Parisian salons during this time of intellectual ferment: "Let the action of natural preferences be unimpeded then, and under their influence let men, conversing together and regarding matters in different lights, gradually develop beliefs in harmony with natural causes." The method of authority wanes, and the a priori method rises to take its place.

Note several features of this new method. First, it's fundamentally permissive: we're expected to "let" people believe what they want. More precisely, we're expected to let the marketplace of ideas sort things out. A kind of implicit faith is at work here: the invisible hand of the ideas market can be counted on to work a beneficent magic: the best ideas will invariably survive, and all will be well. The a priori method, then, is fundamentally laissez-faire.

Under the aegis of the a priori method, liberality about belief becomes a kind of gospel, and interfering with the beliefs of others becomes taboo. Freedom of conscience is exalted, ideational diversity is celebrated, and in principle at least, a thousand intellectual flowers bloom. That's the utopian vision; in reality, ideas still compete for mindshare, just as plants compete for sunlight. Also, the permissive ethos encourages people to stop weeding their mental gardens. It's as if you had a big ideas festival but told your mind's security team to stop screening the participants. The a priori method all but turns off the mind's immune system.

In Peirce's parable, though, the zeitgeist hasn't completely forgotten the lessons of the failed tenacity and authority experiments. With this, he captures a key aspect of cultural history: there's a residual awareness that arbitrary believing isn't quite kosher, that closed-mindedness is problematic, and that our beliefs need to be at least somewhat aligned. Some sort of accountability is needed. That's where the "conversing together and regarding matters in different lights" comes in: the new ethos encompasses a loose expectation of conversational review. Basically, we're expected to take account of the beliefs and feelings of others: to dialogue and adjust our beliefs when it feels like the right thing to do.

Imagine a bunch of philosophers congregating in a Parisian café and enjoying the spirited interplay of diverse opinions. Now imagine the philosophers returning to their respective flats, believing what it pleases them to believe. *That's* the a priori method. On this system, everyone is entitled to their opinion, so no one can tell anyone else what to believe. No one wants to be perceived as reverting to old, authoritarian attitudes, so when real cognitive obligations surface, we downplay them, or treat them as mere suggestions. Timid liberality reigns. The best lack all conviction.

This should sound familiar. It's the system of norms that prevails today. Peirce has revealed the deep logic that created our contemporary cultural ethos.

Peirce claims that this combination of forces yields a system of accountability like that which prevails in "metaphysical philosophy."

Beliefs, he says, are not expected to "rest on any observed facts." Instead, they're adopted because they seem "agreeable to reason." He's alluding here to a long tradition of armchair philosophizing: a process of questioning and introspection that is little constrained by observation. When Peirce talks about the a priori method, he has in mind the way armchair philosophers do business. This suggests a more apt and evocative designation: "the way of the armchair philosopher." Let this "way" join the way of belief and the way of loyalty, then, and let the armchair philosopher join the ostrich and sheep as official mascots.

For those with little experience of armchair philosophers, I offer this handy guide: they ask lots of questions, introspect for answers, and rely heavily on intuition. Simply put, such thinkers test their beliefs against "internal" criteria but seldom test them against "external" reality. (Sometimes, they'll test their beliefs against another person's beliefs, in what we might call the "two armchairs" or "multiple armchairs" method.)

The a priori method is meant to deliver us from "accidental and capricious" believing, but it turns out to be under-constrained. Armchair philosophizing can help make your belief system more coherent, but inattention to actual evidence allows it to diverge from reality. As a result, metaphysical systems go in and out of fashion but never really resolve. (In a cultural ethos dominated by the a priori method, cognitive fads come and go, but we suffer an absence of deep, well-grounded conviction. In a desperate attempt to secure a sense of purpose, many revert to authority-backed doctrines and tenaciously held articles of faith. It seems our culture is substantially shaped by this a priori ethic and its discontents.)

Like its predecessors, the a priori method allows beliefs to be determined by "accidental" causes. As awareness of this defect spreads, some search for a method "by which our beliefs may be determined by nothing human, but by some external permanency." In a word, by something *objective*. This leads to science.

The external permanency we need, Peirce writes, cannot "influence (only) one individual; it must be something which affects, or might affect, every man." Why? Because "the method must be such that the ultimate conclusion of every man shall be the same." A well-designed belief-fixation method, in other words, cannot rely on private revelations, for that would lead to delusion and dissensus. Instead, it should ground its conclusions in empirically verifiable facts.

Distilled to a paragraph, then, here's Peirce's story: The search for an adequate belief-fixation method proceeds through stages. We experiment with tenacity but find that it isolates us. We experiment with blind loyalty but find that it leads to factionalism and tyranny. We try out armchair philosophizing but find that it fails to deliver us from arbitrary and capricious believing. Eventually, humanity hits on science: the one approach that's resolutely committed to responsible, reality-based cognition, and the only one courageous enough to submit to thoroughly "external" accountability standards. Science is thus the only truly civic-minded option: the only one of the four that embodies a truly grown-up approach to resolving cognitive conflicts.

Peirce's "Fixation of Belief" isn't really an argument at all. It's an allegory: a capsule history of humanity's struggle to regulate belief properly. It's also a genealogy, or origins story: one that sheds light on the design wisdom built into science.

## Science Reverse-Engineered

Peirce's parable encodes four important truths. First, a well-functioning belief-fixation method can't be arbitrary. Second, it can't be closed-minded. Third, it must align beliefs without employing coercion. Finally, it must be empirically constrained. Science, Peirce implies, is just such a method.

Science is resolutely nonarbitrary, open-minded, belief-aligning, nonauthoritarian, and empirically constrained. It has these qualities not by accident but by design. And arguably, it is these very qualities

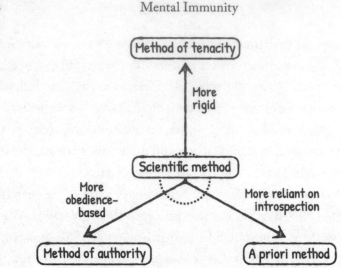

**C.S. Peirce's Four "Methods" of Belief-Fixation**

that make it successful. If this is right, Peirce has accomplished something extraordinary: he's essentially *reverse-engineered the scientific method*. He's revealed the wisdom *behind* the scientific approach to regulating belief. This is brilliant cognitive immunology. It yields the kind of insights that can strengthen mental and cultural immune systems.

Why are there many competing religions but only one science?[2] Because science hitches its wagon to reality, which is unitary. Why do scientists have such a marvelous track record of resolving their differences without resorting to violence? Because they submit their hypotheses and beliefs to the tribunal of evidence. They have shared standards and, for the most part, submit to them.

Science as an institution, of course, has embarrassing lapses. Recently, a shocking percentage of social science studies were found not to be reproducible.[3] But this doesn't diminish my point in the least: we know of such lapses because, time and again, scientists recommit to the ideal of responsible cognition and retest their conclusions.

If you think about it, a scientist's commitment to evidence-based believing involves a kind of submission—a relinquishing of the will to believe. On the account developed here, the accuracy of our factual beliefs, the groundedness of our moral beliefs, even our sense of meaning and purpose—*all of these things* hinge on our willingness to submit not to a deity but to evidence. Talk of faith is sometimes meant to engender an attitude of humble submission, but evidence enthusiasts practice a humble submission of their own—to reality.

The beauty of Peircean pragmatism is that it allows us to extend the scientific method beyond issues of empirical fact. We can test ideas about right and wrong by, among other things, working out their *downstream* pragmatic implications and observing whether they promote flourishing. Take the claim "Society should invest in family planning services." Assessing this claim involves looking at how such services impact teen pregnancy rates, divorce rates, crime rates, the spread of STDs, etc. Such hypothesis-testing is quasi-scientific and consistent with Peirce's conception of science. In effect, Peirce is recommending that we apply critical hypothesis-testing in domains not yet colonized by science.

The method of tenacity generalizes to the way of belief. The method of authority generalizes to the way of loyalty. The a priori method generalizes to the way of the armchair philosopher. In like manner, the scientific method generalizes to the way of inquiry.

Real science, on this conception, is not a grudging encounter with a cold, uncaring reality. It's an attitude fueled by wonder, one that strives for ecstatic but responsible communion with the real. (This attitude is beautifully exemplified in the writings of Carl Sagan.) The scientific attitude involves a kind of humble submission, and by design, it facilitates the noncoercive convergence of belief. If this analysis is right, the general form of science—the way of inquiry—holds the key to building responsible, shared understanding of what *matters* as well as understanding of what *is*. Science—taken now in the broad, Peircean sense—represents nothing less than the path to collective salvation.

## The Politics of Belief

Imagine Peirce's method of tenacity becoming the norm. In this scenario, a large majority adopts the practice of believing whatever strikes their fancy and firmly closing their mind to anything that might disturb such beliefs. What would such a world be like?

The thought experiment is reminiscent of one Thomas Hobbes ran in *Leviathan*. There, Hobbes invited us to imagine a primal condition where selfishness and an utter lack of restraining norms preclude human cooperation. He called this condition "the state of nature" and envisioned it breeding ruthless competition and mutual exploitation. The result, he says, is an anarchic "war of all against all." Such an arrangement, Hobbes wrote, can only afford lives that are "solitary, poor, nasty, brutish, and short."

A belief-fixation regime governed by the method of tenacity would be comparably anarchic. Belief formation would be capricious, and belief maintenance tenacious. Closed-mindedness would prevent reconciliation. Discursive conflict resolution would prove fruitless, and coercion would be commonplace. The simple pleasures of conversation and dialogue would be unknown. Shared outlooks would prove difficult to forge. Manipulative signaling and mutual suspicion would be the rule, precluding trust and much cooperation. Science, technology, and medicine would wither. Our lives would be solitary, poor, nasty, brutish, and ignorant.

In both political and epistemic matters, stubborn individualism makes for anarchy and dysfunction. In fact, epistemic anarchy can pave the way for political anarchy, with tragic consequences. It behooves us, then, to shun the method of tenacity. And avoid its milder cousin, the way of belief.

Now imagine Peirce's *method of authority* becoming the norm. Everyone is expected to loyally believe whatever the chosen religious or political authorities prescribe. Orthodoxies are upheld, and heretical thoughts are condemned. Intellectual freedoms disappear, and dissent is expunged. Such a condition needn't be imagined, for real-world examples abound. Europe's Dark Ages, under the authority of the Catholic Church, provides a salient case. Not surprisingly, it bred a world of ignorance, superstition, violence, and disease. The concept of epistemic authoritarianism, then, picks out a real, honest-to-God phenomenon. In fact, authoritarian political systems invariably find it necessary to regulate belief the way they regulate behavior: aggressively and from the top down.

Now imagine the widespread adoption of Peirce's a priori method. Suppose, that is, that a fundamentally laissez-faire attitude came to prevail vis-à-vis belief. Inward reflection, conversational idea-testing, and heavy reliance on intuition all become pervasive. In a world like this, people ransack their intuitions but never arrive at truly lasting answers. They talk in circles, can't resolve their differences, yet can't be coaxed out of their armchairs. Intellectual fads come and go, and a restless rootlessness prevails. "The meaning of life" becomes a persistent and intractable problem, and people worry it like a loose tooth.

In recent decades, something very like this has become a global phenomenon. First, the right to believe became a kind of orthodoxy: everyone is expected to let others believe what they like. Articles of faith must be respected. Tolerance of ideological diversity is considered mandatory, even when it protects profoundly damaging ideas. The act of challenging another's cherished convictions comes to be viewed as transgressive or at the very least, bad form. Meanwhile, people connect via the Internet and accept things that *feel* reasonable. Far removed from direct evidence, we grow reliant—in fact, overly reliant—on hearsay and intuition. What happens then? Conspiracy theories gain a following. Kooky ideas spread. Propagandists thrive. Fake news becomes profitable. Alternative facts get invented. Memes spread like epidemics. Mental parasites flourish. Ideologies metastasize.

Peirce's a priori method has gone mainstream—with rocket boosters. Houston, we have a problem.

From our current standpoint within the a priori paradigm, though, the very idea of belief regulation appears anathema. It threatens to bring back an authoritarian regime and consequently feels Orwellian. It feels like a step in the wrong direction. The a priori method, though, regulates belief in its own fashion: not aggressively, perhaps, but by letting de facto belief-formation tendencies run roughshod over things we care about.

Philosophers have long observed that unfettered desire leads to a kind of slavery: enslavement, if you will, to the passions. (Addiction is a prime example.) But the same is true of unfettered *belief*: ungoverned by reason, beliefs, too, lead to a kind of enslavement. We're talking here about enslavement to de facto beliefs—or, more precisely, to whatever belief-formation tendencies happen to prevail. This might not seem so bad, until you examine the matter closely. The loss of autonomy is real. And consequential.

The a priori method is similar to a libertarian regime. And just as libertarian politics gives free rein to exploitative agents, a libertarian ethos gives free rein to exploitative memes. In the former, corporations exploit vulnerable workers; in the latter, ideologies exploit vulnerable minds. In both cases, a laissez-faire ideology prevents us from designing well-functioning markets.

Peirce's scientific method is akin to democracy. It's decentralized, distributing epistemic authority the way democracy distributes political authority. (Ideally, of course, it pushes authority all the way out, beyond the subjective inclinations of inquirers, to the objective evidence they possess.) It crowdsources the search for truth, just as democracies crowdsource their search for leaders. Science starts with evidence and builds the system of knowledge from the ground up; democracy starts with the consent of the governed and builds political legitimacy from the ground up. Science treats us as grown-ups, capable of thinking for ourselves, just as democracy treats us as grown-ups, capable of governing ourselves. Science asks us to submit to the force of the better reason, just as democracy asks us to submit to the will of the majority.

Science, though, is not a purely democratic enterprise. It has a meritocratic element too. Training is required, and competence must be demonstrated. Credentials must be earned, and expertise carries clout. Ideas gain a platform by surviving peer review, and incoherent voices are ignored. In this regard, our political discourse could learn a thing or two from scientific discourse.

Belief regulation by means of science also has a quasi-*socialist* aspect. Socialism is based on the realization that, left to themselves, economic and political systems get warped by greed and become exploitative. Science is based on a comparable realization: left to themselves, belief systems get warped by seductive ideas, then come unhinged. Socialism employs regulations to prevent the few from exploiting the many, and science employs evidentiary norms to keep bad ideas from exploiting vulnerable minds.

The way of belief promotes epistemic anarchy. The way of loyalty breeds epistemic authoritarianism. The way of the armchair philosopher yields epistemic libertarianism. The way of inquiry, though, makes for an ethos that is basically democratic and socialist. It seems the parallels between political and epistemic systems run deep.

Plato argued that we can gain a better understanding of the well-ordered mind by thinking about the well-ordered city. A similar strategy yields a richer understanding of mental immune health. It turns out that healthy minds *do* regulate belief, but not with tenacity, authority, or overreliance on subjective criteria. They do it with questions, a collaborative spirit, and a thirst for reliable evidence—in a mix that approximates the sort of hypothesis-testing scientists go in for. Albert Einstein wrote that "the whole of science is nothing more than a refinement of everyday thinking." He was right: we can all learn to think like scientists. The trick is to gain clarity about how reasons work.

How *do* reasons work? What are they, and how does a well-ordered mind wield them? By taking up these questions, we illuminate the workings of the mind's immune system—and uncover the insidious way that ideologies subvert thinking.

# PART III

# Antibodies and System Failures

Man is a rational animal who always loses his temper when called upon to act in accordance with the dictates of reason.

—Oscar Wilde

# CHAPTER 8

# Reason's Fulcrum

*The peculiar magic of reasons*

When the facts change, I change my mind.
What do you do, sir? —*John Maynard Keynes*

In 1882, a Russian atheist stabbed a perfectly innocent starfish larva. He did it in broad daylight and issued no apology. He was not apprehended. Later, investigators identified the assailant, the murder weapon, and the crime scene. The culprit turned out to be a zoologist named Ilya Mechnikov. His weapon was a thorn taken from a nearby tangerine tree. The assault occurred on a microscope slide in an Italian laboratory. Because he reported himself, we know the truth: All along, it was *Professor Mechnikov* with a *citrus thorn* in the *laboratory*. The other suspect—Miss Scarlet—was released when her alibi checked out.

Incidentally, the experiment happened in Sicily, not far from Clifford's shipwreck. (Only a dozen years and a few miles separated the two events.) The starfish never pressed charges, and Mechnikov walked.

Through the lens of his microscope, Mechnikov witnessed an astounding phenomenon. He watched as the larva's white blood cells swarmed to the open wound and surrounded the intruding thorn. He hypothesized what later turned out to be true: the white cells were attacking and destroying infectious microbes. Mechnikov was the first person to observe the immune system in action. Stronger microscopes would reveal white blood cells engulfing and consuming other invading pathogens. They turn out to be a kind of mobile army: microbial shock troops charged with protecting the body's homeland. Today, we call such agents "antibodies." Biologists need a more technical term, so they also classify them as "phagocytes." ("Phage" comes from a Greek word meaning "thing that devours.") Mechnikov was later awarded a Nobel Prize for his discovery of "phagocytosis"—the immune system's process of identifying and devouring dangerous invaders.

Next time you encounter particularly disturbing information—an argument, say, that threatens your religious or political beliefs—pay close attention to what happens in your mind. Examine your thoughts as if you were a scientist peering through a microscope: with care, curiosity, but no moralistic judgment. What do you see? Here's what I often see: doubts and objections swarming to the scene and attacking the offending information. Some challenge the information's veracity. Others probe the reliability of its source. Still others try to work out whether the information can be accommodated without disturbing beliefs I'm fond of.

I trust you're familiar with this phenomenon. If so, you'll see its similarity to phagocytosis. This raises some obvious questions: Is the swarming of objections some kind of immune reaction? Are reasons and objections cognitive antibodies? Are they trying to fight off what they take to be information pathogens? Are they the mind's shock troops? Do they sometimes get confused and give bad ideas a pass? Or attack good ideas by accident? The answer to all these questions, it turns out, is yes.

To really understand the mind's immune system, though, we need to put reasons under the microscope. We need to do this without defensiveness or moralistic judgment and see if we can answer some foundational questions. Questions like: How do reasons work? Why do they so often fail to work properly? And: Why do they sometimes attack good ideas—and rush to the defense of bad ones?

## Lake Wobegon and the Surprising Nature of Reasons

For forty years, fans of Garrison Keillor's popular radio show *A Prairie Home Companion* were treated to weekly updates from Lake Wobegon, a fictional Minnesota town where "the women are strong, the men are good looking, and all the children are above average." Keillor's humor pointed to a fascinating psychological phenomenon, and happiness researcher David Myers coined a phrase for it: "Lake Wobegon effect" now refers to the human need to feel above average. (Psychologists also call it "illusory superiority.") In one study, ninety percent of surveyed faculty rated their teaching as above average. In another, 98 percent of high school students rated themselves at or above average in leadership ability.[1] Ninety-eight percent! That's a huge effect. It's rumored that the remaining 2 percent of high schoolers consoled themselves with thoughts of their analytical geometry skills, which were—you guessed it—well above average.

Keillor wasn't the first to recognize the Lake Wobegon effect. Centuries earlier, the irascible English philosopher Thomas Hobbes made a similar observation about the human need to feel wise. In *Leviathan*, he wrote, "Such is the nature of men: they will hardly believe that there be many so wise as themselves." He then added, with wry wit, that: "This proveth . . . that men are in that point equal (rather) than unequal . . . for there is not ordinarily a greater sign of the equal distribution of anything, than that every man is contented with his share." It's a clever argument, but Hobbes's sarcasm is palpable: if a nearly universal conceit allows you to "prove" equal wisdom, then so much the worse for the conceit. (Hobbes was no egalitarian, and he certainly didn't believe that wisdom is equally distributed.)

His real message would have cheered Socrates: it's unwise to rest content with one's share of wisdom.

Our perceptions of *reasonableness* are similarly skewed. As C. S. Peirce put the point: "Few people care to study logic, because everybody conceives himself to be proficient enough in the art of reasoning already." Peirce detected a double standard in this vanity: "But I observe that this satisfaction is limited to one's own [reasoning], and does not extend to that of other men." Nowadays, we just call for more critical thinking instruction—not for ourselves but for others.

And so, we find ourselves in a world full of unreason, little to none of it of our own making. It's an illusion, of course—one that spawns all kinds of mischief—yet it persists. It persists because we lack an objective measure of reason's requirements. In fact, we lack even a clear understanding of what a reason is. These deficiencies compromise mental and cultural immune systems. But what if we developed such understanding and used it to temper our cognitive conceits? Perhaps then we could become wiser versions of ourselves— less prone to mind infections.

So play along, if you will, with this pop quiz: Which of the following is a reason?

1. Carbon in the atmosphere is trapping heat, causing sea levels to rise.
2. Abortion ends a life.
3. They're gross! (said of overcooked green beans)
4. We're almost out of milk.
5. A low-pressure system is moving in.
6. Because I said so.
7. (A pointing gesture, directed at some salient phenomenon.)

Most people are pretty sure that numbers 1 and 2 count as reasons. Many have doubts, though, about the rest. I'd argue that all of them—and none of them—are reasons. More precisely, none of them is a reason in isolation. Something counts as a reason only if it functions, or might well function, in a certain capacity.

Almost any piece of information can be a reason, given suitable background conditions. For example, imagine someone answering the question "Should I stop at the store?" with "Well, we're out of milk. . . ." The reply provides a good reason to stop at the store—assuming, of course, that running out of milk is understood to be a bad thing. Similarly, "A low pressure system is moving in" is generally a good reason to pack an umbrella. As for "Because I said so," it may be a lousy reason to eat overcooked green beans, but still, it *is* a reason. Of an admittedly authoritarian sort, but a reason nonetheless.

As for the pointing gesture, imagine a hunting party tracking wild boar and reaching an impasse about which way to go. Suppose half the party wants to continue down the river, while the other half thinks the trail has gone cold and wants to cross the ridge. Suppose the party needs to remain together, so progress is temporarily stymied. Then one of the hunters discovers a telltale hoofprint in the mud down by the river. She calls out, gestures to it, and everyone examines what is clearly the trace of wild boar. This resolves the matter, and the group renews its pursuit downriver.

In this scenario, the gesture functions as a reason to hunt downriver. It does this by drawing attention to a salient fact. Is this importantly different from using a sentence, or other verbal indicator, to draw attention to a salient fact? Hardly. The gesture is, for all practical purposes, a reason, and its role in the tribe's decision-making is what makes it so.

Note that a behavior needn't be linguistic to function as, and thereby be, a reason. Sometimes, a simple gesture communicates a reason. Indeed, the mere *fact* that a low-pressure system is moving in constitutes a reason to pack an umbrella, whether or not anyone formulates the corresponding thought. (The philosopher Daniel Dennett calls such reasons "free-floating rationales.")

Conversely, deprive any of numbers 1 through 7 of a suitable context, and its claim to be a reason evaporates. Take number 1: "Carbon in the atmosphere is trapping heat, causing sea levels to rise." In our context, this provides a good reason to reduce our use of fossil fuels. Now imagine this claim appearing not in a debate about climate change but in a routine inventory of global trends. Suppose this inventory is filed by a bored, inattentive functionary left behind by a conquering race of space aliens. Suppose further that humanity is extinct, the list is computer generated, and the fact is promptly relegated to an obsolete database that no one ever consults. Are you still inclined to call it a reason? An *actual* reason, as opposed to a merely *potential* one? If so, mightn't your criteria be a bit indiscriminate?

It seems "reason" is not a natural kind. It's a functional designation: a way of referring to something's *being available for premising*. Put differently, certain facts, ideas, and claims afford a special kind of opportunity, and it's precisely the property of affording such opportunities that makes them reasons. A reason, then, is a possibility-dependent kind of thing. Like football players, words, and money, reasons depend on human practices to be what they are. In this respect, reasons are quite unlike, say, giant squids and asteroids, which are what they are independent of us. Some things can be what they are only because they're embedded in certain practices. And clearly, reasons are of this sort.

This simple fact has far-reaching implications for logic, the science of mental immunity, and the art of thinking. Regarding the first: formal logic can give one an uncanny sense that the so-called space of reasons is some timeless, mind-independent realm. Plato studied the matter and reached precisely that conclusion, and since then, countless logicians have experienced their subject as describing an intelligible but fundamentally mind-independent reality. Logic writ large, though, is about the proper functioning of reasons, and the assessment of a reason's functioning often requires a nuanced appreciation of its concrete purpose or intended role. Add the fact that a reason's usefulness for drawing inferences is highly practice-dependent, and the space of reasons appears quite different.

If logicians wish to understand this space in all its messy, gory glory, they must ask questions like these: Do an argument's premises really afford what they purport to afford? Do they do what the arguer *means* for them to do? Does the argument pretend to show that its conclusion *must* be accepted under *all* circumstances? Or does it mean to show only that it *may* be accepted under *some* circumstances? Are the reasons given meant to *entitle* the reason-giver to the conclusion, or *commit us all* to the conclusion? Or is the argument just meant to rule out certain possibilities? Is it supposed to settle the matter once and for all, or just shade our perception of the likelihoods? Often, the sentences that make up the argument are silent on these matters, and we must look to the larger context to sort things out. There is more to logic than is dreamt of in many philosophies.

Our concept of what reasons fundamentally *are* does more than set an agenda for logic. It also shapes our cognitive dealings in ways both large and subtle. Developing our concept of a reason, it turns out, can pave the way for more capable practice. No, we're not "proficient enough in the art of reasoning already." We can better understand how reasons work and gain insight into why they so often *fail* to work. We can learn to troubleshoot our dysfunctional reason-giving practices, and in this way strengthen mental and cultural immune systems.

## Planet of the Mind-Writing Apes

We've seen that reasons afford possibilities. But what sort of possibility is it that reasons afford? What are they *for*? What sort of functional role must they play—or potentially play—to truly *be* reasons? What is it, exactly, that reasons *do*?

Philosophers often rely on the notion of "support" to answer these questions. The idea is that reasons support conclusions—or at least try to support them. Let's examine this hypothesis. Is the tendency to provide support the defining characteristic of a reason?

Sadly, no. For starters, the hypothesis ignores the fact that we don't just offer reasons *for* conclusions—we also offer reasons *against* them. A reason can show the inadequacy of one hypothesis without doing much to support any alternative. (The previous sentence is an example of this type of reason, as is the next.) We use reasons, not just to *validate* conclusions we *do* favor but also to *invalidate* conclusions we *don't*. We use them to stabilize some thought structures and destabilize others.

Logicians like to frame reasons as arguments before they analyze them. To facilitate assessment of the reason's functioning, they reduce that functioning to a simple relation: a relation between premises and conclusion. This relationship is presumed to be one in which the former support—or mean to support—the latter. This creates a persistent illusion: that reasons are invariably meant to support conclusions. This, though, is just an artifact of the way logicians do business.

There's a second problem with the hypothesis. It doesn't cleanly address the phenomenon of bad reasons—reasons that *fail* to support their conclusions. Put differently, if the supportiveness of a claim is what makes it a reason, then "bad reason" should be a contradiction in terms. But it isn't. In fact, bad reasons exist. "Today is Wednesday because the moon is made of blue cheese" is a lousy argument, but there's no denying that it contains a reason. This shows that *actual* supportiveness is not what makes reasons reasons: sometimes, the mere *intent* to support is enough. The observation that tries but fails to cast doubt has as much claim to be considered a reason as one that successfully proves.

Like mathematicians, logicians like to extract the essential considerations and abstract away the rest. By doing this, they minimize distraction and sometimes gain great clarity. This fundamentally decontextualizing move, though, can obscure important aspects of the functional role that reasons play in our lives. We can gain a richer understanding of this role by examining an ordinary, everyday case. Suppose you and I disagree about the best path to a shared destination. I'm at the wheel of the car and favor a road that you know to be under construction. You inform me that the road is closed, and add that rerouted traffic is experiencing lengthy delays. Not being a complete fool, I change course, in effect conceding that yours is the wiser path. Let's call this the "back-seat-driver case."

Take a moment to appreciate this transaction, for it is both biologically and practically remarkable. Here are its structural features:

1. We start off conflicted about the best way to proceed.
2. You elect to persuade me that your option makes more sense.
3. To that end, you share information.
4. I see your point, and
5. I change my mind.

Clearly, you've given me a *reason* to change course. But what makes your remark a reason? The fact that we disagree in a situation where it would help to agree is part of the story. Your intent to change my mind seems relevant as well. It seems, then, that conditions 1 and 2 transform the informational content of "That road is closed" into a reason. Numbers 4 and 5 indicate that the reason worked as intended, and clinch the case for its being a reason.

You offered the reason in order to change my mind. And it worked. This is a paradigm case of reason-giving. We can even say, quite generally, that reasons are *for* changing minds. In a typical case, we'll use one to get someone else to think or act differently. Sometimes, we'll dwell on a reason in solitude and change our own thinking. This can result in a change of motivational structure, or even behavior. (Note that, in our example, your remark removes my *desire* to take the obstructed road.) We also use reasons to further entrench beliefs we already have. This too represents an alteration of mental condition. Altered mental states, it seems, are what reasons are all about. Could they be what reasons are *for*?

Reasons afford opportunities to change minds. And compared to other species, human beings are highly attuned to these affordances. (Designers call the possibility-creating qualities of a thing "affordances." For example, chairs afford certain sitting opportunities, and money affords buying opportunities.) We inhabit worlds in which reasons—or some of them, anyway—stand out as salient. And we trade reasons like no other animal on Earth. It seems natural selection has wired us for attentiveness to opportunities to change minds. But why? Presumably, a knack for rewiring brains (both our own and others') conferred significant evolutionary advantages.

Reason is an evolved biotechnology for mind writing.[2]

We use reasons to do all kinds of things. Justify our preferences and excuse our lapses, for example. They're handy for explaining, highlighting overlooked commitments, and securing contested permissions. We use them to inform, enlighten, mollify, and impress. We use them to seed and weed our mental gardens: to plant ideas we take to be good, and uproot ideas we take to be bad. We use them to vet the ideas that circulate in and around our minds—to screen out possible troublemakers. For the most part, though, we use reasons to weave and repair complex webs of mutual understanding. There are powerful reasons for thinking that cooperative, alignment-oriented reasoning is the rule, and manipulative, deceitful reasoning is the exception. Were this not so, our reason-giving practices would become degenerate and cease to exist.[3]

*Mind reading* may be an illusion perpetrated by so-called psychics, but *mind writing* is a very real phenomenon. It's so normal, though—so built-in to our way of life—that we fail to see it for what it is. Day in and day out, we use reasons to adjust the thinking of friends, collaborators, and ourselves. We're highly sensitive to signs of divergence in outlook and, countless times each day, take steps to minimize such divergence. We reflexively tend to the common ground that enables collaborative existence and wield many devices to this end: encouraging facial expressions, comforting noises, touch, small talk, gossip, stories, jokes, and religious rituals. (Nowadays, we even use the "share" buttons on Facebook.) It is with *reasons*, though, that we weave the real fabric of our highly social existence.

In the back-seat-driver case, you use a reason to bring my thinking into alignment with yours. Importantly, you also bring our joint behavior into better alignment with circumstances in the world: you target a key belief for revision, and together, we avoid getting stuck in traffic. Such dual alignment is a key enabler of collaborative problem-solving: it helps to understand the world we must navigate together and, for coordination purposes, it helps to think alike. Good reasons are powerful tools for bringing about such dual alignment. When they draw attention to salient objective conditions, they tend to build shared understanding around realistic solutions.

In the case of the wild boar hunt described in the previous section, one hunter used a (gestural) reason to align the thoughts and desires of the tribe. Here too we see a dual alignment: the reason enables the hunt to proceed, and—because the hoofprint in the mud is a reliable indicator of the boar's whereabouts—the hunt is more likely to *succeed*.

Hundreds of thousands of years ago, a relatively hairless breed of terrestrial primate began swapping reasons. This allowed them to weave complex webs of mutual understanding. This helped make us what biologists call "ultrasocial." Psychologist Jonathan Haidt has likened this development to Caesar's crossing of the Rubicon—a fateful step that changed history forever.[4] Historian Rutger Bregman describes social learning—a process that involves swapping reasons—as humankind's "superpower."[5] Could mastery of the affordances of reasons have paved the way for language, culture, and technological prowess? Did facility with reasons allow *Homo sapiens* to outcompete the Neanderthals?[6] The hypothesis has much to recommend it.[7] Reasoning aptitudes certainly gave our ancestors great power.

In any case, we evolved a clever, ultra-collaborative, and highly adaptable way of life, and went on to conquer the planet. Our planet is now the dominion of reason-wielding apes.

It's one thing, though, to wield reasons with cleverness. It's another entirely to wield them with wisdom. To achieve the latter, we must understand a little-appreciated truth about reasons. A fanciful story brings it into focus.

## Reason's Fulcrum

Athena, the goddess of wisdom, and Dionysus, the god of religious ecstasy, give birth to two bright and lively twins. Several years later, they face an important decision. Athena thinks it makes sense to enroll the kids in Plato's Academy, where they can learn the way of inquiry. Dionysus, though, wants to enroll them in the Delphic Seminary, where they can learn the way of belief. As usual, Athena wants to talk it out. She shares her reasons for preferring Plato's. Dionysus listens intently and acknowledges that they are excellent reasons. "Now what about yours?" asks Athena. "Are there good reasons for preferring the seminary?"

Dionysus thinks about it. "No," he concedes. "The good reasons are all on your side." Athena smiles and reaches for the academy's enrollment forms. "Not so fast," replies Dionysus. "You may have the better reasons, but I'm not budging: Delphi it is." Consternation furrows Athena's brow. When words finally come, they're tinged with incredulity: "Why on earth not?" Dionysus shrugs; "I don't know; I just choose to believe in the seminary."

Okay, so it's an unlikely story. In fact, let's call it "The Unlikely Story." Parts of it don't ring true. Still, it's worth pondering. What exactly makes it implausible? Do you find it disturbing? I do. Why?

For one thing, Dionysus's preference for the Delphic Seminary seems strangely arbitrary. Why does he prefer it, if there are no good reasons to? Wouldn't a real person find a way to at least rationalize his preference? So that part doesn't add up. There's something distressing, too, about the male god's refusal to budge: it amounts to a cavalier dismissal of his partner's reasons. It seems basic decency requires us to give weight—indeed due weight—to one another's reasons. But Dionysus doesn't do that. By refusing to yield to them, he implies that Athena's thinking and wishes don't matter as much as his own. He fails to treat her as a coequal parent, and thereby robs her of a measure of dignity. This is no small matter. Nor is it just a cognitive failing; it's a *moral* failing.

Morality, it seems, requires us to yield to the better reason. In some sense, we're ethically bound to submit to the verdict of rational inquiry.

This is an important conclusion, but it stands in need of clarification. How do you know if reason A is "better" than reason B? What if there are more than two opposing reasons involved? How do you distinguish reason from rationalization? How does truly rational inquiry differ from cheap imitations of it? Good questions. In due time, I'll take them up. But they don't arise here: Dionysus doesn't have *any* reasons, so Athena's are automatically better. I've constructed the story to prevent certain questions from diverting our attention from others.

The phrase *force of the better reason* can mislead. It implies that good judgment is a matter of picking out "the better" (or one best) reason, and deciding the question based on that consideration alone. But good judgment isn't like that. It involves considering *all* the reasons for and against (or as many as time and circumstance permit), giving each of them its due, and seeing which way they *collectively* point. The process is more like vector addition: a physicist must add up all the forces on an object to determine the magnitude and direction of its acceleration. In much the same way, we must add up all the reasons for and against to determine a claim's rational standing. The idea is to abide by the verdict that comes from properly aggregating the relevant considerations.

Aggregating sets of reasons, and determining which way they collectively point, can be a nontrivial exercise. Indeed, reasonable-seeming people have been known to look at the same body of evidence and arrive at different conclusions. Later, we'll look at what it means to aggregate reasons properly.[8] In the meantime, I'll use "yield to the better reason" to express what is clearly an important—if still somewhat vague—imperative.

The present point is that Athena has every right to expect Dionysus to yield to the better reason. He fails to live up to that expectation, and this failure constitutes a significant ethical lapse. His stark unwillingness to yield also has a defiant quality, and that, to me, is even more troubling. Dionysus doesn't just violate an expectation; he brazenly defies an elemental cultural norm.

But what norm is that?

When collaborators disagree about the best course for joint action, the expected recourse is to exchange reasons and see which option makes more sense. Thankfully, transactions of this sort are ubiquitous. And typically, they're governed by the understanding that the option backed by the best reasons "wins." Put differently, parties favoring less tenable positions are expected to back down. We're supposed to be persuadable; when the reasons indicate a need to, we're supposed to *change our minds*.

Dionysus' brazen behavior highlights an unwritten rule of discourse: we're supposed to accept what can be shown to be reasonable and give up what is shown to be unreasonable. We're supposed to *yield* to the better reason. It's this rule—and this rule alone—that allows reasons to exert leverage over the disinclined. It is, so to speak, the hinge on which resolution-oriented dialogue turns: reasoning can perform its critical reconciling function, but only to the extent that we acquiesce to this norm. The door of civil discourse swings open on a world of remarkable possibilities—but only if its hinges stay put.

Our unwritten rule merits a name. I propose to call it "reason's fulcrum."

But does reason's fulcrum really function in a fulcrum-like way? Well, reasons *are* like levers, with one arm (what scientists call the "lever arm") in the world of vocalizations, scribbles, and gestures, and another (the "resistance arm") in the world of beliefs and desires. A lever, though, requires a fulcrum: something to brace against. So what is it that allows a reason to exert leverage? Apparently, nothing more than this: our obligation to yield to it, and our willingness to meet that obligation. Where such willingness prevails, reasons can function beautifully. Where it's absent, reasons *can't* function properly. Indeed, they never have.

I've called reason's fulcrum an unwritten rule, and "unwritten" is right. For the most part, it's just a vague expectation—one we don't bother to make explicit. Typically, attention gravitates to the specific reasons on the table and whether they really are better; we fail to notice the rather remarkable fact that, almost invariably, we agree on the underlying premise: the better reason *should* win. This inattention

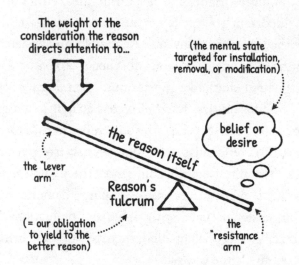

## The Lever Model of How Reasons Work

Reasons are tools for changing minds, but they only work properly if we make a habit of yielding to them.

to the unspoken norm has consequences, among them a collective failure to appreciate the pivotal role it plays in civilized existence. Nearly everything we care about hinges on it in one way or another. Sadly, we fail to recognize how much it's done to educate and civilize us, and otherwise improve human welfare.

We also fail to appreciate how much *more* beneficial it could be, if properly clarified, taught, celebrated, and institutionally reinforced. Its power to enlighten and humanize is truly unparalleled. In fact, it could become a powerful mind vaccine—the centerpiece of a public health intervention that dramatically strengthens mental and cultural immune systems. In a way, it's *the* solution to humanity's ideology problem. To see this, though, we need to understand more fully its role in human practices. What exactly does it do for us?

## The Ungodly Genesis of Moral Norms

Norms have long presented philosophers with a kind of puzzle. Obligations and duties, rights and responsibilities, ethics and values—these are important things, but none of them takes tangible form. Whatever they are, they're invisible, inaudible, and undetected by our best scientific instruments. It won't do, though, to pretend that they're purely imaginary beings, like ghosts or unicorns. For we really *do* have rights and responsibilities. Each of us has a right to a dignified life, for example, and each of us has a responsibility to care for our planet. It follows that it's quite false—and dangerously irresponsible—to say things like "Morality is an illusion," and "There's no such thing as a human right." It made perfect sense to purge demons from our ontologies, but to do the same with rights and obligations would be a huge mistake. We seem compelled, then, to say that norms exist, but in some hard-to-define way.

Similar mysteries arise if we reflect on the goodness of good things and badness of bad things. Or the rightness of moral acts and wrongness of immoral ones. Why is it that these properties etch deep impressions on our nervous systems but leave no trace on our most sensitive scientific instruments? Are they, too, mere imaginings? Or does normative language often point, perhaps indirectly, to real and important features of reality? (If mere preferences don't strike you as important enough to underwrite moral qualities, note that many sorts of goodness can be traced to the *real needs* of sentient creatures.)

The seemingly ethereal character of norms leads many to suspect they're of supernatural origin. Others take this idea further and confidently assert that gods furnish their only cogent explanation. The idea is that the dictates of a god are needed to create *moral* restraints, just as the dictates of human rulers are needed to create *legal* restraints. A simple and popular version of this hypothesis—philosophers call it "divine command theory"—holds that God commanded us to do X, thereby *making* actions of type X morally right. For example, Jesus commanded us to love our neighbors, making it right to love our neighbors. Similarly, Jehovah's "Thou shalt not commit adultery" *made* adultery wrong. *That*, say divine command theorists, is how morality came into being. How else could value come to inhabit a universe otherwise filled with merely natural facts?

Twenty-four hundred years ago, Socrates examined this hypothesis and showed that it doesn't make sense.[9] If you ask the right questions, you can see this for yourself. For why would God require X or prohibit Y if, by hypothesis, neither had any value valence—positive or negative, good or bad, right or wrong—until He said so? If the rightness or wrongness came into being with God's decision, then it wasn't there beforehand to motivate the decision. Such a decision would be the very definition of *arbitrary*.

And morality-by-arbitrary-fiat raises other questions. Suppose God had instead decided that cruelty was a good thing and kindness a sin: Would that have made it so? Does He really have *that* kind of power? Would a divine command to pillage make pillaging okay? Would a divine prohibition on smiling make smiling evil? Clearly not. It seems that something else makes good things good and bad things bad. Divine preferences aren't the right kind of thing to explain the origin of values and norms.

Some argue that God's goodness makes it unthinkable that he'd command us to pillage. Such arguments miss the point: to grapple honestly with the question, you must entertain the hypothetical. Besides, God actually *does* command Moses to pillage Midian. (Really: google "Numbers 31:17" and see for yourself.) Moses and his legions then massacre tens of thousands of men, women, and children. Then they slaughter thousands of farm animals in a bloodthirsty tribute to their lord. For good measure, Moses spares the female virgins and allows his warriors to take them as sex slaves. I mention this story not to trouble the devout but to illustrate how readily supernatural hypotheses about the origins of morality lend themselves to immoral perversions. It's truly important that we motivate the search for alternative hypotheses.

Can we instead understand norms as worldly in origin? It turns out we can. In fact, scientists and philosophers have worked out well-evidenced origins stories that rely entirely on natural entities and forces.[10] Such stories tend to deepen our understanding of right and wrong, and thereby promote moral progress.[11]

The effort to understand morality as a natural phenomenon began, in some ways, with Socrates. The field languished, though, for almost two thousand years. Then, on April 5, 1588, an Englishwoman learned of the coming invasion of the Spanish Armada and went into premature labor. Her name is lost to history, but she birthed a son— Thomas Hobbes—who'd become a brilliant political theorist. The son later wrote that, on that fateful day in 1588, "my mother gave birth to twins: myself and fear." Fear and political instability pursued Hobbes for ninety-one years, and his secular leanings made him one of the most reviled thinkers of his time.

Hobbes, though, pioneered a powerful approach to understanding social norms. It's called "social contract theory," and it sheds light on the origins, nature, and significance of all kinds of norms (including, as we'll soon see, reason's fulcrum). His idea was that cultural, political, and ethical responsibilities are rooted in a sort of agreement. This agreement, or "contract," involves a mutually beneficial exchange. Typically, we each give up certain freedoms in exchange for the benefits that spring from others doing the same. For example, if we agree to forgo pillaging (and thereafter observe that agreement) we give up the spoils of pillaging but gain something of still greater value: freedom from being pillaged. More generally, we give up the freedom to transgress against others, and we gain rights—protections against the transgressions of others. Both sides gain more than they give up; the exchange is, as we say, "win-win."

Importantly, such agreements needn't be explicit. All that's needed are ingredients common in social mammals. First, certain behaviors become normal in the sense of fairly common. Some benefit accrues—either to individuals or the group as a whole—and expectations arise about conformity to the emergent behavioral pattern. As the expectation becomes normal, a standing expectation, or social norm, comes into existence. Finally, individual animals avoid violating the norm so as not to disappoint expectations or earn the disapproval of others, further reinforcing the pattern.

Hobbes grasped that norms have an element of reciprocity: I conform to a certain behavioral constraint, thereby benefiting you, and you conform to the same behavioral constraint, thereby benefiting me. We both come out ahead, but the whole thing is premised on our ability to resist the temptation to cheat. Hobbes saw clearly that a certain instability is thus built-in, not just to moral and political systems, but to all norm-governed social practices.

On this "social contract" account, the most important moral and political norms confer large benefits while requiring relatively small sacrifices. Proscriptions against lying, cheating, and stealing, for example, find their way into the behavioral codes of widely different cultures, not because they're handed down from a deity but because they "pay their way"—they give the members of those cultures far more than they take away. In fact, we now know that cooperative dispositions found their way into the genetic programming of many social animals because, long ago, they paid evolutionary benefits.

This social contract framework sheds fascinating light on our reasoning practices. In fact, it can help us understand how they're supposed to work. It also illuminates the extraordinary centrality and immunity-conferring power of reason's fulcrum.

## A Worthy Prime Directive

"Thou shalt yield to the better reason" didn't make God's top ten list. In fact, it appears nowhere in Scripture. Was it under consideration for inclusion among the Commandments? One presumes so, given divine omniscience. We know for certain, though, that it didn't make the cut. That's unfortunate, for reason's fulcrum is a difference-making bit of moral wisdom. Sacralizing it could have done a world of good. Like "Thou shalt not enslave," it represents a missed opportunity. In God's defense, competition for space on the stone tablets of Sinai must have been fierce. Humanity needs more than a little ethical instruction, and mortal attention spans are limited. Besides, prohibiting other gods was a priority, and graven images could not be tolerated. So it goes.

Should we ever decide to appeal God's verdict—or construct, for ourselves, a more considered behavioral code—the following observations may help us assign the proper weight to reason's fulcrum. First, a simple question: Is mutual willingness to yield to better reasons a "good deal"? Well, sign on to *this* social contract, and you lose the freedom to cling obstinately to irrational opinions. You'll be obliged to concede things you don't like and relinquish some beliefs you find comforting. The steady drip of good reasons frequently compels unwelcome adjustments in outlook. The life of reason is not without sacrifice.

If you take the long view, though, such sacrifices are not expenses, they're investments: investments in a belief system that can serve you, and those you interact with, more reliably. Ignore good reasons, and eventually, you—or somebody else—will pay the price. Either bend to each "better reason" that comes along, or break under the cumulative strain of irrational denial. We rationalists aren't insensitive to human emotional needs: we just play the long game.

Anyway, the costs of reason's fulcrum pale next to its benefits. The norm anchors rational discourse, and *that* activity opens a world of possibilities. When allowed to function properly, reasons allow us to build shared understanding. This facilitates friendship formation and constructive conflict resolution. It makes complex collaboration exponentially easier and brings the fruits of such collaboration—including just about everything humanity produces—within reach. A joint commitment to reason's fulcrum represents a very special kind of reciprocity: one that allows those committed to build, share, and test remarkably sophisticated mental models.

*Star Trek*'s beloved Spock character could perform a tricky operation called the "Vulcan mind meld." He'd carefully place his fingertips on the temples of an alien being, then close his eyes. He'd enter a trancelike state, and somehow sync up the two minds. In this way, he'd gain deep insight into the thinking of another. I'm claiming that we humans do this kind of thing all the time. Only in our case, the linking cables are reasons, not fingers. Mind melding is real, and it takes the benefits of relationship to a whole new level. To gain the benefits, though, you have to reason with others.

Also, the benefits of *general* observance—as opposed to mere *reciprocal* observance—are enormous. A social world structured by rational accountability is one where persuasion can systematically displace more coercive means of wielding influence. Where we can resolve our differences with words, we can replace more destructive means of waging conflict. And reasons, of course, are especially useful for forging shared understanding. With the normalization of reason's fulcrum, then, something like civilization emerges, and freedom from constant fear becomes a real possibility.

Also, where reason's fulcrum stands firm, collaborative *inquiry* becomes possible. It lets us put our heads together and figure things out. We've already seen that good, evidence-based reasons tend to align our beliefs with circumstances in the world. Researchers have also found that collaborative reasoning is surprisingly truth-conducive when we require one another to justify our claims.[12] Rational accountability, in other words, is a tremendous aid to inquiry and discovery.

Without reason's fulcrum, there'd be no science, no mathematics, and no philosophy. There'd be no engineering. Learning would be hamstrung, and our understanding of the world would be rudimentary. Medicine would be underdeveloped. Disease and suffering would be widespread. Ignorance and superstition would flourish. Ideological demons would run rampant. Procedural justice would be arbitrary. Problem-solving aptitudes would be primitive. Mental immune systems would be weak. Life under such conditions would surely be solitary, poor, nasty, brutish, and short.

Reason's fulcrum also passes the other great test that philosophers have proposed for moral norms. I speak of Immanuel Kant's celebrated *categorical imperative*. This principle instructs us to ask, of any candidate moral rule, "What if obedience to it became normal? What if *everyone* acted that way?" In effect, Kant urges us to conduct a thought experiment: imagine a world where the norm in question is universally upheld.

Give it a try. Imagine a world where everyone always yields to the better reason. (This is decidedly not the same as imagining a world drained of passion, reverence, love, or spontaneity, for those elements of the good life turn out to be compatible with a commitment to reason.) Would *you* want to live in such a world?

I would. If you're not sure, focus first on an easier question:

Which world would you rather inhabit: World A, where *everyone always* yields to the better reason, or World B, where *no one ever* yields to the better reason? We know the answer to this question: World A would afford us vastly better lives.

Fans of empirical research methods rightly celebrate the value of A/B testing. Comparing two conditions that differ in only one particular allows us to isolate the effects of a single variable, generate "clean" evidence, and (in principle at least) arrive at reliable conclusions about cause and effect. Understandably, though, research ethics watchdogs won't let us expose real test subjects to World B. More generally, the testing of normative hypotheses requires thought experiments and intellectual honesty—simulation without dissimulation.

Before long, I think, we'll have computer simulations that vividly demonstrate the systemic effects of strong rationality norms. Until then, we need to rely on thought experiments: simulations we run in imagination. I know people who distrust intuition and, for this reason, think little of thought experiments. They're surely right to recommend caution when it comes to intuition. It would be a mistake, though, to conclude that thought experiments have no place here. (Indeed, ethics watchdogs need them to do what they do.) It's easy enough to make out the basic contours of a society structured by universal adherence to reason's fulcrum, and the intuitions that support such a conclusion turn out not to be capricious: they withstand scrutiny. Conversely, the large-scale consequences of universal *nonobservance* of reason's fulcrum can also be reliably predicted.

It's a bit harder to compare World A—where reason's fulcrum is observed without fail—to the world we actually have: where people respond to reasons, but inconsistently. Psychologists have demonstrated that, to a surprising extent, we reason opportunistically: we bow to better reasons when it suits us but are not above ignoring them when convenient. When asked, we express commitment to reason's fulcrum, but in practice, we can be pretty half-assed about it.

Fortunately, a little practice can move us from half-assed to three-quarter-assed. Or from, say, 93 percent responsive to 96 percent responsive to the better reason. Whatever the numbers, it's a mistake to scoff at marginal improvements. For small differences in level of commitment to reason's fulcrum can yield large improvements in collective well-being. It's truly that pivotal.

Evidence for this lies all around us. Examine the root causes of contemporary social and political dysfunction, for example, and you'll find that disdain for reason is a primary culprit. Consider also the case of the Enlightenment. Human nature didn't change appreciably from 1600 to 1750 CE, but something else did: philosophers celebrated reason, faith-based believing waned, and Europe reached a kind of inflection point. The concept of human rights was invented, violence declined by almost an order of magnitude, and human welfare improved dramatically.[13] Apparently, marginal improvements in our level of commitment to reason triggered huge changes in the world.

It should be noted that the Enlightenment failed to bring well-being to everyone. Slavery, colonization, and economic exploitation continued, in defiance of both decency and reason. Still, the Enlightenment established a fulcrum—reason's fulcrum—that abolitionists, champions of women's suffrage, civil rights reformers, union organizers, and gay rights activists would later use to beautiful effect. Since then, the critical examination of unjust arrangements has time and again inspired moral awakenings.[14]

Marginal *declines* in our collective commitment to reason's fulcrum can also have huge impacts. Remember W. B. Yeats' poem "The Second Coming"? It captures the frightening dynamic that plays out whenever a people's commitment to reason wanes. Reason's centripetal pull is lost, and we're no longer drawn back to common ground. Amity succumbs to partisanship; partisanship curdles into factionalism; and factionalism stokes tribal hatreds. The unreasonable are filled with passionate intensity, and the reasonable fall silent. If the cycle isn't interrupted, all hell breaks loose.

Yeats wrote "The Second Coming" in the wake of the First World War. He'd watched unreason spread and observed the resulting carnage with horror. As I write this, the social fabric in the United States is fraying rapidly. It's clear to all that some basic social contract has fallen into disrepair, but no consensus exists as to the root cause.

The three great social contract theorists of the Enlightenment—Hobbes, Locke, and Rousseau—sought to understand the fundamental conditions that allow well-functioning social norms to form and persist. They understood that civilized coexistence requires a complex scaffolding of such norms, and sought to understand how such scaffolding works. In fact, two of the three—Locke and Rousseau—tried to identify the form of reciprocity that lies at the very foundation of civilization.[15]

According to Locke, the social contract forms when a group of individuals submits to a sovereign, or civil authority. The originating act is a joint renunciation of the individual's right to judge and punish. People cede this power to a civil authority, which then has a monopoly on violence. Ideally, representatives of the civil authority use this monopoly wisely, and mostly to safeguard citizens' rights. Usually, they're constrained by the need to maintain the consent of the governed, so they institute discourse-based procedural justice mechanisms (trials, basically). Uncorrupted, these mechanisms go some ways toward protecting life, liberty, and property. The basic or "original" deal, though, is quite simple: give up vigilantism, respect the authorities, and gain some protections for your basic rights. That, argues Locke, is the key step away from barbarism.

It's a nice story, but it overlooks something important. Discourse-based conflict resolution (not just formal jury trials, but also informal let's-work-things-out conversations) work only if reason's fulcrum is *already* in play. Otherwise, reasons exert no leverage, and talk-it-out mechanisms aren't available to supplant vigilante justice. In this sense, Locke's "original contract" is not original at all, but derivative of reason's fulcrum. The same goes for Rousseau's "first convention." In the complex scaffolding of social norms we call civilization, reason's fulcrum occupies a foundational stratum.

In fact, reason's fulcrum has a strong claim to be considered the real "original contract" of civil society. For it is precisely our capacity to reason together that makes it possible to forsake uncivilized modes of dispute resolution. Conducted properly, reason-giving dialogue affords a near-optimal mechanism for adjudicating disputes, and nothing civilizes people like the recognition that this is so. Becoming civilized is, at bottom, a matter of submitting to the force of the better reason.

Every belief system, no matter how informal, has a center of gravity. We prioritize whether we mean to or not, and our priorities have implications for the well-being of self and others. Grasping this, philosophers have always sought to order their thoughts. Hobbes, Locke, and Rousseau had their respective original contracts. Jehovah had his First Commandment: "Thou shalt have no other gods before me." Descartes had his *cogito ergo sum*, or "I think, therefore I am." (Intriguingly, Descartes characterized this idea as the "Archimedean point" of "first philosophy"—a reference to the science of leverage; apparently, Descartes viewed his first principle as fulcrum-like.) Euclid had his axioms. Kant had his categorical imperative. *Star Trek*'s Federation of Planets had its Prime Directive.

Reason's fulcrum compares favorably to *all* of these. As a norm, it's more fundamental than those nominated by the social contract theorists. It's more practical and less self-serving than Jehovah's First Commandment. It's every bit the Archimedean point that the Cartesian *cogito* is (in fact, it functions as a fulcrum!). "I think, therefore I am" loses significance when you outgrow artificial fears about the existence of reality outside of your mind; reason's fulcrum has no comparable defect. Reason's fulcrum is methodologically prerequisite for all kinds of inquiry, and indispensable for all sorts of civil dispute resolution. It's simpler, more obvious, and more substantive than the categorical imperative. And unlike Euclid's fifth axiom, we don't suspend reason's fulcrum when we think about curved space!

Notice that we can examine the functional role that reason's fulcrum plays in our lives, reach evidence-based conclusions about its importance, and assign it a central place in our system of values. This means that we needn't take it on faith—or exempt it from critical scrutiny—for it to serve as a moral touchstone for us. We can subject it to rigorous examination, and as long as it continues to *survive* such scrutiny, it can remain quite basic or foundational.

It's always dangerous to treat something as sacred, especially if doing so places it beyond the reach of critical questioning. But the more carefully I examine "Thou shalt yield to the better reason," the more reverent my attitude toward it becomes. As a moral touchstone and prime directive, we could do a *lot* worse. For the purposes of building mental immunity—and resilient communities—it's hard to do better.

Hard, but not impossible. Let's see if we can fine-tune it.

## The Paradox of Rational Commitment

*Thou shalt yield to the better reason* isn't going to win any popularity contests. Like "Thou shalt not covet," it runs against the grain of human nature. Its religious vibe and imperative tone probably don't help matters: human sensibilities have evolved in recent millennia, and authoritarian dictates have lost much of their appeal. Expressed in this imperious way, reason's fulcrum is, and will probably remain, an exceedingly tough sell. Put differently, "authoritarian rationalism" won't be a significant player in the mindshare sweepstakes any time soon.

These days, *I'll yield to your better reasons if you yield to mine* is more apt to gain an interested hearing. The prospect of others responding to your reasons has appeal, and the price of gaining that advantage—your own persuadability—seems eminently fair. It's easy to imagine benefiting from such an arrangement, and the costs appear quite manageable. As we've seen, additional reflection reveals it to be a remarkable bargain: the benefits of belonging to a community of inquiry include many of the finest affordances of civilization, and the cost of yielding to better reasons is essentially that of having to *learn*. (A sufficiently devoted lover of wisdom, I think, will not view this as a cost at all.) So here's a better sales pitch for rationalism in the modern age: "All this can be yours—and for the low, low price of being open to learning new things!"

The very qualities that gain the "I'll yield if . . ." formulation a hearing, though, make it a poor candidate for moral principle. To be sure, "I'll yield to your better reasons provided you yield to mine" seems prudent; but since when is morality so . . . transactional? Is it really a matter of selling a bit of this to buy a bit of that? Isn't conditioning one's responsiveness to good reasons in this way kind of . . . self-serving? Is genuine morality really so . . . provisional? So tit-for-tat? So nakedly driven by self-interest?

For that matter, is genuine rationalism only conditionally responsive to reason? Or does it instead require a more unwavering commitment to follow good reasons where they lead? The question, I think, cannot be avoided: Is it really a good idea to frame reason's fulcrum in such a conditional, what's-in-it-for-me kind of way?

For *explanatory* purposes, the answer appears to be yes. Scientists have found that, if we want to understand the origins of human morality, there's really no alternative to analyzing it as an evolved form of reciprocity—as a kind of social contract. Moral sensibilities and systems of rules have precisely the characteristics one would expect if they had to survive a Darwinian winnowing process. In fact, the instabilities of rule systems are just what the emerging moral sciences (particularly evolutionary game theory) would predict.[16] Systems of norms are the product of biological and cultural evolution, and they bear the stamp of their evolutionary origins. This much is now settled science.

By extension, the same is true of human reasoning propensities:

they had to evolve under conditions that sometimes favored self-serving breaches of reciprocity. Ditto for reasoning *practices*: they had to sustain themselves under shifting biological and cultural pressures, some of them selfish and shortsighted. Our reasoning practices have precisely the vulnerabilities one would expect, given that being unreasonable was sometimes advantageous. In fact, it's *still* the case that being unreasonable can pay dividends, and still the case that selfish and shortsighted actors compromise our reasoning practices. The tragedy of the reasoning commons is a real thing.

We humans, though, do more with language than just explain things. We also use it to express ourselves, undertake commitments, exhort, and inspire one another. And for purposes like these, the transactional formulation of reason's fulcrum—"I will if you will"—appears suboptimal.

Consider the matter in this light: reciprocity is an important part of marriage, but at weddings, brides and grooms don't say, "I will if you will." The situation calls for a more resolute and categorical commitment, and the commitment needs to be expressed in an unwavering way. So soon-to-be-newlyweds leave off the "if" part and say "I do," preferably with some fervor. The ritual is designed to imbue the commitment with an aura of sacredness.

Certain circumstances, then, necessitate the adoption of a more resolute or unconditional attitude. So here's the question I want to pose: Doesn't it make sense to adopt a more resolute attitude toward reason's fulcrum? Doesn't its pivotal importance for our collective well-being create a moral imperative to adopt a more categorical stance? And if the human condition generally doesn't create such an imperative, can we at least agree that our present predicament does—a predicament where reason-defying thinking threatens to wreak planetary devastation?

The Quaker meetinghouse where I was once a member now sports a banner over its front entrance. It reads LOVE YOUR NEIGHBOR—NO EXCEPTIONS. The slogan gained currency in recent years as a way of pushing back against intolerance. An analogous version of reason's fulcrum might read: *Yield to the better reason—no exceptions.*

This slogan expresses a view we might call "exception-free rationalism." Does such a view merit serious consideration? I don't think so. For starters, it demands an inhuman degree of mental discipline. Our biases, passions, and limited conscious bandwidth pretty much guarantee that we won't live up to its standard. In fact, it would be quite *un*reasonable to expect any human being to adhere to such a rule for long. On this standard, the most resolute rationalist would count as an abject failure. Worse, its imperative tone suggests that those who fall short always deserve condemnation. But that can't be true. At best, it represents an unattainable ideal.

So how about this: *I will, to the best of my ability, yield to better reasons in all things.*

Here we have a comparatively unconditional statement of resolve. The "I will . . ." expresses not a commandment but a commitment. One who undertakes and keeps such a commitment might be called a "resolute rationalist."

It's not hard to imagine undertaking such a commitment voluntarily, under no duress whatever. In this sense, it's perfectly consistent with personal autonomy. That's a big plus in my book. Perhaps that makes it a better fit for modern, nonauthoritarian sensibilities. I certainly hope so.

I know many people who make this commitment, and do so not grudgingly but with enthusiasm. Interestingly, these cheerfully dedicated friends fancy themselves *freethinkers*. Though they undertake a commitment that binds and constrains them, the voluntary nature of the undertaking appears to change the character of the limitation. Because it's *self*-imposed, it doesn't feel like an imposition. My rationalist friends don't *resent* rational restraints; they welcome them and experience them as *freeing*.

Or do their best to welcome them. If the welcoming attitude doesn't come spontaneously, they sometimes make do with mere toleration of unwelcome reasons—submitting to them without any fuss. With practice, you can get very good at welcoming unwelcome reasons. In fact, you can learn to be even-handed in your treatment of welcome and unwelcome reasons. (I'll explain how in chapter 9.) Indeed, fair-mindedness and objectivity demand no less, and the lesson goes a long way toward mitigating the biases to which we are prone.

For thousands of years, philosophers have argued that rational self-discipline is the very essence of freedom. You don't have to accept this, though, to see that a world structured by the voluntary undertaking of rational constraints is hugely preferable to a world crisscrossed by arbitrary, irrational, and coercive constraints. Give resolute rationalism a try: it feels—and quite possibly is—liberating.

Is it a good idea, though, to be a resolute rationalist? Is it wise to so bind oneself? There are really two questions here. One is: Should *we* be resolute rationalists? The other is: Should *I* be a resolute rationalist? I've tried to show that the answer to the first question is a complete no-brainer: *of course* we should be resolute rationalists. Simply stated, it's the best way to put our reasoning practices—and so much else that matters to us—on a solid foundation.

If you focus on the second question, though, it's easy to construct a case *against* being a resolute rationalist. After all, a binding commitment to yield to all better reasons means you can't be opportunistically irrational. When you focus on the opportunity costs of being a resolute rationalist, in other words, your resolution is likely to waver. When "Should I?" takes the place of "Should we?" cracks begin forming in the foundation.

In Roman myth, Ulysses had his sailors tie him to the mast of a sailing ship, then plug their own ears with wax. He did this because they were about to sail past the fabled island of the Sirens. The Sirens were bewitching water nymphs that would lure unsuspecting sailors to their doom. They'd mesmerize their victims with enchanting song, and entranced sailors would hurl themselves overboard or sail directly onto the rocks. The shoals of the island were said to be littered with the rotting hulls of once-proud ships and the bleached bones of weak-willed sailors.

Ulysses contrived to escape this fate. The wax made his crew impervious to seductive song, and his bonds kept Ulysses himself from jumping ship. The plan worked: Ulysses was the first to hear the Sirens' song and live to tell the tale.

This ancient tale contains important insights about commitment: choose to bind yourself in some fashion and, for better or worse, relinquish certain freedoms. Tie yourself to the ship, and you can't indulge the urge to jump overboard. The decision to become a resolute rationalist is just such a commitment: undertake and keep it, and you bind yourself to the ship of reason. The winds of evidence and reason-giving discourse will thereafter determine your course. The seas can get rough, but the resolute rationalist will remain aboard.

The stance of the resolute rationalist bears a passing resemblance to faith. It involves steadfast commitment. It involves trust—in this case, trusting reason. It involves voluntarily depriving yourself of future options. Like Ulysses, the resolute rationalist surveys the dangers that lie ahead and takes steps to ensure that he or she won't jump ship when faced with temptation. Intriguingly, these steps might include something that seems antithetical to reason: plugging your ears against the Siren songs of unreason.

Plato's classic account of his mentor's final days stressed the latter's unswerving devotion to reason. Awaiting his execution, Socrates receives an offer that most would find irresistible: the jailer has been bribed, and his friends stand ready to spirit Socrates to freedom. Astonishingly, Socrates doesn't jump at the chance. Instead, he pins his decision on the outcome of inquiry and begins examining the reasons for and against. He comes to the conclusion that escape would be wrong, and—in an impressive display of rationalist resolve—decides to accept his sentence. Even in the face of death, Socrates took a stand for reason's fulcrum. In so doing, he set an example that has echoed through the ages.

Curiously, Plato depicts Socrates as deaf to counterargument. The reasons that compel me to stay and die, Socrates admits, "murmur in my ears like the sound of a flute in the ears of a mystic; the voice hums in my ears, and prevents me from hearing any other. Anything you say, Crito, will be in vain." He doesn't plug his ears with wax, exactly, but something strangely similar happens. He succumbs to an almost religious devotion to reason, and he martyrs himself for the cause.

Does the truly reasonable person constantly reevaluate his commitment to the life of reason and jump ship when it's in his interests to do so? Or does she instead maintain her commitment "in good faith," remaining aboard even when the seas get rough? There is cleverness in the former option, but wisdom in the latter.

# CHAPTER 9

# Reason Unhinged

## *How thinking becomes ideological*

The moment you declare a set of ideas
immune to criticism . . . thought becomes
impossible. —*Salman Rushdie*

*T*he mind is born free, but everywhere it is in chains.* These words
make up the terrific opening line of *The Social Contract*, Jean-
Jacques Rousseau's classic work of Enlightenment political philosophy. I changed it a little bit.

By "chains," I mean ideological chains. Consider this fact: no
one is born an ideologue. Now combine it with another: ideological rigidity is common among the elderly. Conclusion? Worldviews
harden over time. Or tend to. Say what you will about old dogs and
new tricks: in humans, mental inflexibility is *acquired*.

Of course, ideologues rarely experience their ideologies as chains.
From the inside, their views just seem deeply, obviously right. From
without, though, it's often clear that the ideologue has a blind spot.
Or—to pick a better analogy—a deafness: an inability to hear certain
kinds of reasons. For example, a free market ideologue might be unable to appreciate a nuanced case for regulating economic activity. A
devout Marxist might be unable to process certain critiques of Marx.

In both cases, an ardent philosophical commitment makes it hard to think straight. Incidentally, these cases are perfectly representative of the entire class: ideologues generally are trapped in a way that prevents them from hearing certain sorts of reasons. The falcon cannot hear the falconer.

## The Road to Cognitive Perdition

We need a better understanding of what I'll call the "road to cognitive perdition." How does thinking *become* ideological? What's the mechanism? Why are some, but not others, entrapped?

Let's begin with a well-established fact: our minds are riddled with biases. We're prone to confirmation bias, motivated reasoning, and groupthink. We're self-righteous, suggestible, and too often, hypocritical. We rationalize and can fool ourselves. All this is true, and exhaustively researched.[1] Unfortunately, many learn of this research and conclude that rationality is a lost cause. Others conclude that fair-mindedness is impossible, or that objectivity is nothing but a false and oppressive ideal.

These conclusions are deeply problematic. For starters, they aren't true: sometimes people manage to be reasonable, fair-minded, and objective—about certain things anyway. For example, you want the entire remaining slice of pie but understand the need for fairness; so you divide it neatly in half and share it with your sister. Or consider the case of the scientist who fervently wants her pet theory to be true; when evidence shows it not to be, she graciously concedes and moves on. This is what real fair-mindedness and objectivity look like. Such things happen all the time, and it's misleading to suggest otherwise.

Perhaps it's true that our brains can't shape a perfectly objective outlook. So what? *Imperfect* objectivity is still worth striving for. To declare objectivity, fair-mindedness, and rationality false ideals, or to suggest that we abandon their pursuit, is patently counterproductive. It matters greatly that we make progress toward them—even if they prove, in the end, to be like asymptotes: things we can approach but never quite reach.

When we take psychology's findings of built-in bias and interpret them as innate, a certain resignation can kick in. Why bother striving for something that isn't in the cards? The answer is that "innate" doesn't mean "uncorrectable." Think about it: the human retina has a blind spot—the place where light-sensitive cells are missing because the optic nerve gets in the way. This defect is as innate as it gets, yet astronomers invent ways to prevent it from hiding the telescope image of a sought-after star. Cars sport mirrors that shrink a driver's blind spots. A friend can help you see the log in your eye. Dialogue with a detractor can broaden your perspective. As for our penchant for self-serving thinking—we find ways to correct for that too. You can entertain an inconvenient hypothesis and give it a real chance to win you over. You can welcome unwelcome reasons and honor their potential to broaden and correct your point of view. In these and other ways, we lessen confirmation bias.

The partial undoing of our biases may leave us partial; still, mitigated partiality is better than unmitigated partiality.

Scientists are trained to mitigate their biases. So are philosophers, judges, and many journalists. No one's perfect, but that's not the relevant standard: the important thing is to be more reasonable than we would otherwise be. Besides, bias mitigation shouldn't be the exclusive province of professional inquirers: all of us—politicians, journalists, jurists, voters, citizens—must strive to limit the impact of bias. Only so will we overcome the scourge of ideology.

When we paint the mind as innately ideological, the important question—How do we *become* ideological?—tends to go unasked. So I'll say it again: we aren't born ideological; mental rigidity is acquired.

Nor should we assume that involuntary tendencies of thought are always the culprit. True, a tendency to discount the arguments of a rival can become automatic, thereby skewing one's judgment. But *willful* departures from rationality norms are also implicated.

Deliberate inattention to certain sorts of reasons (those that make you uncomfortable, say) can become a habit of mind, sowing the seeds of ideological thinking. Willful dishonesty can have similar effects. Sometimes, we're culpable for becoming ideologues.

If we want to mitigate humanity's ideology problem, we need to take an honest look at the discretionary contributors to ideological thinking. For these are the things we can do something about. It's hard to acknowledge our failings in this area, but nothing else will confer the needed self-determination. It's hard truths about our mental habits that will set us free.

So here's the question I want to ask: What is it that the strongly immune and the highly susceptible do differently? To answer this question, we must zoom in on the machinery of the mind's immune system.

## The Damaged Fulcrum Model

Viruses hijack living cells. We know how they do it: a virus will circumvent a cell's defenses, commandeer its copying machinery, and use it to create copies of itself. These copies go on to hijack other cells. We call the result an infection. If it jumps to other hosts and continues to spread, we call it an epidemic. Ideologies do something similar: they hijack minds. Typically, an ideology will circumvent a mind's defenses, commandeer its copying machinery, and create copies of itself. These copies then go on to hijack other minds. The result could be called a mind infection. Or when it spreads, an *ideodemic*.

Scientists have a detailed understanding of the machinery of viral hijacking. This gives us real power to fight disease. To date, though, we lack a comparably detailed understanding of the machinery of ideological hijacking. We know *that* ideologies subvert thinking, but we don't yet know *how*. In fact, we lack a credible working model of the process.

Fortunately, the lever-like functioning of reasons points to just such a model. Here's my hypothesis: reasoning done right functions to "sync" our mental states—to reconcile them with one another and (when they convey evidence) with conditions in the world. But this can happen only where the norm I've called reason's fulcrum prevails. Damage this norm, and you effectively decouple mental states from rational checks and balances. That, I claim, is how thinking comes unhinged.

The beliefs and desires of others are important features of the world we must sync up with. I mean this in a weak sense: it's not that we must adopt others' beliefs and desires; it's that we need to take account of them to live in harmony. Collaboration and coexistence require it. When reason's fulcrum is working properly, we have a shot at resolving several types of conflict: conflicts among our beliefs, conflicts between our beliefs and our desires, conflicts between our mental states and conditions in the world, and conflicts between our mental states and those of others. When reason's fulcrum becomes damaged, though, we lose a powerful way to resolve such conflicts, and thinking becomes disordered. I call this the "damaged fulcrum model" of the descent into ideological thinking.

But what role does the ideology itself play in this process? Picture an unstoppable force applied to one arm of a lever, while the other arm is obstructed by an immovable object. What happens? Well, the lever snaps. Or the fulcrum disintegrates. Either way, the mechanism is damaged. Now imagine compelling evidence pushing hard against a nonnegotiable belief. What happens? Something's got to give. Either you give up the discredited belief, or you find a way to live with it. Usually, this means discounting the evidence or living with contradiction. If you *won't* give up the belief, and you can't discount the evidence (or fault the logic), then invariably you damage the fulcrum.[2]

Past encounters with reasons shape a person's response to challenging information. Make a habit of evading your cognitive responsibilities, and next time, it becomes a little easier. In effect, you can degrade reason's fulcrum, thereby compromising your mind's immune system. Importantly, you can also *reinforce* reason's fulcrum, effectively *strengthening* your mind's immune system. A person with a healthy mental immune system can easily fight off ideologies that mentally cripple others. Often, the condition of the fulcrum is what makes the difference.

"Reason's fulcrum," as I use it here, can refer to a social norm or an individual's internalized resolve to conform to that norm. You can expect *others* to yield to better reasons, and you can expect *yourself* to yield to better reasons. And each expectation establishes a kind of fulcrum: a way for evidence to apply leverage to thinking. My point is that such expectations can erode bit by bit: damage to reason's fulcrum can be incremental. A given incident can weaken reason's fulcrum to a negligible degree, but the cumulative effect of many such incidents can be dramatic. I offer Robert Bowers as Exhibit A. He wasn't radicalized overnight; he went down an ideological rabbit hole, defied reason's fulcrum repeatedly, and eventually became deranged.

For Exhibit B, take the increasingly ideological nature of modern American conservativism: on issue after issue—taxes, the climate, the economy, church-state separation—its responsiveness to better reasons has eroded. This exhibit, of course, contains millions of data points. In May 2020, Thomas Friedman authored an Op-Ed that finally connected the dots. His conclusion? America is suffering from a massive breakdown of our culture's immune system.[3] A month later, his Nobel Prize–winning colleague Paul Krugman described America as suffering from a "plague of willful ignorance."[4]

The erosion of reason starts off imperceptible. But at a certain point, a tipping point is reached. The mechanism becomes noticeably unreliable, and the affected mind (or minds) deteriorate rapidly. When this happens, a person—or entire community of people—can become effectively unreachable: beyond the reach of rational appeal. As I write, such deterioration is on vivid display in the unhinged presidency of Donald Trump. In August 2020, a reporter asked Mr. Trump what he thought of QAnon, the theory that a "satanic cult made up of pedophiles and cannibals" was conspiring to overthrow his presidency. His answer? He offered to "help" the conspiracy theorists.[5] His tenuous grasp on reality doesn't seem to dent his approval ratings: some 40 percent of the American electorate consistently approve of his job performance.

A recent book labeled science deniers "the unpersuadables."[6] It makes a compelling case that people can become impervious to scientific persuasion. The label, though, can be used to describe a much broader phenomenon, one where minds become resistant to *many* kinds of reasons. In fact, unresponsiveness to scientific reasons is just a fragment of the problem. The bulk of the problem consists in unresponsiveness to moral, political, and economic reasons. If we include these sorts of reasons, and partial as well as total unresponsiveness to them, we're talking about a pervasive and influential phenomenon—one we might call "ideological rigidity."

Remember, unresponsiveness to better reasons isn't just a function of being *unable* to see their force. It's also a function of being *unwilling* to yield to them. We grow attached to our beliefs and willfully resistant to changing them. Obstinacy-induced irrationality is a real thing, and it plays a role in the formation of ideological attitudes. C. S. Peirce didn't call it the "method of tenacity" for nothing.

We're talking, then, about an acquired unresponsiveness to better reasons—one fed by willful irrationality. Sometimes, people simply refuse to yield to better reasons. It does no good to pretend otherwise: the road to cognitive perdition is paved with intentions.

To truly reduce susceptibility to ideological thinking, we must honestly confront, and somehow combat, willful irrationality. We must understand the atrophy of rational resolve. Most of all, we need to understand how norms work: what they are, how they form, and how they lose their power over us.

## The Unmaking of Social Norms

Norms don't spring into existence fully formed. They don't descend from Mount Olympus or Mount Sinai. They're rarely written in stone, and perfectly rational actors don't simultaneously opt in. The origins of norms are more mundane. They usually start out as agreeable behaviors: a tendency, say, to extend a hand upon greeting. We're prone to mimicry, so sometimes the behavior gets copied. As the behavior becomes more common, expectations begin to form. In this case, a friendly handshake is increasingly expected when people meet. In this way, shaking hands can come to seem normal, and the failure to extend a hand can come to feel abnormal. And by *abnormal*, I don't just mean *unusual*: the failure to extend a hand begins to feel *inappropriate*. With this, a norm has come into being.

A norm, then, is a kind of standing expectation. Or better: a self-perpetuating set of expectations. Norms are, at bottom, a dynamic social phenomenon: they're born, they live, and they die. To persist, they need to be renewed—generation after generation, year after year, and instance after instance. They need to embed themselves in habits, sensibilities, and practices, or they perish.

Put differently, norms need us to replicate: to take root in new minds, an expectation must, with some reliability, induce expected behavior. That's how expectations sustain themselves: they induce conforming behavior, and each new instance of conformity reinforces the expectation. We do what's expected of us, and the expectation gets stronger. Adherence strengthens norms.

Sometimes, we make norms explicit. For example, we can codify into law the expectation that one drive on the right side of the road. Most norms, though, remain tacit—essentially unwritten rules. For example, when listening to a friend, one should stand at an appropriate distance. Standing too close is inappropriate. Even tacit norms like this are encoded: they're written into our brains in the form of expectations—the expectations we have of one another, and the expectations we have of ourselves. Expectations are literally the stuff of norms.

And here's the thing about norms: that's all there is to them. A norm is *nothing but* a self-perpetuating pattern of expectation. No more substantial basis exists. Norms are fragile, insubstantial beings, utterly reliant on us. Without our compliance, they wither and die.

Some basic features of human nature, though, serve to stabilize them. We're social animals and generally anxious to fit in. We're hardwired to notice how others act, and generally, we're inclined to behave "as one does." We have a gift for imitation and a pronounced tendency to conform. So clever-but-anxious monkey see, clever-but-anxious monkey do—often enough, at any rate, to sustain the social patterns we call norms.

Norms also lapse. This happens when the underlying expectation erodes to the point of being inoperative. Generally, it works like this: someone deviates from the norm, and others take note. For example, a blowhard defies the norms of accountable talk: he makes stuff up, say, and ignores requests for evidence. Others follow suit, and the aberrant behavior—in this case, unaccountable talk—begins occurring with greater frequency. This causes expectations of conformity to wane. In other words, a feedback loop can develop: noncompliance weakens a norm, and the weakened norm commands even less compliance. If nothing halts this spiral, the pattern of expectation simply ceases to be. That's how norms die.

Fortunately, norms can also recover. Instances of compliance can strengthen a norm, leading to more compliance. If this is right, each instance of accountable talk does a little to reinforce the norms of accountable talk. Adherence strengthens accountability norms, violation weakens them, and, in a very real sense, it's up to us whether they live or die.

Arguably, every failure to observe a norm does a little to weaken it. Other things can weaken a norm—denouncing it, say—but nonobservance is the phenomenon to reckon with. It also matters *how* a norm is violated. Norm violation is often covert: embezzlers, for example, steal on the sly. But other times, people violate norms openly, defiantly inviting others to follow suit. Such defiance can cripple a norm. For example, Gandhi openly defied the unjust laws of British occupiers, inspiring others to do likewise. The resulting movement fatally compromised British colonial rule. Deliberate norm violation helped India win its independence.

Brazen defiance can also weaken *good* norms. The Prohibition-era mob boss Al Capone employed violence in ways that flouted fundamental moral and legal norms. In so doing, he did great damage to civil order and the rule of law. Present-day drug cartels use similar tactics to defend their reputations and business interests, with comparably damaging effects. When white-collar criminals brazenly commit fraud and settle lawsuits for pennies on the dollar, they send a signal to others: white-collar crime pays. This tears at the social fabric. Again, we see defiant nonobservance damaging a social norm.

The fate of a norm can hinge on whether people are held accountable for their violations. In recent years, white cops have shot and killed dozens of unarmed black men. Many of these killings were caught on camera, but even when the evidence is conclusive, the shooters are rarely held accountable. This is both morally inexcusable and shortsighted. When norm violation draws no sanction, a web of civilizing expectations can unravel.

These facts about norms apply to the norm we're concerned with here. Reason's fulcrum is at bottom a pattern of expectation—the expectation that we yield to better reasons. Because we can expect this of others, and expect this of ourselves, there are, in a way, two fulcra here: the collective expectation that we *all* yield to better reasons—the social norm—and our individual expectations of *ourselves* in this regard: something more like a personal commitment.

To persist, the expectations underlying reason's fulcrum must be renewed, and renewal requires adherence. Every time we submit to a good reason, then, reason's fulcrum gets a little stronger. Every time we don't, it gets a little weaker. You can fail to comply with reason's fulcrum privately—by quietly discounting a good reason, say, or neglecting to revise a belief. Sometimes, no one finds out, and the damage to the social norm is minimal. Even then, though, private violation weakens personal resolve. The will to be rational is like a muscle: fail to exercise it, and it atrophies. Every concession to unreason, then, does some damage to the norm that keeps us "hinged."

It's also possible to defy reason's fulcrum publicly. Ken Ham did this in his debate with Bill Nye, proudly advertising his defiance with the words "No one is ever going to convince me that the word of God is not true." This proclamation enhanced his reputation in evangelical circles but also contributed to the unraveling of our reasoning practices. Donald Trump now flouts reason's fulcrum daily, causing incalculable damage to what is arguably the most civilizing norm of all time.

Many of Trump's supporters seem to regard this as a feature of his candidacy, rather than a flaw. Why were Trump's digs at "political correctness" among his rallies' most effective applause lines? Because his base experiences the norms of accountable talk as oppressive.[7] In online forums, defying the norms of reason to "own the libs" has become a popular way for conservatives to signal their virtue.[8] Willful defiance of reason doesn't get more blatant than that.

If we hope to place our emerging global civilization on a sustainable footing, we must attend, with special seriousness, to the blatant disregard of "better" reasons. But let's press the inquiry further: What makes us prone to such disregard?

## A Thumb on the Scales

Thinking doesn't become ideological the moment it's exposed to an ideology. It happens as the ideology renders its host progressively unresponsive to certain sorts of reasons. A biological metaphor gives us one way to understand this process: the ideology compromises the mind's immune system, making it unable to fight off bad ideas. A mechanical metaphor provides additional insight: ideas can lodge in the mind, obstruct the lever-like functioning of reasons, and thereby degrade the fulcrum-like expectation that allows *other* reasons to function properly. This degradation is often gradual, but given time, it can thoroughly addle a person's wits.

This "damaged fulcrum" model suggests a continuum between everyday failures of rational self-control and advanced stages of ideological derangement. It highlights the plain fact that the former can pave the way for the latter. It also explains the empirical finding mentioned earlier: accepting that beliefs should change in response to new evidence is "robustly associated" with several dimensions of healthy cognitive function.[9]

I want to shine a spotlight on some of the primary ways we damage reason's fulcrum. First, we can reason with what amounts to a thumb on the scales. Second, a cherished belief can lodge in the psyche and degrade rational resolve. In both cases, the lever-and-fulcrum metaphor sheds light on the underlying dynamic.

Unscrupulous merchants used to cheat customers by covertly depressing one side of a pan balance. This would cause the scale to deliver a false reading. (The expression "thumb on the scales" became an all-purpose metaphor for illicitly skewing results.) We do something similar with reasons: faced with a question, we'll make a show of weighing up the reasons for and against. Sometimes, though, we play favorites with the reasons and tip the scales in favor of the answer we want to get. We can grow quite adept at this—and good at fooling ourselves. It can then feel like you're reasoning fairly, when in fact you're not.

We're all prone to confirmation bias. We seek out confirming evidence and tend to overlook, downplay, or explain away information that might force belief change. It seems we prefer not to change our minds, and we bend reasons to the task of bolstering the beliefs we have. When this tendency goes unchecked, it can damage reason's fulcrum.

Philosophers employ several strategies to prevent this from happening. We celebrate epistemic humility. We tell stories that glorify the work of asking questions. We take objections seriously. We enjoy the process of testing ideas and turn the process inward—on our own beliefs. We turn the process into a game, and sometimes play with powerfully corrosive doubts. We try not to become too fond of our beliefs. We learn to live with uncertainty. In these and other ways, philosophy combats confirmation bias.

But confirmation bias isn't the only form of skewed thinking. For an idea needn't be *already on board* to receive favorable treatment. If we want to believe something, or are otherwise motivated to find it true, we'll often reason about it in tendentious ways. Here's an example: you want to do something that others might object to. Cheat on your taxes, say. An impulsive person might simply do it, but you're more circumspect. So you ask yourself: "May I cut corners on my taxes?" Then you look for a justifying reason. Reasons prove easy to manufacture, so soon, you have the permission you want. You file it away for safekeeping: if someone challenges you later—or audits your taxes—you can produce it to justify your corner-cutting, and maintain your reputation as a reasonably decent person.

Your desire to get a big tax refund, though, might cause you to overlook the reasons why cheating on your taxes is *not* okay. (Among them, of course, is this reason: doing it makes you a tax cheat.) You divert your attention away from such considerations and get the verdict you want. In this example, you do things with reasons, but you're not truly reasoning: you're rationalizing. You aren't reasoning to find out, you're reasoning to provide social cover. Psychologists call this tendency "motivated reasoning," and it's akin to—indeed a kind of—wishful thinking.

Motivated reasoning can be used in the other direction too.

Suppose you're expected to do something you're not inclined to do. Vote, say. You have the presence of mind, though, to engage in a little reflection. So you ask yourself, *"Must I go to the trouble of voting?,"* and begin looking for a reason why you shouldn't have to. As before, it proves easy to come up with an excuse, so you file it away. Should someone call you on your failure to vote, you can produce this reason and create the impression that you did due diligence. As before, though, you don't look very hard at the reasons on the other side. Again, this is not reasoning proper but rationalizing. Real reasoning seeks to find out, not rubber-stamp a predetermined conclusion.

Motivated reasoning is thought to reduce cognitive dissonance. Typically, it does this by bringing belief into alignment with desire. The dissonance can disappear, but often, the "solution" is problematic. First, the desire might be an unhealthy one: acting on it could harm you or others. Second, the resulting belief might not be true; motivated reasoning fuels delusions. Third, the process involves overlooking relevant considerations, which can lead to unwise decisions and actions. Finally, there's an almost willful unfairness in it: a failure to treat reasons *for* and reasons *against* in an even-handed way. Indulge in motivated reasoning enough, and skewed thinking becomes habitual.

It's a bit like putting your thumb on the scales and cheating your customers. Do this enough, and you lose your integrity. You can also damage your pan balance, rendering it incapable of giving an accurate reading. In just this way, habitual indulgence in motivated reasoning can decalibrate the mind. You can lose your ability to think straight.

For thousands of years, philosophers have counteracted these biases with questions like these: *Do I really know this? How do I know it? Is my source reliable? Do my reasons bear scrutiny?* These questions are fundamentally antibodies: the mind's way of protecting itself against bad ideas. They only protect your mind, though, if you make a habit of asking them. Remember this too: real reasoning is not about lining up reasons for a preordained conclusion, it's about examining reasons—pro *and* con—to find out what's true. Don't reason to win, reason to find out.

Imagine dropping a bowling ball into one pan of a delicate pan balance. Or placing a bowling ball in one pan, then applying a great force to the other pan. Imagine weighing a sticky, glue-like substance and finding a thick layer of it adhered to the weighing pan. Imagine grit fouling the mechanism. Our capacity to reason, I think, can be damaged in corresponding ways.

To see this, consider the phenomenon of *identity-protective cognition*. Dan Kahan, a decision scientist at Yale, has shown that we're averse to thinking thoughts that threaten our chosen identities.[10] Become a professor, and you'll find yourself more reluctant to criticize academics. Join a political party, and the party's fundraising—which looked like straightforward corruption from the outside—takes on a new aspect. When you start looking for identity-protective cognition, you find it everywhere: patriots who reflexively dismiss criticisms of their country; Marxists who can't admit that markets do some things rather well; fundamentalists who perform intellectual contortions to protect their faith. The list is easily extended. Importantly, though, identity-protective cognition isn't just found among flagrant ideologues.

Just by coining the phrase, Kahan opens our eyes to a widespread phenomenon. Identity protection appears to underlie many of our most egregious failures to think well. When your identity is at stake—or even feels as if it's at stake—you're likely to reason in dishonest, evasive, or self-serving ways. Identity protection can become an ideology trap.

The philosopher Rebecca Goldstein has a hypothesis that can further expand our awareness of ideology traps. She conjectures that human beings have a deep need to matter: we need to understand our lives as significant, as difference making.[11] The thought that we might not matter is profoundly uncomfortable, and we'll do almost anything to avoid that discomfort. We devote ourselves to causes, risk our lives, even *give* our lives. We kill and die, cheat and lie in order to feel that we matter.

At my urging, Goldstein has labeled this need "the mattering instinct." We both think that it's an underappreciated driver of human behavior. It's certainly a major driver of religious ideation. Religions are full of ideas that reassure people that they matter: *God loves you*; *We are God's chosen people*; *God sacrificed his only son for you*; *You have an important role to play in God's cosmic plan*; etc. What do all these ideas have in common? They all shout (or at least whisper) "You matter." In a world that affords too few opportunities to *really* matter, is it any surprise that we cling to mattering myths?

Importantly, the mattering instinct has secular as well as religious manifestations. Like believers, nonbelievers cling to delusions about their significance. For example, I cling to the hope that this book will somehow defy the odds and become widely influential. The thought gives me solace. Perhaps someday my work will be discovered and leave a lasting imprint on the world. Maybe I'll have mattered in something other than the small, everyday ways I try to matter: helping a friend here, providing an encouraging word there, inspiring the occasional student.

We all accumulate beliefs that bolster our sense that we matter, and we're loath to part with them. Question the value of a person's work, and expect a defensive reaction. If we marry Kahan's and Goldstein's ideas, we get the idea of *mattering-protective cognition*, or MPC. MPC is probably universal: doesn't everyone indulge in less-than-scrupulous thinking to protect their sense that they matter? Our need to matter clashes, time and again, with our commitment (however weak) to reason in fair-minded ways; and frequently, the former overrides the latter. As with Kahan's identity-protective cognition, when you start looking for it, you see it everywhere.

Existential needs, then, play a role in compromising our collective commitment to rational belief change. But more mundane needs also play a role. The author Upton Sinclair observed that "It's difficult to get a man to understand something when his salary depends on his not understanding it." The point applies to reasoning as well as understanding: a well-paid industry lobbyist can be counted on to reason in self-serving ways about the industry's ethical lapses. And clearly, the prospect of a billion-dollar windfall can compromise an oil baron's ability to think clearly about climate change. Sadly, we often sacrifice reason at the altar of economic self-interest.

When political or economic self-interest damages reason's fulcrum, moral reasoning also tends to go haywire. A learned unresponsiveness to good reasons can be very good for the corporate bottom line. It comes in handy if you need to screw with the planet's capacity to sustain life and feel like a decent human being in the morning. Sinclair's dictum, then, is just a corollary of what I'll call Norman's Law: *It's difficult to reason well when you need to reason poorly to feel like a decent human being.*

We sell out reason for fame too. And power. Indeed, the damaged fulcrum model suggests that every need, inclination, belief, desire, habit, norm, or institution that creates a stubbornly resistant counterweight to "better" reasons helps to weaken reason's fulcrum—thereby contributing to the unhinging of thought.

All of us, then, are implicated in the unhinging of reason. Religious and secular, conservative and liberal, we're all in it together. So let's put aside the accusations and instruments of cultural warfare; let's work together to enhance our immunity to ideological thinking. We can disarm Medusa, but only with mirrored shields.

But this, too, is true: we'll never complete this process if we don't take an honest look at religion. For religions appear to play a key role in weakening cognitive immune systems. Researchers have found, for example, that when people endorse religious worldviews, they're more susceptible to conspiracy thinking.[12] Religiosity correlates with anti-intellectualism and political intolerance.[13] Some researchers think the effect is mediated by what scientists call moral or coalitional rigidity—a tendency to sacralize things central to group identity, and thereafter refuse to compromise.[14] In fact, the embrace of sacred values may itself be motivated by tribal resistance to moral progress.[15] If this is right, secular and political allegiances can also produce such rigidity. Whether religiosity is a root cause or a contributing factor, either way, the question must be asked: Do religious habits of mind weaken mental immune systems? To my knowledge, the question has not been investigated empirically. In the meantime, we can explore it philosophically.

## The Problem with Faith

Years ago, I was enjoying conversation with a religious friend. The subject of gay marriage came up, and he asserted his opposition to its legalization. This surprised me. So I asked him: "Why would you want to interfere with the happiness of consenting adults—especially those who want to sanctify their commitment?" He replied that homosexual union runs counter to God's will: our Creator evidently meant for men to marry women, and women men. I took a slow breath. Careful to keep the incredulity out of my voice, I affected a tone of sincere curiosity. "How do you know that?" I asked mildly.

My friend shrugged. He couldn't really explain it, he said. It was just one of those things he knew. Men aren't meant to marry men, and women aren't meant to marry women: that was just an article of faith for him. It wasn't the kind of truth you could argue for, he said. It was too basic, too fundamental for that.

My friend said this with no hint of apology. For him, it seemed quite proper to have articles of faith and to invoke them in a debate over public policy. I was surprised at this and asked if he recognized the problematic nature of his stance. "Problematic?" he replied. "How so?" I was tempted to answer directly, but I wanted him to discover the reason for himself. So I asked questions instead. "Do you agree that we should treat others the way we want to be treated?" I asked.

"Of course," he replied. He seemed confident that the Golden Rule put him on firm argumentative ground.

"Well," I asked, "would you like it if someone invoked an article of faith to limit *your* freedom?" The question gave him pause. "What do you mean?" he replied. I clarified: "Suppose a Muslim invoked his articles of faith to justify imposing sharia law where you live: Would you be okay with that?" No, he admitted. I gave another example: "What if a person of another race invoked groundless beliefs to justify policies that oppressed you and your race?" My friend fell silent. I gave him a good minute to think about it. "Play the 'faith' card if you want," I said, "but then you can hardly object if others do the same."

Later, in another conversation, my concern came out as a kind of grievance. Why is it that people of faith—often the loudest champions of the Golden Rule—so often exempt their own convictions from basic norms of accountable talk, but don't extend the same exemption to people of other faiths? How is that not a double standard? My counterpart in this conversation, though, had a more ecumenical attitude: "I wouldn't dream of denying others their articles of faith," she affirmed. I tried to explain my issue with that stance, and it came out like this: "How does that not carve out a huge loophole in rationality norms—one that allows all kinds of irresponsible thinking, saying, and doing?" She had no reply.

When we all make ourselves persuadable, dialogue holds real potential to resolve our differences. When we retreat to nonnegotiable articles of faith, though, dialogue breaks down. How, then, can faith-based thinking *not* do damage to our prospects for dialogue-based conflict resolution?

At the time, I couldn't explain how the damage is done. Now I can: what I have called "bad faith" damages reason's fulcrum. It quite literally unhinges us. It weakens our capacity to think together in constructive, accountable ways. It compromises our best methods of civilized dispute resolution. The prevalence of faith-based thinking makes it exceedingly hard for humanity to forge a shared, reality-based understanding of what is. Or for that matter, a shared understanding of what matters. If the argument of this book is sound, the persistence of bad faith substantially diminishes our collective prospects.

I know many well-meaning people of faith. Most of them think of faith as a good thing. And the religious circles they inhabit tend to be humble, generous, and compassionate. When these folks cling to an otherwise baseless belief, they usually do so quietly, without ostentation or condemnation of others. My plea to well-meaning people of faith is this: take an honest look at the way the concept of faith functions. In your faith community, does it function as a blank check for unaccountable believing? If so, is it compromising reason's fulcrum? Could it not, as an unintended side effect, weaken mental immune systems? And if so, is it really a good idea to promote faith-based believing?

In 2018, a researcher studied the recent resurgence of Flat Earth theory. He attended a Flat Earth convention and found that "Flat Earth ideology appears to [involve] a merging of Young Earth Creationism and conspiracy thinking." When asked whether the Bible was meant to be interpreted literally, a conference attendee replied, "Yes, almost all of it [the Bible] is meant to be literal. And now I can take more of it literally as a Flat-Earther, which is satisfying."[16] Notice the conspicuous role here played by willful believing. The fact that conspiracy theorists, science deniers, and political extremists are often religious shouldn't surprise us; faith, like good intentions, can pave the road to a very bad place.[17]

A faith-based belief in God, of course, doesn't automatically produce evidence-defying attitudes about other things. You can believe in God and still believe in vaccines, evolution, and climate change. You can still be an exceedingly decent person. Evidence is mounting, though, that wishful thinking in some domains can "spill over" into other domains.[18]

Also, I'm not talking here about "good" faith: prosocial attitudes like trust and hope remain fundamental to human well-being, and the willful adoption of a positive attitude is a permissible coping strategy. Nothing I say here should be interpreted as denying this. If you want to refer to this coping strategy as "good faith," go ahead; just be careful not to confuse it with "bad faith"—the willful defiance of sensible epistemic standards. For those who flout reason's fulcrum damage a hugely civilizing social norm, and do us all a great disservice.

The good faith/bad faith distinction may prove useful, especially in the near term.[19] But in the end, I think, we'll conclude that it makes sense to dispense with a concept that, century after century, blurs an important line: between maintaining a resolutely positive attitude (a very good thing), and pugnaciously refusing to yield to better reasons (by my lights, a very bad thing). To avoid confusion, in other words, it might be best to relinquish the word *faith* to those who promote tenacious closed-mindedness. Let's use words like *hope*, *trust*, and *resolutely positive attitude* to denote the attitudes that are genuinely worth promoting. Let's secularize good faith and leave the rest behind.

Many, I expect, will resist this conclusion. Such reluctance must be met with patience and compassion. For anyone can become invested in their beliefs. Religious beliefs are notoriously change resistant, and belief change can't be forced. Perhaps an unusual exercise in cognitive immunotherapy can help.

## A Saboteur's Guide

You know those TV images of crash dummies driving shiny new cars into walls? They represent something engineers often do: *stress-test* their creations. Go out of your way to break something, and you can learn how to make it more robust. A similar approach can help us understand why human reasoning practices so frequently break down. We'll soon have computer models for this sort of thing. In fact, researchers are already subjecting virtual reasoning practices to simulated stresses.[20] In the meantime, we can perform an important experiment in imagination.

The experiment I have in mind is like the stress tests that information security professionals perform. Those who build sensitive online systems hire hackers and challenge them to break into their system. These "white hat" hackers help identify the system's vulnerabilities, so they can be patched up—preferably before malicious, "black hat" hackers do real damage. These white hat hackers are essentially friendly saboteurs: they stress-test systems in order to strengthen them.

Imagine yourself part of a team charged with stress-testing civilization's all-important reasoning practices. The team has an initial meeting, and the question is posed: How can we best disrupt human reasoning practices? The task is then clarified: How can we cause not just temporary disruption but lasting damage?

"We" would probably begin with a little reverse-engineering: we'd take apart the mechanism and see how it works. This would lead us to the lever-like functioning of reasons and the key role of reason's fulcrum. We'd come to realize that our reasoning practices hinge on a norm that requires us to accommodate ourselves to good reasons. Then we'd ask: How can we disable this norm?

We might start by creating a loophole in the requirement. Specifically, we could grant that yielding to better reasons is often a good thing, but deny that it's *always* a good thing. Certain beliefs, we might argue, are too important to be hostage to rational fortune. Then we'd carve out an exemption and insist that convictions X, Y, and Z belong to a special, protected class. We might call these convictions "articles of faith."

Then, we could spread the good news that this exemption exists. We'd probably appeal, first, to those who resent rational constraint and explain that, on certain subjects, it's okay to believe and assert things without evidence. From there, we could extend the exemption to claims that fly in the face of evidence—things made unlikely by, or directly contradicted by, facts. Claims about miracles and virgin birth, for example. Of course, we might need to traverse this path gradually, giving people time to acclimate to each expansion of the rationality exemption.

We could hasten the decline of rational standards by making some articles of faith mandatory: not just permissible, but required. In fact, we could make them nonnegotiable—the mental equivalent of the immovable object. The beauty of this approach is that, once such articles of faith are installed, efforts to dislodge them further degrade reason's fulcrum. The lever is obstructed, and something's got to give. A glance at history confirms that we're on to something here: reasoning practices are highly vulnerable to such stresses.

Next, we could sell people on the idea that credulity is a virtue. We could promise fantastic rewards for those who believe and threaten terrifying punishments for those who doubt. We could invent a being capable of delivering such rewards and punishments and make people fear him. Why can't you see this being? Because he's invisible. Why does he need you to believe in him? Never mind: just take our word for it. Why can't we see others experiencing their rewards and punishments? Because all that happens in the afterlife.

If all of this seems patently ridiculous, so much the better—by which I mean, so much the worse for rationality norms. As the Red Queen told Alice in Wonderland: believing impossible things takes practice. A saboteur of rational accountability norms must take this to heart. To wreak real havoc, you've got to think big. Go big or go home. Tepid irrationalism is for chumps. Real saboteurs wield *patently* unreasonable claims. When called on it, they double down on the delusion: that's the way to do *real* damage to rationality norms.

We can also stigmatize those who take epistemic standards seriously. If they're outspoken, we can demonize them. We can label them, say, infidels, heretics, heathens, apostates, or blasphemers. We can teach believers to shun and hate them. We can instruct believers to kill nonbelievers (as sacred texts sometimes do). Only a few believers need to follow through: the rest of the nonbelievers usually get the message and stop enforcing rationality norms. A little intimidation goes a long way.

We could also harness identity-protective cognition. The idea, again, is that people will usually bend rationality norms in order to protect their identity. The thing to do, then, is get people hooked on one or another ideological identity—preferably before they're old enough to understand the consequences. We could saddle children with the identities of their parents. Install an ideological identity early enough, and identity-protective thinking will often be with that person for life. From then on, challenges to identity-defining beliefs will feel offensive and somehow unfair. This is sure to damage reason's fulcrum.

We can also harness humanity's tribal instincts. We can build communities around arbitrary doctrinal differences and have the members of these communities validate each other's defiance of rationality norms. Us-versus-them stories can be counted on to stir deep emotions and skew rational judgment. We can exploit humanity's "mattering instinct"—our need to feel that our lives matter. To do this, just sell a group on the idea that they're God's chosen people. Or better yet, that God has some mysterious mission for them. Faced with temptation like that, rational resolution often crumbles. Mattering myths are highly seductive—and useful for subverting rationality norms.

We could exploit the evolved brain's penchant for kin sympathy. Those who share the tenets of the faith, for example, could be called "brother" or "sister." We could exploit our natural deference to authority. Authority figures in the community could be called "father" or "mother superior." The sky-being at the center of the big myth could be referred to as "lord" or "king."

We could confer status on the most aggressive champions of the faith, calling them "reverend," "holy father," "guru," or "ayatollah."

We could give these champions a platform and an audience—a "pulpit," say, and a "flock." They could use this platform to publicly violate rationality norms and celebrate the defiant disregard of such norms. Stories glorifying the sort of blind faith that Abraham had for God would be especially useful. (The founding parable of the so-called Abrahamic religions involves a father, Abraham, willing to sacrifice his son to prove his devotion to God.) See Abraham's breathtaking willingness to sacrifice not just his reason but also his son? The clear implication is that *that's* the sort of faith to aspire to.

We could develop a concept of the "sacred" or "holy" that paints certain things as too precious to question. We could label entire lines of inquiry profane. Or sacrilegious. We could promote contempt for intellectual virtues and deride rationality norms as "scientism run amok."

The most important thing, however, is to have a concept that blurs the line between keeping a positive attitude (something we all admire, and rightly understand to be good) and resolute closed-mindedness (something we should all have qualms about). One word—say, *faith*—should be used to refer to both phenomena. An effective campaign will sow confusion by suggesting that there's really no difference between the two. To accomplish this, we must use the word *faith* when we really mean everyday hope, trust, confidence, commitment, or resolve. This will give the word positive connotations. These associations will then carry over and help us rebrand the obstinate dogmatism needed to subvert reasoning practices. If we do this right, even well-meaning people will become resolutely unpersuadable yet believe themselves to be paragons of rational virtue.

Of course, religious ideas and practices are not the only way to damage our reasoning practices. We could use similar tactics to generate irrational obstinacy about other things. A fervent patriotism, for example, can also work to compromise rational resolve. This "stress test" of our reasoning practices, however, has revealed something quite striking: a deliberate effort to sabotage our reasoning practices would probably settle on tactics similar to those wielded by the world's most successful religions. In fact, many of religion's most distinctive features seem eerily well designed to protect core beliefs, damage reason's fulcrum, and thereby subvert the belief-modifying power of our reasoning practices.

To be clear: I'm not suggesting that the religious *deliberately* sabotage rationality norms. Some probably do, but the religious are usually well meaning, and the harm is inadvertent. But that doesn't make the damage any less real. Bad faith really does damage reason's fulcrum, gradually unraveling our capacity for rational self-transformation. And many good people—religious and secular—are unwittingly complicit in the harm.

Again, I'm not suggesting that the rationality-defying features of the world's religions are the sinister product of malevolent design. The idea is rather that cultural evolution has shaped religious ideas and institutions into things that persist in the face of evolving rationality norms. As our reasoning practices mature, they threaten irrational ideas and institutions. Some of these ideas and institutions die out: for example, we no longer sacrifice goats to Zeus. Other ideas and institutions, however, evolve countermeasures: ways of shutting down, or at least caging, the rational inquiry that threatens them. Prominent among these are ideas and expectations that degrade reason's fulcrum. In some ways, the world's faith traditions represent organized opposition to our reasoning practices.

Stress tests are meant to measure fault tolerances and, yes, find faults. The point, however, is not to cast blame. I'm not faultfinding in that sense. Scapegoating the religious won't solve the problem, and anyway, secular thinkers make comparable errors. I understand that there are excellent health-related reasons for reducing my sugar consumption, but time and again, I opt for just one more cookie. This is a failure of rational will, and I know it. So I won't be casting any stones.

The point is to better understand our reasoning practices and their vulnerabilities so we can make them more robust. If my argument is sound, this must be done in a collaborative spirit. We all need to acknowledge our rational shortcomings, roll up our sleeves, and help each other strengthen rational resolve. Working together, we can safeguard the reasoning practices that do so much to promote human and planetary welfare.

## Temple of the Future

In his 1971 song "Imagine," former Beatle John Lennon and his co-songwriter Yoko Ono invited listeners to imagine a world without religion. The song struck a chord. Its guileless lyrics, hopeful tone, and disarming melody made it a hit on both sides of the Atlantic. It went on to become one of the best-selling singles of all time. *Rolling Stone* magazine later described it as Lennon's "greatest musical gift to the world"—exceedingly high praise, considering the output of the Beatles. The recording industry consistently ranks "Imagine" among history's most significant musical accomplishments.

The song encourages us to conduct a thought experiment: in imagination, subtract religion from the world and see what you get. Since its release, countless people have performed the experiment and found that the resulting world—one untroubled by arbitrary religious divisions—is quite probably a better world. Others, though, get different results. Sensitive to the *costs* of subtracting religion, they draw different conclusions. The experiment, it turns out, is highly sensitive to what one understands religion to be.

I've just argued that major religions have features that damage our reason-giving practices. To some, these are the defining features of religions. To others, fellowship and congregational life are what's essential, and the reason-hostile features are merely accidental. The two camps often talk past each other. The path to shared understanding here involves adopting each of the proposed definitions in turn, running *both* thought experiments, and combining the results.

So let's concede—tentatively, and for argument's sake—a concept of religion as inherently hostile to reason. Now suppose that we subtract religion in this sense from the world. What kind of world results? If, as I have argued, our collective well-being is highly dependent on the health of our reasoning practices, the answer seems plain: subtract reason-hostile religions and get a vastly better world.

Now suppose we take other features of religions to be defining—features like congregational life, values-based community, social bonds deepened by shared commitment, and meaningful fellowship around some kind of "larger" (that is to say, self-transcending) purpose. We know that such involvements are important. For some, they provide relief from existential anxiety, making religion a sort of antidote to despair. For others, religions are fundamentally institutions that promote love, trust, hope, integrity, and moral accountability. If we concede—again, for argument's sake—that *that's* what religions are fundamentally about, and we imagine doing away with such institutions, it's not at all clear that we get a better world. In fact, the resulting world might be much worse. Lennon's thought experiment, it turns out, is highly sensitive to one's concept of religion.

I want to urge a different thought experiment. Imagine a world where religions haven't been *expunged*, but instead *reformed* into thoroughly reason-friendly institutions. What might *that* world be like? The astrophysicist Carl Sagan ran a similar thought experiment:

> How is it that hardly any major religion has looked at science and concluded, "This is better than we thought! The Universe is much bigger than our prophets said, grander, more subtle, more elegant?" Instead they say, "No, no, no! My god is a little god, and I want him to stay that way." A religion, old or new, that stressed the magnificence of the Universe as revealed by modern science might be able to draw forth reserves of reverence and awe hardly tapped by the conventional faiths.[21]

In *Zen and the Art of Motorcycle Maintenance*, Robert Pirsig's central character—a professor he calls Phaedrus—delivers a lecture arguing that the modern university is essentially a "church of reason." There's something to this claim, for universities are relatively reason-friendly institutions. *Imperfectly* reason-friendly, to be sure, but in principle committed to nurturing our reason-giving practices.

Pirsig's language suggests that universities are just another kind of religion. This way of speaking creates problems for any society that means to maintain church/state separation. For such a society would violate church/state separation every time it used academic research to formulate public policy. The perversity of *that* result should persuade us not to confuse universities with churches, or categorize a commitment to reason as just another religious commitment. Still, Pirsig's suggestion can help us imagine what it would be like to belong to a reason-friendly religion: it would be a bit like belonging to a university community.

Felix Adler's Ethical Culture movement sought to build religious congregations around secular ethical principles. Unitarian Universalism is a noncredal religion that promotes "the free and responsible search for truth and meaning." Today, congregational humanists meet regularly to build community around reason-friendly values, and Sunday Assemblies provide semireligious services without the God-talk. All of these are reason-friendly, quasi-religious institutions.

I direct a Humanism Initiative at Carnegie Mellon University. The initiative builds community around the values central to science and, more generally, honest inquiry. I work closely with our student-led Humanist League. The League is by no stretch a religion, but we do provide fellowship and a sense of belonging. We practice collaborative inquiry, promote reason-giving dialogue, and celebrate compassion. We encourage people to adopt reason-friendly identities like "humanist," "rationalist," and "freethinker," but welcome all comers.

My friend James Croft is the outreach director for the Ethical

Society of Saint Louis. I once invited him to Pittsburgh and gave him a tour of a remarkable local building: the University of Pittsburgh's thirty-five-story (and genuinely cathedral-like) Cathedral of Learning. James was instantly alive to the symbolism of the structure: rather than build cathedrals to entrench change-resistant beliefs, why not erect cathedrals to *learning*, i.e., the possibility of enlightened belief *change*?

Later, James spoke to the Humanist League and about a hundred guests. He gave a lovely tribute to Carl Sagan, and shared an inspiring vision. If memory serves, it featured something James calls "the temple of the future." His idea, I think, is to build institutions that are both quasi-religious and reason-friendly: institutions that can serve emotional and spiritual needs, while also nurturing and strengthening our reason-giving practices. I think he's on to something.

The Israeli historian Yuval Noah Harari has argued that every society needs to posit an "imagined order" that "confers superhuman legitimacy" on its ordering principles. I'm not sure he's right about this, but a well-functioning society may need to sacralize certain things to sustain itself. (One study showed that, on average, religious communes survive longer than secular communes.[22] I think this finding should give secular debunkers pause.)

With apologies, then, to John Lennon and Yoko Ono, I offer an "Imagine"-inspired invitation to help design the temple of the future. Perhaps a real artist can render the prose poetic, or even set it to music.

## Imagine 2

Imagine the world's religions re-formed as communities of *inquiry*. Imagine them teaching accountable talk. Imagine them dispensing healthy attitude adjustments, unencumbered by magical thinking or baldly improbable metaphysics. Imagine houses of worship becoming cathedrals of *learning*—places to practice the art of enlightened belief *change*.

Imagine a religion that seeks to untangle good and bad faith. Imagine devotional practices that work to strengthen, rather than weaken, mental immune systems. Imagine a religion that teaches the epistemic golden rule: "Observe the same standards of belief you would have others observe."

Imagine a religion that doesn't exploit the will to believe, but instead celebrates the will to find out.[23] What if religious education taught children to meet uncertainty, disagreement, and conflict with friendly collaborative inquiry? (Such inquiry deserves a cheeky, informal designation; I humbly propose "let's find out mode"—a designation conveniently abbreviated, in text messages, with the letters "lfom." Of course, it would be quite unfortunate if "lfo"—a shorthand invitation to inquire together—were mistaken for "lmfao"— shorthand for "laughing my effing posterior off.")

Imagine a religion that afforded identity options—like "seeker" or "rationalist"—that serve to loosen our attachments and mitigate our cognitive biases. What if the concepts of the sacred and the holy were used sparingly, and only to instill reverence for things that genuinely merit reverence: things like facts, evidence, and truth; compassion, kindness, and human dignity?

What if we used the power of myth to instill curiosity, wonder, and rational resolve? Can we use the story of Perseus and Medusa to teach the way of inquiry? Can the tale of Ulysses teach us to tune out the Siren song of unreason?

I'm inviting you to contemplate reforms that probably seem unrealistic. Perhaps they *are* unrealistic. But cynicism about the possibility of needed change won't get the final word here. I wanted to end this chapter by sharing the inspired closing refrain of "Imagine." There, Lennon and Ono remind us that reformers are invariably derided as "dreamers"—until the day we shrug off our cynicism, join them, and thereby *make* the needed change happen. Their artless lyrics would have made a better coda to this chapter, but alas, copyright law forbids me from reproducing them here. Still, you can summon the tune from memory (or google it). And nothing prevents us from heeding its timeless call to rise above cynical realism.

# PART IV

# Inoculating Minds

Science is like an inoculation
against charlatans.

—Neil deGrasse Tyson

Education, whatever else it
should be, must be an inoculation
against the poisons of life.

—Havelock Ellis

# CHAPTER 10

# Mind Upgrade

*Can we update the brain's
operating system?*

The illiterate of the 21st century will not be
those who can't read or write, but those who
can't learn and unlearn. —*Alvin Toffler*

What would a mind vaccine look like? In the chapters that remain, I mean to develop one. The concept is to move past an
influential but ultimately dysfunctional standard of reasonable belief
and replace it with a better standard—one capable of reducing our
susceptibility to bad ideas. By doing this we essentially update the
mind's antivirus software. But that's not all: because our understanding of reason's requirements plays a pivotal role in our thinking, such
an update can be compared to an *operating system upgrade*: a mind
upgrade, if you will. If I'm right, we can inoculate minds against
morally disorienting ideologies and become wiser versions of ourselves. The trick is to engineer a certain shift in the way we think
about reason.

Step one is to understand how vaccination works.

## Manufacturing Immunity

In 1796, an English doctor named Edward Jenner infected his gardener's eight-year-old son with the relatively harmless cowpox virus. As he'd hoped, the child developed an immunity to *smallpox*, a far deadlier disease. To test his hypothesis, Jenner then exposed the kid to smallpox. (Creepy? Ethical? You be the judge.)

The experiment confirmed that the boy was immune, so Jenner coined the term *vaccine*, and news of his discovery spread across Europe. England began offering vaccinations for free. Spain organized a massive vaccination campaign in the Americas—the same continent its conquistadors once ravaged with disease. In France, Napoleon had his troops vaccinated, then declared Jenner "one of humanity's great benefactors." It would take almost two hundred years, but Jenner's vaccine would essentially eradicate smallpox—a disease that, all told, has probably killed almost a *billion* human beings. Jenner may have been ethically challenged, but Napoleon wasn't wrong.

Jenner wasn't the first to inoculate people, but the method he pioneered—vaccination—is arguably one of humanity's most consequential innovations. The cowpox he used was a naturally occurring inoculant—something that evolved on its own. Today, though, vaccines are distinctly artificial—the product of an intricate development process. Before a vaccine can be administered, someone must isolate the infectious agent, weaken or kill it, then purify, stabilize, preserve, and enhance it. Vaccines must be tested for effectiveness, checked for safety, and mass-produced. A good one will motivate the immune system to produce disease-fighting proteins called antibodies.

There are certain things everyone should know about vaccines. The heartwarming story of Jonas Salk contains many of them.

As a teenager, Jonas Salk had a nerdy dream. In it, he was a medical scientist making discoveries that would benefit humanity. It was a dream facing long odds. First, college was expensive, and Salk's family was poor. Second, his age (fifteen) was a red flag for college admissions officers. Finally, he was a Jew at a time when colleges used quotas to screen out Jews. The kid had three strikes against him, but he applied anyway. Happily, college admissions isn't baseball: New York's City College gave him a shot, and Salk enrolled in 1929. Barely a month later, the US stock market crashed and America entered the Great Depression. Dire economic conditions would last for the rest of Salk's formative years, and cripple many a career.

But Salk persisted. He impressed his teachers, got his degree, and enrolled in New York University's medical school. There, he got a chance to study the newly discovered influenza virus. He learned that a virus stripped of its "infectivity" can be used to immunize people. With this, he grasped a basic principle of immunology: the right biochemical compound can teach the immune system how to spot and neutralize a pathogen. In a very real sense, the immune system can *learn*. Intrigued, Salk dedicated his life to immunology.

In 1950, polio was a widespread and terrifying disease. So Salk set up a lab and got to work. Year after year, he put in long hours. He isolated the virus and worked out how to kill it. He purified, preserved, and enhanced the resulting serum, then tested it on lab animals. He tried, he failed, and he tried again. Eventually, he found something that worked and tried it on human subjects. It performed beautifully, and in 1955, his discovery became headline news: *Polio Vaccine Proved Safe and Effective*. Overnight, Salk became a scientific celebrity. Millions of kids were vaccinated, and polio was all but extinguished. Salk became a nerdy kind of folk hero, lauded wherever he went. For the rest of his life, he'd regret his loss of anonymity. (Apparently, *recognition* for benefiting humanity was not part of the dream.)

In a TV interview, the journalist Edward R. Murrow asked Salk who owned the patent on his vaccine. Salk looked puzzled, then stammered: "Well, the people I would say. There is no patent. Could you patent the sun?" Incredibly, Salk viewed the substance he'd painstakingly *designed* as common property. Half a century later,

*Forbes* magazine estimated that a patent on the vaccine would have been worth about seven billion dollars. There's no evidence that Salk mourned the lost windfall: he'd realized his dream, and that was enough.

## How Vaccines Work

Salk's story illustrates some key points. First, vaccine development involves a lot of trial and error. Second, a vaccine is more than an inoculant. In most cases, it's a carefully engineered biological compound. Usually, it involves an active ingredient and one or more complementary ingredients. Scientists call the active ingredient an "immunogen," and its job is to profile the pathogen for the immune system. Typically, a dead or weakened form of the dangerous microbe is used to "teach" the immune system what to guard against. It essentially uploads a profile of the disease into the immune system's "database." For simplicity, I'll call this active ingredient the "inoculant."

Scientists call the complementary ingredients "adjuvants," and their job is to prime the immune system to deliver a more decisive response. They help the immune system "draw the right lesson" from the inoculant. That way, when the actual pathogen comes along, the body knows what to do: produce antibodies and fight off the disease. Combine the right inoculant with the right adjuvants, and you can manufacture immunity.

Immunologists have ample reason to describe the immune system as capable of "learning" how to "recognize" pathogens. For it has two major subsystems. One of them—the *innate* immune system—employs inherited biochemical profiles of infectious agents. This is the system that acts on microbes the genome recognizes as pathogenic. Simply put, the innate system handles pathogens the gene line "knows" to be dangerous. By contrast, the *adaptive* immune system responds to unfamiliar pathogens. It essentially learns from experience by developing brand-new profiles of harmful parasites. *A vac-*

*cine, then, is a compound we deliberately manufacture to help the adaptive immune system learn how to handle an unfamiliar disease.* It sounds odd to put it like this, but vaccine development amounts to a kind of instructional design.

With this in mind, we can ask the essential question: How might a mind vaccine work? Apparently, it would *instruct*—that is, teach the mind how to identify and rid itself of (some) parasites. Presumably, this means equipping it with a profile: a "picture" of what a bad idea looks like. (Or alternatively, something that conveys what a *good* idea looks like; a screening mechanism can use either sort of profile.) The idea is to outfit the mind's security team with a better, more discriminating set of criteria, so it can keep out cognitive troublemakers.

Here's what makes the task difficult: we can't afford to be indiscriminately critical. We want to increase our resistance to bad ideas without compromising our openness to good ones. We need the mind's gatekeepers to be smart and selective. They need to know their stuff. At some level, they need to understand what makes bad ideas bad and good ideas good. They need to be *appropriately* discriminating.

One of my favorite bumper stickers reads DON'T BELIEVE EVERYTHING YOU THINK. This is arguably the founding insight of philosophy: some thoughts are worth accepting and relying on; others aren't. But a question follows in its wake: Which of our thoughts *should* we rely on? We philosophers have been working this problem for a long time. We call it the search for wisdom. The idea is to equip the mind with the profiles it needs to distinguish right from wrong, real from imaginary, true from false, and knowledge from mere opinion. In short, to tell good from bad.

Philosophers embarked on this quest long ago and quickly realized that reasoning together is a powerful way to enhance judgment. We've seen that, to benefit from this strategy, you need to do certain things, among them: adopt a collaborative mindset, listen intently, and try to learn from the objections of others. You need to express reservations, test ideas for viability, and try not to rely on untested opinions. Above all, you must yield to "better reasons." When we do these things, judgment tends to improve.

But like the bumper sticker, it raises a more difficult question, namely: What does "better reason" mean, exactly? What is the relevant test? What kinds of reasons and considerations signal that an idea is worth relying on? When we critically examine an idea, what exactly should we be looking *for*? The presence of some distinctive configuration of supporting (upstream) reasons? A proof, perhaps? The absence of countervailing reasons? Evidence of some kind? If so, what kind of evidence? And how much? Or should we be looking at (downstream) implications? When is a belief's pragmatic fallout disqualifying, and when is it not? When you train your mind's eye on the relevant considerations, what does a reasonable judgment look like?

These questions can be rolled into a single, beautiful question, specifically: *What are reason's requirements?* Or if you prefer: To what standard should we hold our opinions? In the book's remaining chapters, I mean to sketch a novel answer to this question—one meant to enhance mental immune function. A mind vaccine, if you will.

Two caveats. First: I don't imagine that the vaccine developed here will confer full immunity to all bad ideas. That's a very high bar, and I don't claim to clear it. That's why I say "enhanced" immune function: for now, it will be enough to fashion a *better* understanding of reason's requirements. If we're successful, we can continue to refine the standard. There are at least two kinds of improvement in play here: you can get better at screening out bad ideas, and you can get better at letting in good ones. Cognitive immunology, in other words, gives us a preliminary answer to the question "What does 'better' mean in this context?" Second caveat: a better understanding of reason's requirements is more inoculant than vaccine. By itself, it can't impart robust immunity. Immerse that understanding in the right "serum," though, and you can equip the mind to better protect itself. It's the combination that produces results.

So here's the plan. In chapter 12 I'll modify an ancient picture of reasonable belief and show how the result can boost mental immune response. This is our inoculant: the active ingredient of what could become a powerful mind vaccine. (The vaccine itself is new, but its core idea is recycled.) First, though, I need to give you a guided tour of philosophy's mind-vaccine lab. On this tour, you'll learn how cognitive immunologists test their proposed inoculants (this chapter), and see for yourself why prevailing conceptions of reasonable belief are bankrupt (chapter 11).

Yes, I expose such bankruptcy in chapter *11*. Happy accident.[1]

Incidentally, chapter 11 also tells a remarkable tale. For a hundred generations, philosophers have sought wisdom and proposed candidate standards of reasonable belief. Time and again, their ideas have leaked out of the lab, updated mental and cultural immune systems, and changed the course of history. Time and again, they've gained cultural prominence and altered the way civilizations evaluate ideas. If we examine this history through the lens of cognitive immunology, we gain fresh insight and come to understand how philosophy's wisdom quest lost its way. I think this story—recast as the quest for a wisdom-conducive mind vaccine—can boost our immune response to bad ideas.

In a way, chapters 10 and 11 constitute a cognitive "serum." Their job is to prime you to benefit from the inoculant developed in chapter 12. If I do this properly, the lesson will "take" and confer enhanced immunity to bad ideas.

## The Mindset of the Morally Incurious

Long ago, Plato noticed a major pitfall on the path to wisdom. He realized that it's easy to fall into, hard to climb out of, and a major obstacle to moral growth. So he planted a warning sign, then skipped off down the path. He left me far behind, but there's a silver lining in that: I can alert folks to the danger. That's my goal in the remainder of this chapter: to flag this "wisdom trap" and guide you safely past it.

Here's the problem: several clever-but-superficial arguments breed an incurious attitude about important things. This in turn interferes with learning and critical thinking. Sadly, many of us get suckered in by the arguments and develop a condition I call the "mindset of the morally incurious." In the rest of this chapter, I hope to dismantle the arguments and kindle a particularly philosophical form of curiosity.

The exercise should also confer a measure of cognitive immunity. For the mindset of the morally incurious is a major mental immune disruptor: it prevents the removal of problematic assumptions about what matters. (Direct evidence for this claim remains scarce because the concepts are so new; a growing body of research on moral rigidity, though, provides plenty of indirect evidence.[2]) Meanwhile, curiosity is essential to healthy mental immune function. These facts make the remainder of this chapter another form of cognitive immunotherapy—a key ingredient of the mind vaccine our world so badly needs.

Before we step into philosophy's mind-vaccine lab, here's what you need to know about our testing methodology: we like to pick out a concept with distinctly positive connotations—say *good, right, fair, honest, true, known,* or *reasonable*—and ask what it means. Then, we ask whether there's a *better* understanding of what it means. We try to define the concept, then run a thought experiment: we imagine a world where people rely on the proposed definition to sort the good from the bad, the right from the wrong, the fair from the unfair, or the reasonable from the unreasonable. Then we ask ourselves: What would such a world be like? Would it be *better* than the world we have, or would it be *worse*? We find that such thought experiments reveal fascinating things.

Now, a clever thought experimenter can usually show that a proposed definition is imperfect—that it misclassifies something, or otherwise creates problems. And our tendency is to interpret such findings as failed experiments. This contributes to a persistent illusion: that philosophy fails to generate results.

Here's what philosophy's detractors fail to see: even the failed experiments teach us something about the phenomenon of interest. *For thousands of years, philosophers have regarded failed thought experiments as significant negative results.* They welcome the opportunity to learn from such failure and use it to refine and deepen moral understanding. But it's addition by subtraction—what I've called "subtractive learning." For example, we can imagine a world where everyone defines "justice" the way a selfish child might: as "more of the good stuff for me." It's not hard to see that such a world would devolve into infighting, and a diminished life for all. In his dialogue *Republic,* Plato has Socrates argue just that. He also examines a more refined conception: justice involves everyone getting what they deserve. Socrates shows that even *that* definition is problematic, and we learn not to rely on it overmuch. Imagining a world with different standards and seeing for yourself why things don't work out are staples of moral learning.

If you learn to perform this operation, your moral sensibilities can evolve rapidly. This can put a philosophically adventurous person on the cutting edge of moral progress. It's no accident that the concepts of human rights, women's rights, animal rights, empirical evidence, and distributive justice were all boundary-pushing philosophical proposals before they seeped into common sense: in each case philosophical argumentation revealed the concept to be promising, so its use spread. But many feel threatened by this process: the privileged find the concept of equal rights threatening; some men find the concept of women's rights threatening; most faith traditions find the concept of scrupulously evidence-based believing threatening; and resource-hoarding rich people find the concept of distributive justice threatening.

So philosophical inquiry has a long history of making people uncomfortable. To many, philosophical investigations feel like accusations of moral backwardness. So instead of learning from them, they tend to react defensively. Historically, insecure traditionalists have chosen moral ignorance—willful belief—and lashed out against moral progressives. (The conservative backlash against progressives in our own time—with its disdainful references to "political correctness," "bleeding hearts," "libtards," and "liberal elites"—is just the latest example of a morally regressive backlash.) When moral progressives seek to bend the arc, the privileged and the morally backward fight back.

It almost never helps to accuse someone of moral backwardness, but make no mistake: moral backwardness exists. It's a real thing. Those who opposed the abolition of slavery were morally backward, and those who oppose a more enlightened distribution of the planet's wealth are equally backward.

In fairness to conservatives, progressive proposals can be poorly thought out. Often, they have unintended consequences. China's Great Leap Forward, for example, was anything but. Also, it led to tens of millions of unnecessary deaths. At its best, conservatism employs reasons to counteract the excesses of progressivism and reduce the risk of rash reform—just as progressives employ reasons to spur needed change. But when either stance adopts the aggressive demeanor of the culture warrior (or for that matter, the defensive posture of the true believer), it loses the moral high ground. Hey conservatives: we liberals aren't the enemy. And fellow liberals: our conservative brothers and sisters aren't the enemy. The real enemy—our common enemy—is unreason.

## Curiosity Killers

We have a moral incuriosity problem. Tribal emotions are a big part of it, and readily available excuses are too. Here's what I mean: it's easy to convince yourself that value inquiry is a waste of time. Especially if philosophy has been portrayed as useless, impractical trifling. In a culture disdainful of philosophy, it becomes easy to talk yourself into the mindset of the morally incurious.

Plato articulated the bones of the problem in a dialogue titled *Meno*. In it, Socrates and Meno are about to inquire into the nature of virtue (good moral character, basically), and Meno is suddenly struck by an apparent difficulty. There seem to be two possibilities: either we begin the inquiry with the knowledge we seek, or we don't. If we *do* have such knowledge, the inquiry appears pointless, for why seek for something you already have? On the other hand, if we *don't* have such knowledge, inquiry appears to be equally pointless, for how would you know where to look? And how would you recognize the answer as correct? Either way, Socrates points out, moral inquiry appears to be a waste of time. Philosophers call this argument "Meno's paradox."

So why bother? Why seek to deepen your understanding of right and wrong? Why not stand pat and cling tenaciously to the moral opinions you have? That way you can feel good about yourself and not risk learning that, morally speaking, you have room to grow. In this way, the way of belief beckons.

Socrates responds that Meno's pointless-either-way argument is clever but superficial. In the end, it's an excuse—one that breeds moral incuriosity. He goes on to advance an alternative model of moral learning. On this model, learning is fundamentally a matter of re-membering what the eternal soul has partially forgotten. Philosophers call this Plato's "Doctrine of Recollection," and it's meant to explain how questioning and introspection—philosophizing, basically—can deepen our understanding of right and wrong.

Socrates confessed to having doubts about the Doctrine of Rec-ollection but concludes that, true or false, it's probably useful. If it can prevent us from concluding that value inquiry is pointless, and laps-ing into a morally incurious mindset, he tells Meno, it might prove learning-conducive. Unfortunately, almost no one thinks it's true, and this compromises the idea's utility.

Plato did as much as anyone to save us from moral incuriosity, but after twenty-four hundred years of building on the foundation he laid, genuine craving for moral wisdom remains rare. As a result, folly and unreason plague humanity. Religious zealotry inspires senseless violence. Stupid wars cause terrible suffering. Poverty, hunger, and injustice afflict billions. We plunder the planet for short-term gain, strain ecosystems, and court environmental collapse. Everyone knows that greater wisdom will be needed to develop a sustainable future, but even so, the will to acquire deep wisdom is barely in evidence. Plato would be appalled by our lack of progress along this dimension.

I think a better model of moral learning can help. We also need to be conscious of several things that deaden curiosity:

1. *Conceit*—The smug assurance that one's understanding of reasonable belief is already adequately developed. (This one has come up before: it proved to be a product of illusory superiority—the so-called Lake Wobegon effect.) We tend to think: "I use the word *reasonable* with adequate facility. Every time I check my understanding against particular cases, it checks out. So no thanks; no need for a better understanding here." Consequence: incuriosity about the nature of reasonable belief.

2. *Lack of imagination*—The inability to imagine how much more a well-developed understanding of reason could be doing for us. Consequence: more incuriosity. (I hope this book is convincing you that a better understanding of reason's requirements can do all of the following for us: strengthen our reasoning practices, confer cognitive immunity, reduce ideological thinking, improve judgment, advance science, cultivate problem-solving, streamline dialogue, resolve conflicts, reduce violence, stimulate progress, and afford meaning. The truth is that small improvements in our capacity for reasoned judgment can yield large benefits.)

3. *Incomprehension*—The inability to comprehend how upgrading your understanding of reason's requirements might work. After all, where would you look for a better standard? And how would you recognize it? Wouldn't you have to assess any new standard using the standard that's already on board? And wouldn't any new standard have to appear *sub*-standard, relative to the old standard? After all, nothing can match the operative standard as well as it matches itself! What's the point, then, in seeking a better understanding of reason? Consequence of such reasoning: more incuriosity.

4. *Apparent lack of a factual basis*—Can there even be an objectively correct understanding of reason's requirements? Surely there's no fact of the matter as to what "reasonable" *really* means. For where would such a fact live? Is there any room, in a scientific universe, for facts like that? Apparently not: the search for a correct understanding of reason's requirements, then, looks a lot like a unicorn hunt. Why seek something that's not there? Apparent lesson: moral curiosity is unwarranted.

5. *Relativism*—Standards of reasonable belief are invariably subjective. You have your standards of reasonable belief, and I have mine. Insisting on mine would amount to imposing my will on you, and that's wrong. Meanwhile, we have our standards and they have theirs. Who's to say that ours are better? Doing so would amount to cultural imperialism. Dwell on considerations like these, and it can seem intolerant to have any conviction at all. On this warped logic, moral incuriosity starts to look like a virtue! (Yet another reason "the best lack all conviction.")

6. *Moral Cowardice*—The only facts that might ground a given opinion about the true meaning of "reasonable," it seems, are the word-usage norms that happen to prevail. But who's to say that the prevailing norms are the right ones? Wouldn't

assuming so beg the question against other conceptions? You need to rely on some concept of reasonable belief to inquire, so inquiry is invariably tainted by bias. Best to be scrupulously neutral and simply avoid the question. Consequence: more incuriosity.

It turns out we can do more—a *lot* more—to cultivate moral curiosity. We can puncture arrogant conceits. We can fire imaginations. We can combat relativism. We can inspire moral courage. We can expose the flaw in Meno's paradox. We can develop a concept of learning that promotes rather than inhibits moral growth. We can dismantle all six of these curiosity-killing arguments. In fact, we can replace the rhetorical questions that animate them with better questions. Questions like:

- When it comes to standards of reasonable belief, what does "better" even mean?
- If standard A is better than standard B, what makes it so?
- How can we know that standard A is better than standard B?

Finally, we can use the tools of cognitive immunology to answer these questions. The combination adds up to powerful cognitive serum.

## How Moral Learning Works

Many of us harbor a flawed mental model of learning. We imagine it works like this: you come across a new fact, and add a discrete bit of knowledge to the knowledge receptacle that is your mind. *That*, we tend to assume, is what learning fundamentally is. Following Karl Popper, I call this the "bucket" model: on it, the mind is like a bucket, and learning is like gathering pebbles and putting them in the bucket. Educational practices today are largely built around this model. (Its preconceptions are embedded in the tests we teach to, not to mention the architecture of our lecture halls.) When you treat a kid as a passive knowledge receptacle, though, that's what they become.

But Meno's paradox *shows* us that the bucket model is flawed. For it makes nonsense of active learning—something we know to exist. Moral education—the process of learning right from wrong—becomes especially problematic, for it's not clear that there are any moral facts to gather.[3] Let's sidestep the question of moral facts, though, so we don't get bogged down. The real key is to replace the bucket model with a better model of learning.

We talk about knowledge as if it were quantized—as if it came in discrete chunks, like pebbles. For any given piece of knowledge, you either know it or you don't. But Meno's paradox should shake this conviction. For if knowledge were fundamentally discrete, research would be pointless. You'd either have what you seek already ("Relax, it's in the bucket!") or you'd lack the means of seeking it ("You don't know what you're looking for, so why try?") If knowledge were truly quantized, research wouldn't be a thing. But it is.

A scientist I know taped these words to his office door: "If we knew what we were doing, it wouldn't be called 'research'!" This hand-printed provocation put me in mind of Meno's paradox, so I tapped on his open door. "About this," I said, pointing to his sign. "Suppose we had *no idea* what we were doing—that we were stumbling about randomly—would we call it research then?" He thought about it, laughed, and admitted, "Probably not." I told him about Meno's paradox, and we spent half an hour trying to unravel it. Our conclusion? Research happens only where there is partial understanding.

Consider replacing talk of *knowledge* with talk of *understanding*. For understanding is never an all-or-nothing thing—it's always a matter of degree. To quote the philosopher Ludwig Wittgenstein, understanding is about "seeing connections"—a process whereon "light dawns gradually over the whole." For practical reasons, then, moral inquiry should be reconceived: it's not about amassing discrete moral facts, it's about the iterative refinement of partial understanding.

Incidentally, we needn't presume that objectively correct answers to moral questions are out there, waiting to be discovered, the way pebbles are out there, waiting to be tossed into a bucket. All that's required are better and worse ways of conducting our affairs. If we have standards, and those standards can function more or less well, it makes sense to ask whether they stand in need of refinement. If you like, think of it as a *design* process: a process wherein we create something new, rather than discover something preexisting. Make this gestalt shift, and the motivational obstacle to pursuing deeper understanding evaporates.

Each of us harbors a kind of half-baked understanding of what's reasonable. These conceptions form in idiosyncratic, impressionistic ways. They tend to be vague and not terribly useful for judging hard cases. They aren't particularly useful for teaching critical thinking. They're invariably partial (in both senses: shaped by self-interest and incomplete). As any philosopher can tell you, pre-theoretical ideas about reason are vulnerable to the simplest objections (as we'll see in the next chapter). Significantly, our concepts of what's reasonable *differ*, which dramatically complicates our efforts to resolve our differences with words. Consequently, our collective capacity for reason-guided conflict resolution remains underdeveloped, and our capacity for moral inquiry remains stunted.

Imagine replacing such half-baked understanding with understanding that is three-quarters baked. Or seven-eighths baked. What if we came up with a clear, explicit, defensible, and useful standard of reasonable belief—one that's properly vetted, suitable for sharing, and worth relying on collectively? Such a conception would fill a yawning gap in critical thinking instruction and accelerate efforts to make critical thinking a way of life. Instead of relying on subjective guesswork, we'd have something like an objective standard.

I hasten to add that "objective" here means nothing like "the final, ultimate answer—the one that makes it unnecessary to continue learning." It means something like "well tested, nonarbitrary, better than anything else we have at present, hence worth relying on until we find a better one." Even with an *explicit, vetted, useful,* and *shared* standard of reasonable belief—even then there'd be room for improvement.

How often does dialogue break down for lack of a shared measure of reasonableness? How often does inquiry run aground, or problem-solving fail to bear fruit, for want of the same? Start looking for such instances, and you find them everywhere.

A better understanding of reason would also help inoculate minds against ideological infection. It would help us reason more capably not just about what *is* but also about what *ought to be.* It would allow us to build shared and responsible "mattering maps" and think together with real clarity about right and wrong.[4] With such a standard in hand, ethical and political discourse would become markedly more fruitful.

"What makes reasonable things reasonable?" is very much a philosophical question. But it's the exact opposite of impractical. A good answer would in fact be hugely useful.

## What "Better" Means

Consider again this rationale for harboring the mindset of the morally incurious: I know what's reasonable. My conception works for me. I use the word *reasonable* with some facility. When I check my judgments about what's reasonable against the only measure I have—my intuitions about what's reasonable—they check out. So you see, I have no need for an understanding upgrade.

Note the self-validating circularity of such thinking. Note its sad lack of humility. It's oblivious to all the ways our conceptions of reason are deficient, and all the ways our understanding might develop. If an immunologist or network security specialist exhibited similar complacency, they'd merit immediate dismissal.

The real challenge here is to help people imagine how much more a conception of reason could be doing for us. Why settle for a vague, inchoate standard when we could have one that's clear and explicit? Why settle for one that's untested when we could have one that's been carefully vetted? Why settle for each of us harboring an individual, subjective standard when we could share an objective (or nonarbitrary) standard?

When I speak of a "better" understanding of reason's requirements, I mean one that is clear, explicit, vetted, defensible, well functioning, and shared. What makes these the right qualities to focus on? Well, look at the way reasoning works, and think about ways to improve that functioning.[5] Do this, and it quickly becomes apparent what "better" ought to mean in this context.

The immunology frame gives us a simple and useful way to think about improvement along this dimension. We can get better at screening out bad ideas and better at letting in good ones. Notice again that getting better at one can involve getting worse at the other. For example, if you traded in your everyday concept of a bad idea for one that classifies all ideas as bad, you'd get very good at screening out bad ideas but very bad at letting in good ones. This would not be a progress-conducive replacement. The opposite extreme—treating all ideas as good ones (aka believing everything you think) would be indiscriminate and dysfunctional, too, but in a different way.

When we clarify the role that a normative concept plays in our lives, we come to understand its functional requirements. This puts us in touch with nonarbitrary measures of adequacy: Is the standard clear and explicit? Is it impartial? Is it defensible? Is it useful? Does it help us discriminate properly between good stuff and bad stuff? There's a practical alternative, in other words, to circular self-validation: instead, we can understand the concept's role, then extract and apply functional requirements. With this realization, we get a framework for answering the question: "What makes reasonable things reasonable?" (A comparable process yields a framework for answering "What is virtue?" The same goes for other normative questions.) And with this, Meno's paradox dissolves.

We've done more here than resolve an academic puzzle. We've shown how to uproot moral incuriosity. Simplistic conceptions of mind, knowledge, and learning cause real-world mischief. They make it hard to see how moral comprehension upgrades work and sap our motivation to learn. They block individual growth and slow collective progress. But It doesn't have to be this way. Instead, we can adopt conceptions that are more useful, more learning-conducive, and closer to the truth. And in this way, make meaningful progress toward collective wisdom.

## Why Philosophical Progress Is Inconspicuous[6]

A final word to equip you for the rigors that lie ahead. It's easy to glance at the history of philosophy and think: two and a half millennia on, and still no final answers to life's big questions? Where are the definitive findings? Why is there no recognized inventory of solved philosophical problems? Philosophy, it seems, is a fruitless enterprise.[7]

This complaint is triply blind. First, it's blind to the vast bulk of philosophical findings. Often, philosophical idea-testing doesn't leave us with a definitive answer to the question of what something (like justice, goodness, or reasonableness) is. Instead, it leaves us with insights about what the thing *isn't*. In this way, philosophical inquiry is a bit like sculpting: you carve away the marble that doesn't look like David, and you end up a bit closer to a statue of David.

Second, the complaint is blind to the way philosophical findings seep into the larger culture and become unobtrusive features of common sense. The concept of human rights, for example, was originally a philosophical invention. In just over a century, it blossomed into mainstream thinking, changed modes of governance,

and dramatically improved human welfare across Europe.[8] Because
the concept is now woven into our culture, we don't need textbooks
to convey the basic idea. People absorb it, to the extent they do, by
osmosis.

Many philosophical findings are like that. Basic truths about
women's rights, civil rights, and animal rights were once derided as
impractical philosophizing; now, they're pillars of common decency.
The concept of evidence was once a philosophical innovation; now,
it's an integral part of common sense. The operating system gets
an upgrade, and soon, it's just the taken-for-granted backdrop for
thinking. The arduous path that conceptual inquiry took to create
the upgrade is erased, like a trail of breadcrumbs left to the birds.

Finally, the idea that philosophy is fruitless is blind to the many
philosophical findings that are locked away in dusty, abstract vol-
umes written for specialists. The professionalization of the discipline
has had many unfortunate side effects; one is that potential upgrades
to our mental operating systems remain trapped in hyper-technical
language. To address this concern, philosophers need to change their
approach—or arrange for the translation of their findings. We can
jump-start cognitive immunology by doing just that.

Next up: a capsule history of philosophy's search for a mind
vaccine.

# CHAPTER 11

# Seductive Misconceptions

### *How rationalism lost its way*

Human history in essence is the
history of ideas. —*H. G. Wells*

Ideas have unhinged the gates
of empires. —*Paul P. Harris*

For twenty-four hundred years, we philosophers have sought a
better understanding of reason's requirements. We've tested hundreds of possibilities and learned something important: common assumptions about reason don't withstand scrutiny. In fact, the criteria
folks employ in their day-to-day lives fail the most basic tests.[1] Works
of epistemology are full of such demonstrations, but philosophers
rarely translate these findings into terms the rest of us can appreciate.
That's where the language of cognitive immunology comes in. For it
allows us to explain, simply and directly, why common conceptions
of reason are problematic: at best, they fail to induce healthy cognitive function; at worst, they create serious *dys*function. Some of
them make mental immune systems *underactive* and vulnerable to

the mind-parasites we call bad ideas; others make them *overactive* and prone to attack good ideas.

With the tools of cognitive immunology in hand, though, we can reinterpret philosophy's wisdom quest: epistemology amounts to a laboratory—a testing ground for mental inoculants. And the history of epistemology amounts to an epic, quasi-scientific investigation. In this chapter, I want to tell its story. I'll proceed chronologically, highlight essential discoveries, and show how assumptions about reason have time and again altered cultural immune health. The immunology lens lets us see, with startling clarity, how the quest for wisdom lost its way.

Now the actual history is messy and complex: full of false starts, wrong turns, and dead ends. So I won't attempt completeness. Instead, I offer an overview: a tale of four influential concepts of reasonable belief, and how each one shaped prevailing reasoning practices. In some cases, the favored concept damaged humanity's prospects; in other cases, it substantially improved them. All along, though, the failure to achieve a fully adequate conception has cost us dearly.

So welcome to philosophy's mind-vaccine lab. Feel free to interact with the experiments.

## Socrates' Dialogical Picture

Socrates devoted his life to seeking wisdom and showed that we need a better understanding of, among other things, reason's requirements. He never articulated a standard of his own—not that we know—but his actions do suggest one. For when he wanted to determine the worthiness of a claim, he'd test it with questions and see how it fared. The implied standard in such an approach is this: judgments that can survive critical questioning might merit acceptance, but those that can't, don't. To count as reasonable, a belief must run a gauntlet of questions and emerge in reasonably good shape. The essence of being reasonable, in other words, is to think, say, and do things that

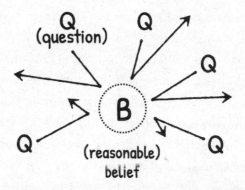

### The Socratic Picture of Reasonable Belief:
#### Reasonable beliefs can withstand questioning.

are *dialectically defensible*. ("Dialectic" is a form of conversation where participants test ideas together.) I call this the "Socratic" or "dialogical" model of reason.

This idea was in the air in classical Athens. That's why Socrates was able to delight and outrage his contemporaries with mere questions: he leveraged a prevailing expectation that claims be able to withstand questioning. Socrates wielded questions with consummate skill and showed that much of what passed for common sense wasn't in fact tenable. In the process, he demonstrated the need for epistemic humility. Dogmatic and mentally inflexible Athenians found this infuriating and, after a famous trial, condemned Socrates to death. The entire drama inspired a young playwright to write a series of dialogues. Plato's dialogues immortalized his mentor and dramatized the power of his "Socratic method."

Socrates' conception of reason has much to recommend it. Skilled thinkers find it intuitive and plausible: it fits their experience of how thinkers should conduct themselves. They recognize that, to evaluate ideas, we need to consider challenges. (As I use the term, a *challenge* is a question that takes issue with a claim.) Socrates understood that the wise seek out such challenges: they take them seriously, but not personally.

When responsible thinkers encounter a challenge they (or the relevant experts) can't answer, they cease to insist on the claim at issue.[2] Or rely on the corresponding belief. In this sense, the Socratic model is well functioning: embrace it and you'll go about the task of assessing ideas in roughly the right way: you'll look at the questions that it makes sense to ask and see whether they can be answered. We see this approach at work in the empirical hypothesis-testing that's so central to science. We see it in the stress-testing performed by designers and engineers. We see it in the cross-examinations of trial lawyers. And we see it in the everyday idea-testing performed by capable critical thinkers.

The Socratic model implies that we need to pay attention to the clues that indicate that something is questionable. It recommends that we take time to focus on these (often subtle) clues, and make the resulting questions explicit. Teach this model to a young person, and he or she will grasp that questions play an important role in idea-testing. Properly taught, the model will infuse the pupil with the Socratic spirit: the habit of peppering hypotheses with questions and seeing what happens.

Educators speak of the Socratic method of teaching and envision a classroom where the teacher fires questions at students, requiring them to think on their feet. I think this misses the mark: the important thing is for *students themselves* to wield the questions. For this reason, I prefer to think of the Socratic method as an approach to *learning*—one the instructor models and pupils emulate.

The Socratic model also reinforces an important kind of epistemic humility. For it implies that no judgment should be treated as settled once and for all. For no judgment is immune from questioning. Suppose that a highly plausible hypothesis has faced hundreds of challenges and objections, and survived them all. Suppose that it has passed every test with flying colors. Even then, the model says, we can't treat the matter as forever settled, for an unforeseen objection might arise tomorrow and force us to reconsider. For example, Newton's theory of gravity—perhaps the most celebrated scientific accomplishment of all time—was nevertheless overturned, almost two hundred years later, by the unforeseen challenges raised by relativity theory. In this way, the Socratic model sanctions a key element of the scientific attitude, whereon every finding is regarded as (in some sense) provisional.

The Socratic picture, though, also faces difficulties. These difficulties arise when you try to think it through. Which questions, exactly, must a hypothesis withstand? Must it withstand *all* of them, most of them, or just some of them? What if it faces questions that are silly, impossibly demanding, or unfair: must it withstand them as well? Can you defend a claim by showing that a challenge to it is misguided? What if no one asks the truly important questions? And what does "withstand" really mean?

If we outfit the Socratic model with some clarifying distinctions, we get satisfying answers to all of these questions. That part of the story, though, comes later. First we must look at the idea's actual historical uptake.

Socrates' contemporaries were quick to point out one implication. It seems that, at a minimum, a claim must be able to survive the question "How do you know?" Suppose a friend says "It's going to snow tomorrow," and we want to know if that's a reasonable thing to believe. So we ask "How do you know?" and she shares supporting information: precipitation is likely, the temperature will surely remain below freezing, etc. Our friend, in other words, produces *reasons*—claims that support the prediction of snowfall. Each reason, though, is similarly open to questioning. For each of them, we can ask "But how do you know *that*?" thereby generating a demand for another reason. Our friend's supply of reasons is assuredly finite, but our supply of follow-up questions is in principle inexhaustible, so it's hard to see how her claim could survive rigorous questioning.

It gets worse. For anyone with a little persistence can in this way defeat *any* claim to knowledge: just iterate the question "How do you know?" until the claimant gives up. Some beliefs and claims, then, may *appear* reasonable, but that, it seems, is just an artifact of our customary complacency. Any fully rigorous testing of a claim's credentials will be characterized by persistent questioning, so in the end, nothing is really, objectively reasonable. Or so it seems—if we embrace the Socratic model of reason.

Philosophers call this the "regress" problem. Some parents encounter a real-world version of it. Typically, their child discovers the power of why-questions, and turns asking them into a kind of game. It goes like this: a parent says something, and the child asks "Why?" Delighted that the child wants to understand, the parent produces an answer. Then the why-child asks her go-to question again. And again. Genuine curiosity often initiates the game, but at some point, it becomes about getting parents to jump though explanatory hoops. I confess to having tormented my parents in this way. My mom, though, learned to turn the tables; she'd say something like "I don't know, what do you think?" At the time, she seemed like a spoil-sport; but I've come to see her table-turning trick as rooted in a rare wisdom.

The prospect of an infinitely persistent questioner setting out to undermine all claims to knowledge strikes many as ludicrous. Rightly so: no one is in fact that patient, and clearly, no one should be handed a simplistic formula for defeating any claim whatever. Any such formula could be used to defeat calls for justice as well as claims about ghosts; calls for climate action as well as claims about alien abduction.

Why, then, should we take the regress problem seriously? The point is not to mollify children who won't stop asking why. Nor is it to gird ourselves against tireless, metronomic skeptics. The real point is that a genuinely promising conception of what's reasonable— the Socratic model—seems to saddle us with a radical, all-corrosive skepticism: one that obliterates any meaningful distinction between what should and shouldn't be accepted.

The regress problem shows that the Socratic conception can inject dysfunction into our reason-giving practices. Unadorned by the distinctions I'll introduce later, the Socratic model makes skeptical debunking trivially easy, and conclusive demonstration all but impossible. It rigs the reasoning game in favor of challengers, making it unduly hard to secure sensible claims.

It helps to put the point in immunological terms. Apparently, a mental immune system that relied on the Socratic standard would be hyperactive. It wouldn't just screen out bad ideas, it would also wipe out a lot of good ones.

The ancient Greeks, though, didn't have the tools of cognitive immunology. Instead, they faced a fascinating philosophical conundrum: either we treat everything as open to question, or we don't. If we do, there's no way to halt the regress, and the skeptic succeeds in undermining every claim to knowledge. If we don't, though, we essentially place some things beyond the reach of questions, and end up de facto dogmatists. Either we're thoroughly open-minded—and the bottom falls out—or we elect to be closed-minded about certain things, and rationality proves relative to whatever we refuse to question. The former option might be attractive to a nihilistic debunker, and the latter might appeal to an apologist for a certain dogma, but neither option should appeal to a genuine rationalist. Both prove fatal to the prospects of thoroughgoing rational accountability.

Commit to the Socratic model, and it seems you're stuck with cognitive immune dysfunction either way.

Plato was rightly concerned about this defect. He knew that, without a more practicable standard, cynicism about reason would grow. He understood that all-corrosive skepticisms undermine faith in reason, subverting our reason-giving practices. He understood that the apparent alternative breeds relativism, which also subverts inquiry. And he knew that, when our reasoning practices atrophy, all kinds of things go haywire. So he set out to find an alternative.

## Plato's Mathematical Picture

Plato lived in turbulent times. A protracted war with the fiercely independent Spartans had left Athens depleted, its empire a shadow of its former self. The wise governance of Solon had given way to decidedly unwise democratic rule. Professional educators taught that right and wrong are relative, and critical thinkers lacked the courage of their convictions. Meanwhile, the uncritical were full of passionate intensity and prone to support unwise policies. Riven by partisanship, Athens descended into political infighting. (Any of this sound familiar?)

Like his mentor, Plato understood that irrational thinking is a major impediment to harmonious existence. So he followed Socrates into the wisdom-cultivation business. Both men understood the need for a clear and workable standard of reasonable judgment. We've seen that Socrates found one in a norm that had some currency at the time: if a belief or claim can't withstand questioning, disavow it. This standard perfectly suited his purposes, and he leveraged it to the hilt.

Plato admired this criterion's power to dislodge groundless opinions and dismantle ideological conceits. His dialogues pay reverential homage to the critical application of this standard. Plato saw something, though, that Socrates seems to have missed: while useful for combatting confused and mistaken judgments, the Socratic picture is less than ideal for building common knowledge.

Actually, this understates the problem. The Socratic conception turns out to be profoundly corrosive of the very *possibility* of positive knowledge. Combine it with a sensible taboo against exempting any judgment from critical questioning, and naysayers can defeat any claim they please. Meanwhile, builders of positive knowledge find it prohibitively difficult to establish much of anything. As a result, both good and bad ideas get swept away.

Socrates was known to insist that he had no knowledge whatever, but why? The simplest answer is best: he'd adopted an overly stringent standard of reasonable belief. (His claim to know *nothing* was a needlessly provocative show of humility; it expressed an *indiscriminate* skepticism, thereby flouting linguistic norms that help us differentiate between worthy and unworthy ideas. Socrates' critics sensed that any standard of reasonable belief that wipes out all knowledge is far from well functioning. They weren't wrong.)

Socrates was fundamentally a debunker. He focused on combating bad ideas. For this, he needed a *necessary* condition on sound judgment—a recognized standard he could use to pry loose unreasonable beliefs. He had little interest, though, in building positive knowledge. Consequently, he had no need for a *sufficient* condition: a way of demonstrating that something *does* pass muster. Plato, though, understood that we need both necessary *and* sufficient conditions: necessary conditions for combating bad ideas, and sufficient conditions for validating good ones. So he set out to find a more workable model.

To better understand real, positive knowledge, Plato needed uncontroversial examples. He found them in mathematics. Math, he realized, was chock-full of utterly unassailable propositions. If anyone disputes a theorem, the proof can be provided, and that settles the matter. You can then build on that theorem with utter confidence that it is reliable. Mathematicians, it seemed, had figured out a surefire way to resolve their differences and establish knowledge. And as they built on one another's findings, their field progressed.

Mathematics also seemed to capture timeless and unchanging truths: truths that are related in precise, orderly, and sometimes beautiful ways. The axiomatic systems that would later evolve into Euclidean geometry seemed the pinnacle of intellectual achievement: *here*, Plato realized, was knowledge that would stand the test of time.

Also, the clear, orderly thinking of mathematicians stood in stark contrast to the disordered thinking of fools and ideologues. Surely there were lessons here for anyone interested in wisdom. Suppose we approach questions about right and wrong the way mathematicians approach questions about triangles; imagine starting with a small number of moral "axioms," and reasoning carefully, building an edifice of moral "theorems." Perhaps such an approach would transplant the harmony and stability of mathematics into the chaotic free-for-all we call moral and political discourse. Mightn't we thereby cultivate currently unimagined levels of moral wisdom? Why not build an actual *science* of right and wrong?

A beautiful but impossible dream? Perhaps. At the time, though, there were reasons for optimism. Several centuries before, Greek scribes had borrowed the twenty-two-symbol Hebrew *alefbet* and added symbols for the vowel sounds. The result was the first fully phonetic alphabet. This turned out to be a revolutionary information technology; for the first time, literacy was relatively easy to achieve. In ensuing generations, human brains were rewired by the written word, then networked as never before. Pioneer users of this new technology, the Greeks developed a surprisingly advanced society. For the first time in human history, ideas had a somewhat stable existence outside of human minds.

Until then, ideas were ephemeral entities that could evaporate with a shift in attention, but *with* written language, they took on an objective aspect. It became impossible to deny that certain ideas are more than merely subjective. Indeed, if you focused your attention in the right way, the world of ideas—what Plato called "the intelligible realm"—manifested a definite order and stability. (In the twentieth century, the philosopher Wilfrid Sellars gave us another way to talk about this realm; he called it "the space of reasons.")

Concrete, worldly conditions are always in flux. But the abstract principles *behind* the flux? These change more slowly, if at all. Why? It seems the logic binding them together persists and holds them in

place. So why not map the world of abstract ideas the way mathematicians map the world of geometric truths? Perhaps by doing this we
can replace the scattered confusion of everyday thinking with judgment that is clear, cogent, ordered, purposeful, and wise.

Plato was rightly captivated by the prospects. When he founded
the Academy—an ancient forerunner of the modern university—he
had the words LET NO ONE UNVERSED IN GEOMETRY ENTER HERE
inscribed above the door. This was no idle remark: Plato believed
that the clarity and rigor of mathematical thinking was the key to a
well-ordered mind. In this, he was following Pythagoras, the mystic
whose mathematical discoveries inspired an actual movement for as-
cetic, communal living.

But what is it, exactly, that makes mathematical theorems worthy
of our acceptance? The answer seems obvious: in each case, it's the
existence of a proof. In math, genuine knowledge is distinguished
from mere conjecture by the fact that a conclusive argument exists.
Now suppose we generalize this answer to domains where conclusive
proof is impossible—that is, relax the requirement that the argument
*guarantee* the conclusion's truth. In this way, we arrive at an appealing mental picture of reasonable belief: beliefs and claims are reasonable (and therefore candidates for knowledge) just in case they're
supported by sufficiently good reasons.

Plato was quite taken with this picture. In *Meno*, an elegant inquiry into the nature of moral knowledge, he had Socrates float this
very hypothesis. Perhaps knowledge differs from mere opinion by
being "tethered"—literally tied down—with a *logos* or reason. (*Logos*
is a Greek word meaning "reason," "account," or "logical argument.")
Put differently, reasonable judgments differ from unreasonable ones
by being *anchored* or *logically grounded*.

This is one of the most natural and intuitive thoughts one can
have on the subject: reasonable judgments count as reasonable because
they're backed by good reasons; such backing is what *makes* sound
judgments sound. I call this the "Platonic picture" of reasonable belief.

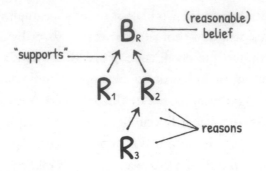

## The Platonic Picture of Reasonable Belief:
### Reasonable beliefs are supported by good reasons.

The Platonic picture has many appealing features. First, it's simple and intuitive. Indeed, many find it hard to imagine what else "reasonable" could possibly mean. Second, it's built atop a baseline skepticism: you're not supposed to accept anything that can't be argued for. This makes it useful for debunking baseless claims: just ask for the justifying argument, and if it proves inadequate, you can reject the claim. Third, the Platonic picture captures the intuition that you can build new knowledge atop old knowledge: new findings become part of background knowledge, and become available for premising. We deploy these premises in new arguments, and eventually add *their* conclusions to the stockpile of knowledge. In this way, we get an appealing picture of scientific progress. Fourth, the Platonic picture has always promised to bring something like scientific rigor to everyday thinking and judging: perhaps it really *is* the key to promoting wisdom. Finally, it explains the classic case of knowledge transfer: someone (call her the claimant) makes a claim and someone else (call him the questioner) asks how she knows. She produces her supporting reason, essentially showing that her claim is well grounded. And in this way, he comes to know too. If learning the supporting reason is enough to impart knowledge, surely the reason is the very thing that *makes it* knowledge.

If you think through the Platonic model, though, you encounter a difficulty. Plato noted it himself in the dialogue *Theaetetus*. For what must the reasons that underwrite rational conviction be like? We've already said that the justifying reasons must be "good" ones, but what does that mean? Can any old premise confer rational legitimacy? Clearly not: patently unreasonable premises shouldn't carry that kind of weight. The claim "Everyone drives a blue sedan" entails that the defendant drives a blue sedan, but that doesn't mean it *justifies* it; the premise is unreasonable, hence useless for this purpose.

It seems, then, that reasons must themselves be reasonable if they're to provide genuine support. But notice what this entails: on the model under consideration, the only way a supporting premise can *be* reasonable is if it stands at the receiving end of its *own* justifying inference—another argument underlying the first. The premises of *that* argument are in precisely the same boat, and it becomes difficult to see how this chain or "regress" of reasons can come to a satisfactory end.

Again, resist the urge to dismiss this argument as sophistry. Instead, draw this lesson: the Platonic model leads us in an explanatory circle. Remember, the goal is to understand what "reasonable" means. The Platonic model sets forth this hypothesis: a supporting argument is the very thing that makes reasonable beliefs reasonable. Ask how an argument can be genuinely supportive, though, and we're back to the idea that its premises must be reasonable. It's as if we were to say: *Claims are only as good as the arguments that* back *them up*, then add: *Arguments are only as good as the claims that* make *them up*. The prospect of an endless chain of reasons is merely a symptom; the real problem is that two components of the Platonic picture each pass the explanatory buck to the other.

The difficulty is precisely analogous to the famed causal regress problem, which goes like this: It seems nothing happens without an antecedent cause, but before such a cause can cause anything, it must itself happen. And that requires yet another, even earlier cause. Thus, it seems an impossibly long chain of causes is needed for anything at all to happen. How, then, can the origins of the universe, or indeed anything else, be fully explained? Plato's most gifted pupil—a man named Aristotle—was much impressed by these arguments. In answer to them, he developed parallel pictures of the causal and epistemic realms. He reasoned that a *first cause* must preside over the causal order, imparting motion to all that moves, and that *first principles* must preside over the rational order, imparting validity to all knowledge.

The words *first principle*, though, don't solve the epistemic regress problem, any more than the incantation "prime mover" solves the causal regress problem. In both cases, Aristotle had simply given a name to our ignorance. The key question remained: By what right do we treat any premise as "first" or basic? In mathematics, we just assume a set of axioms and get to work. But what are the rightful "axioms" of everyday knowledge? And if such axioms aren't based on anything—and "basic" means "not based on anything more basic"— then what makes them anything more than arbitrary? What good does it do to derive conclusions from premises that are themselves baseless? Given that they are baseless, by what right do we treat them as solid enough to base knowledge upon? Suppose, on the other hand, that we come up with a clever way of showing that certain "basic" beliefs aren't in fact arbitrary: doesn't that very demonstration render them demonstrated, hence *non*-basic?

I call this the "quandary of basic belief." Within the paradigm created by Plato's picture, it arises with a vengeance. Note the irony here: concerns about regress skepticism led Plato to set aside the Socratic model and seek an upgrade. But the alternative made the regress problem even more acute. For where the former opens the door to ridiculously persistent questioning—a possibility, but not a necessity— the latter generates a regress by pure, inexorable logic.

In retrospect, it's possible to see that the Platonic picture makes basic belief both necessary and impossible: necessary because justifying arguments must start somewhere, and impossible because the logic of the view entails that basic beliefs can't do what the paradigm needs them to do.[3] (I've spelled out the logic of this argument in the endnote.) The easier way to see the problem, though, is to view the Platonic picture through the lens of cognitive immunology. For the picture's fatal flaw then leaps into focus: it overgeneralizes, and teaches us to demand a warrant for *every* belief and claim. This makes it like an autoimmune trigger: conducive to hyperactive immune response. If the body's immune system attacked microbes indiscriminately, it would quickly kill us; how then can a mind that challenges ideas indiscriminately be healthy?

But again, ancient philosophers didn't have the tools of cognitive immunology. So the quandary of basic belief persisted. Though it generated a regress (and created cognitive autoimmune disorders), the Platonic picture maintained its viselike grip on the philosophical imagination. As a result, philosophers failed to resolve the quandary. As we're about to see, this failure was enormously consequential.

## Uneasy Accommodations

When Plato founded his Academy, the misconception that would confound the rationalist enterprise had its foot in the door. The project was barely out of the gates, and its Trojan horse was already inside them. Ironically, philosophers have failed to examine this subversive gift. Instead, they've clung to it and undergone intellectual contortions.

The story of Western epistemology is largely one of philosophers making uneasy accommodations to the Platonic picture of reason. Yes, we philosophers have dreamed up clever ways to halt the regress. Yes, some highly technical accounts of basic belief seem to secure the possibility of knowledge. To date, though, we've not achieved an understanding of basic belief that is tenable, well functioning, and wisdom conducive. Or, for that matter, conducive to cognitive immune health.

To see why, we must resume the story. Socrates inspired Plato, and Plato mentored Aristotle. Aristotle in turn tutored Alexander the Great, who built one of the largest empires the world has ever seen. By the age of thirty, Alexander ruled an empire stretching from Greece to India. The resulting civilization—called Hellenistic for its basis in Hellas or Greek culture—lasted for three centuries. It gave way to a Roman Empire deeply influenced by Greek philosophy. That empire lasted another five centuries; its eastern part would last ten more.

Here's the point: a curious confluence of philosophical, military, and political firepower allowed the ideas of Plato and Aristotle to exert enormous influence across much of Europe, Asia, and the Middle East. And they did so for the better part of *eighteen centuries*: from 300 BC to 1500 CE. For much of the Middle Ages, in fact, Aristotle was known, in educated circles, as simply "the philosopher" (as in, "the one and only non-Christian philosopher you need to know"). Tutor the right emperor and your ideas can spread far and wide.

During this extended period, three basic epistemologies gained and lost influence: Aristotle's, that of the Academic skeptics, and that of Christian philosophers. Each made an uneasy accommodation to the Platonic picture of reason. Each developed an influential standard of reasonable belief—one that gave rise to a distinctive set of reason-giving practices. And each of these epistemologies—initially a "solution" to the quandary of basic belief—went on to shape Western civilization in ways both subtle and profound. Abstract ideas about reason, it turns out, have concrete and far-ranging implications.

I've mentioned that Aristotle opted for an epistemology based on first principles. First principles, he argued, are needed to bring the regress of reasons to an end.[4] Fair enough, said his contemporaries: But what are these first principles, and why do they merit our acceptance? Aristotle's answer was clever but evasive: our apprehension of first principles is "immediate"—that is, direct and unmediated. In other words, we simply behold them and know them to be true.

We know this answer to be problematic. Yes, we seem to know certain things quite directly. The wrongness of cruelty, for example. The immediacy, though, is just a fact about the way we experience them, and no guarantor of truth. After all, the rage that makes vengeance feel just is equally visceral and direct. The revulsion some feel at the idea of gay marriage is immediate but morally misleading: How do we know that our revulsion at cruelty isn't like that? Direct, intuitive immediacy, in other words, doesn't eliminate the need for a reliability-ensuring warrant. We want credence that can withstand critical scrutiny.

To his credit, Aristotle grasped that his initial answer was insufficient. So he supplemented it with another. Our ability to apprehend the truth of first principles, he asserted, is built up over time, from perceptions and our ability to generalize from them.[5]

Aristotle was saying that first principles are warranted by *induction*—the process of inferring from specific instances to general principles. Clearly, though, an inductive argument is a kind of supporting argument, which makes Aristotle's first principles . . . not "first" after all! By shifting attention from deductive demonstration to inductive corroboration, Aristotle was playing a kind of shell game, hiding his lack of a deep solution to the regress problem.

The philosophers of Plato's Academy quickly identified the problem with Aristotle's solution. They saw that it must be possible to query even first principles. You can call a principle "first" if you like, but that shouldn't exempt it from critical scrutiny. They also understood that, whether you *justify* a first principle directly, or merely *explain* its rational merits from some lofty perch, either way you deprive it of primacy. When you stamp down a wrinkle in the rug and it pops up elsewhere, you can't claim to have solved the problem.

The Academy philosophers concluded instead that rigorous reflection on the nature of reason leads invariably to skepticism. And the conclusion stuck. According to leading scholars, Academy philosophers employed a skeptical strategy that ". . . attempted to show that all claims are groundless." "For over two hundred years," writes one of them, 'Why do you believe that?' became the leading question in philosophical discussion. 'You can have no reason to believe that' became the skeptical refrain."[6]

Clearly, Plato's early followers were in thrall to his concept of reason. Some of them discovered that it could be wielded as a skeptical axe. With its ceaseless demand for supporting reasons, it proved easy (and, frankly, formulaic) to clear away dogma and false belief. Of course, the strategy turned out to undermine conviction of *all* kinds—true and seemingly reasonable beliefs among them—but what could one do? The logic seemed airtight. The Academy skeptics settled on making a virtue of (apparent) necessity. They set about purging themselves and others of conviction and viewed such humbling reflections as a kind of spiritual exercise.

Many a critical thinker is skeptical in the sense of having a healthy appetite for evidence. But this was skepticism of a different order. We're talking now about a *radical* skepticism, one that obliterates the distinction between reasonable and unreasonable belief, thereby undermining healthy mental immune function. Prior to Socrates and Plato, such skepticism was unheard-of. After them, it became commonplace. Early Roman thinkers, for example, were very much in the grip of the Platonic picture. One of them—a man named Agrippa—reasoned as follows: "We say that what is brought forward as a warrant for the [claim] needs another warrant, which itself needs another, and so on ad infinitum; so that we have no point from which to begin to establish anything, and suspension of judgment follows."[7]

Similar reasoning led another influential Roman philosopher to conclude that conviction in any form represents a rational failing. Almost six centuries after Plato, Sextus Empiricus mounted a crusade against mathematicians, medical researchers, religionists, and others in the habit of making positive knowledge claims. To Sextus, it was axiomatic: they weren't radical skeptics, so they were dogmatists. The Platonic conception had made dogmatism appear the only alternative to radical skepticism. From the standpoint of serious researchers in other fields, though, such "academic" (or Academy-based) skepticism seemed ridiculous. (Indeed, this is the likely origin of the disparaging phrase "merely academic.") Epistemology had painted itself into a corner and made itself all but irrelevant to practical thinkers.

Naturally, this "academic" skepticism proved unstable. The pragmatic need to distinguish between more and less reasonable claims soon reasserted itself. This led early Christian thinkers to try a different tack: questioning can't go on forever, they reasoned, so we must accept some things on faith. In the same way that God can halt the regress of *causes* (by being the Creator, or Prime Mover), faith in God can halt the regress of *reasons*. Just as God provides the true basis for existence, faith provides the true basis for knowledge.[8]

This faith-based understanding of the space of reasons would prevail, with minor alterations, for more than a thousand years. It helped entrench an orthodoxy that discouraged challenges to church teaching. It excused stubbornly dogmatic thinking and compromised mental immune systems across Europe. Medieval epistemology reached its fullest expression in the twelfth-century writings of the Italian priest Thomas Aquinas. As Aquinas saw it, "All knowledge proceeds from first principles"—principles themselves underwritten by faith.[9] This view held sway well into the sixteenth century.

Let's take stock. Aristotle, the ancient skeptics, and leading medieval thinkers all began with Plato's picture of reason. But they came to different and uneasy conclusions. In retrospect, it's easy to see why. Faced with the prospect of infinite regress, you have three basic options. First, you can throw up your hands and conclude that objectively reasonable belief just isn't in the cards. That's the option the Academy skeptics took.

The problem with this view is that it effectively neuters the rationalist project. As a theoretician, you say that nothing is truly reasonable, but in practice, you keep treating some words and deeds as more reasonable than others. Others see that you're keeping two

sets of books—one intellectual, the other practical—and decide that
your intellectual standards are a sham. Often, they conclude that rationalism, or academic inquiry generally, is bunk. This is no way to
defend reason and inquiry. In fact, it breeds anti-intellectualism. In
late Hellenistic times, it effectively marginalized philosophers and
other academics. For centuries thereafter, academic skepticism made
it hard for the well educated to have the courage of their convictions.

Your second option is to halt the regress with dogmatic beliefs:
you simply refuse to question certain things and insist that, contrary
to appearances, they somehow qualify as reasonable anyway. This
represents capitulation to an especially destructive kind of irrationalism: one that revels in selective closed-mindedness. It also makes rationality relative to whatever you or your faith community takes to be
basic. It subverts reason's power to adjudicate interfaith disputes, and
renders reasoning an essentially tribal exercise. The resulting epistemology fills dogmatists with passionate intensity. When this option
gained the favor of those in power, it led to an exceedingly dark age:
a thousand years of ignorance, superstition, disease, and suffering. It
compromised the cultural immune system of Western civilization.

Your third option is to try and steer a middle path between skepticism and dogmatism. The idea here is to argue that certain beliefs
really are properly and objectively basic, or foundational, for us all.
Aristotle was arguably the first proponent of this view—the first
post-Plato *foundationalist*. He would not be the last. Most serious
philosophers have followed in his footsteps. There are now hundreds
of variations on Aristotle's "middle way" solution.

Such "solutions," though, invariably turn out to be problematic.
To see this, note that a foundationalist must engage in selective defiance of the Platonic standard: their basic beliefs are invariably *exceptions* to the "reasonable only if supported by something more basic"
rule. If you're going to go that route, though, you owe us an explanation of what those beliefs are, and why they deserve to be treated

as exceptions. But if it's worth its salt, such an explanation ends up *justifying* the basic beliefs, and this renders them nonbasic. A validating explanation is also a justification—something that renders a belief derivative.

When pressed with questions like these, foundationalists have tended to wave their hands and employ techniques of distraction. This has diminished rationalism and prevented it from becoming an influential movement. As it happens, foundationalist accounts of basic belief compromise mental immune systems and hamstring our reason-giving practices. More on this soon.

By the time modernity was taking its first wobbly steps, Plato's picture had dominated attempts to understand reason's requirements for close to two *thousand* years. The European Enlightenment was about to turn the worldview of the West upside down, but the Platonic conception wasn't through. In fact, it was about to harness a fascinating mechanism to embed itself yet more deeply in our collective consciousness.

## Gravity's Cradle

Recall that a faith-based picture of knowledge and reason ruled European intellectual life for a thousand years. From the fall of the Roman Empire to the dawn of the Italian Renaissance, powerful institutions rewarded faithful obedience and punished impious questioning. The dogmatic acceptance of some things seemed epistemologically necessary, and many accepted that centralized authority was needed to reinforce basic commitments. The dominant orthodoxy in Europe was Christian, and heretical opinions could get you burned at the stake. Inquiry was discouraged, science languished, and medicine remained primitive. Ignorance and superstition reigned, while warfare and disease killed hundreds of millions. It was truly a dark, dark age, because in Europe, the light of reason had been largely extinguished. (During this time, freedom of inquiry found more fertile ground in the Arab world. In fact, historians credit it with sparking the so-called Golden Age of Islam.)

And then, somewhat abruptly, things changed. Historians differ about the root causes, but a sea change in epistemological attitudes was surely a key factor. The Black Death hadn't spared the devout, and people noticed. Revelations of Church corruption—the sale of indulgences, for example—emboldened critics, and even the faithful were forced to adopt a more skeptical posture toward Church teachings. Protestants challenged the Church's authority to interpret God's will, the Church fought back by persecuting heretics, and for more than a century, religious wars wracked the European continent. By 1600, faithful obedience no longer appeared necessary or benign; instead, it looked like a formula for closed-mindedness, tribal thinking, and sectarian conflict.

These developments dealt a serious blow to the epistemology of faith. Apparently, even fundamental commitments merit scrutiny; reason must play a role in resolving even basic differences. The ancient "pagan" philosophers were rediscovered, and once again discussed openly. Heretical thoughts were increasingly expressed, and the spirit of critical inquiry sputtered back to life. The printing press dramatically expanded the reach of ideas; prevailing expectations shifted, and so did the norms of reasoned discourse.

Italy experienced a dramatic rebirth of intellectual ferment. The epistemological issues came to a head in the person of Galileo Galilei. This impudent polymath trained a telescope on the heavens and discovered Jupiter's moons. He treated the venerable teachings of Aristotle as hypotheses to be tested. He devised ingenious experiments and showed that falling bodies obey mathematical laws. He wrote beautifully and made it cool to think scientifically. He even championed Copernicus and helped turn the solar system inside out. Thanks to Galileo, the Earth, long the stable center of the physical universe, was suddenly careening wildly through space. Meanwhile, the anchor of the *moral* universe—religion—seemed to have lost *its* center of gravity too. It was a time of profound intellectual vertigo.

By the 1630s, the epistemology of faith was in full retreat. It was apparent that observation, experimentation, and mathematical reasoning could yield real knowledge. Compared to that, faith-based conviction seemed like thin gruel. A return to the radical skepticism of the ancients, though, just wasn't an option, for clearly, knowledge wasn't just possible: it was actual. The Platonic picture of reason, though, hadn't relaxed its grip on the philosophical imagination. Consequently, that imagination had only one place to go: knowledge exists, and it must have a rational basis. Among philosophers, "On what is true knowledge based?" became the central problem of the age.

It fell to the French philosopher René Descartes to frame the problem in its distinctively modern form. If we hope to establish anything "firm and lasting in the sciences," Descartes wrote, we must first raze the foundations of received opinion, and build all of knowledge afresh upon beliefs that cannot be doubted. His candidate for foundational belief (the famous *cogito ergo sum*, or "I think, therefore I am") would become a topic of lively dispute but in the end, furnish too slim a basis for a robust system of knowledge.[10] It wasn't Descartes' solution, though, that would prove decisive; it was his framing of the problem. His clever use of a fundamentally *architectural* metaphor would set the agenda for modern philosophy and decisively shape all subsequent attempts to understand reason's requirements.

Descartes' architectural metaphor gave modern thinkers a convenient way to cast the central philosophical problem of the age: On what foundation does true knowledge rest? But it also did something more subtle and far-reaching—something that has, until now, escaped notice: *it projected a gravitational field onto the space of reasons.*[11] In other words, the idea that knowledge *needs* a foundation only makes sense if, absent support, beliefs gravitate to their demise. And this is precisely what Descartes presupposed. Indeed, he declared it a "fact" that "the destruction of the foundations [of opinion] of necessity brings the downfall of the edifice." Claims are not to be upheld unless there is something to hold them up; "baseless," "groundless," and "unsupported" claims are unworthy. These thoughts presuppose what we might call "epistemic gravity." But what is this mysterious force, exactly? Where does it come from? Why should we suppose that it exists, let alone that it pervades the space of reasons?

It was implicit, all along, in the Platonic idea that reason requires support. The idea that support is the hallmark of rational judgment had been projecting a gravitational field onto the space of reasons for centuries. As we might say today, the Platonic picture gives that space a distinct curvature. Descartes' most decisive contribution was to grasp this and make it explicit. More precisely, he popularized the foundations metaphor, thereby giving generations of philosophers an intuitive, almost visceral sense of the "physics" of Plato's space of reasons. He depicted it as a place where nothing merits acceptance unless something *else* supports it. (It must be something *else* because an idea can no more support itself than a weighty object can levitate itself; gravity rules out bootstrap levitation.[12]) Of course, Descartes didn't see that epistemic gravity was an artifact of Plato's model; to him, it was a "fact" about the space of reasons, and an obvious one at that.

The metaphor proved irresistible. It caught on and generated an entire idiom for thinking and talking about reason. Gravitationally loaded terms like *baseless*, *grounded*, *unfounded*, and *supported* gained currency, and people's intuitive sense of how things work in the space of reasons adjusted accordingly. In this way, the Platonic picture became embedded in our language, making it difficult to imagine that rational merit might depend on anything other than a solid support structure. This is how foundationalism—the doctrine that knowledge rests on a stratum of "basic" beliefs—ensnared many of the greatest minds of the modern era.[13]

Nor was this assumption incidental to the philosophies of these thinkers. In each case, basic belief became *the* central problem. The Platonic concept of reason, in other words, decisively shaped Enlightenment philosophy.

Descartes managed to give the Platonic conception significant influence outside of academic philosophy. How? By providing a simple and compelling metaphor that embedded itself in everyday language. Immersed in a language that treats "unfounded" and "groundless" as synonyms for "lacking rational merit," we tend to take epistemic gravity for granted—just as denizens of a massive planet tend to take physical gravity for granted. Since Descartes, it has seemed mostly obvious that bits of knowledge are like the bricks that make up a cathedral: supported by foundations, and locked into place by neighboring bricks.

Notice, by the way, that we tend to use terms like *baseless* to signify that a claim is lacking in rational merit, even when our grounds for such a claim have nothing to do with an *absence of reasons for* (the literal meaning of "baseless") and everything to do with the *presence of reasons against*. For example, we'll call astrological claims baseless, but not because no one has experiential evidence of an apparently confirmatory nature; we call them baseless for other reasons.[14] Just as physical gravity is an invisible and pervasive fact, the Platonic concept of reason became an invisible and pervasive feature of the modern worldview. This feature has frustrated the search for a mind vaccine.

I'll note here that Descartes' *Meditations* had a second important effect on the rationalist project. By entertaining doubts about the world outside of his mind—mightn't it be wholly different from how it appears?—Descartes created a problem that would distract generations of thinkers. The real problem is to understand reason's requirements in a way that makes sense and promotes wisdom. The so-called problem of the external world takes that inquiry down a rabbit hole.[15]

One assumption, though, has enjoyed a nearly free ride. An undetected stowaway on the ship of language, the Platonic picture—the idea that reasonable beliefs are invariably supported by reasons—has for hundreds of years enjoyed the appearance of a definitional truth.[16]

Enlightenment devotion to reason was, of course, a huge and salutary step in the right direction. It doesn't follow, though, that modern philosophers succeeded in understanding reason's requirements. Nor did modernity banish the difficulties that had long plagued rationalism. In fact, professional philosophers now generally accept that David Hume followed the modern problematic through to its logical conclusion, the result being a radical skepticism about the possibility of causal knowledge.[17]

In sum, the Platonic picture not only survived the Enlightenment, it traversed it in grand style. It was borne along by the foundations metaphor and its attendant assumption of epistemic gravity. It helped generate one of the defining problems of the age, a difficulty that modern philosophers ultimately failed to solve.[18]

Only now can we see why: the Platonic picture has long created cognitive immune problems. It leads many down the garden path to an extreme and impractical skepticism, which again and again compels reactionaries to embrace a ferocious dogmatism. In this way, it renders some mental immune systems hyperactive, and others underactive. Modern thinkers tried to find a path between these extremes of immune dysfunction. Typically, they did this by taking axiomatic proofs as their model, and muttering incantations about "axioms," "first principles," and "rational foundations." In this way, they tried to conjure a solution to the quandary of basic belief. But they failed to grasp what the tools of cognitive immunology make so clear: *the Platonic picture is itself the root of the problem.*

Modern thinkers deserve credit for their renewed commitment to reason; it's clear, though, that they failed to untangle the conceptual knot that Plato had tied. Indeed, they had drawn it tighter.

## Hume's "Empiricist" Picture

Descartes noticed that "I think, therefore I am" has a peculiar property: it can't be coherently doubted. This observation inspired an entire school of thought: perhaps all basic beliefs are like that, self-evident or impossible to doubt. So on the European continent, a school of thought arose to build on this idea. The plan was to identify a comprehensive set of foundational propositions, all of them utterly self-evident to the faculty of reason. This turned out to be a dead end: there simply weren't enough undoubtable beliefs to build a viable edifice of factual knowledge.

So another school of thought arose, this one in the British Isles. From John Locke in the 1600s to David Hume in the 1700s, British philosophers explored a competing idea: that genuine knowledge differs from mere opinion by being grounded in sensory evidence. In 1748, Hume neatly summed up this "empiricist" view as follows: "If I ask why you believe any matter of fact, which you relate, you must tell me some reason; and this reason will be some other fact, connected with it. But as you cannot proceed after this manner, *in infinitum*, you must at last terminate in some fact, which is present to your memory or senses; or allow that your belief is entirely without foundation."[19]

In this passage, Hume generates the regress problem and puts forward sensory evidence as the solution to that problem. Clearly, the suggestion is that perception can halt what might otherwise be an endless search for stable grounding. On this view, observed facts are uniquely suited to bringing factual reasoning to a close.[20]

Such thinking creates what I call the Humean picture of reasonable belief. The idea is that beliefs formed in the direct presence of the fact they depict form the foundation of factual knowledge.[21] For example, you look at a nearby tree and think, "There's a tree." Beliefs like *that*, the thinking goes, are solidly based on sensory evidence, hence eminently reasonable and worth building upon. At the same time, they're truly "first" in the order of justification, for no one in their right mind would demand a verbal justification for something they can plainly see. (And if they did, one could reply by simply pointing.) On this view, sensory evidence supports perceptual beliefs, and they in turn support the rest of factual knowledge.

Empiricism has its attractions. Its baseline skepticism (don't believe anything unless it can be validated by evidence) is useful for combating ideology, prejudice, and dogma. This feature can be used to dispense with the highly suspect business of armchair metaphysics, and Hume wielded it in just this way. Empiricism also answers the question of where the modern natural sciences get their authority: they get it from careful observation and patient reasoning. Arguably, empiricism gave the sciences cultural legitimacy and helped to bring about modernity. These are significant accomplishments, and empiricism merits recognition for them.

Empiricism also gave us a solution, of sorts, to the problem of basic belief. It reminds us that an argument needn't build on dogmatic or arbitrary premises. For a directly observed fact is neither dogmatic nor arbitrary. Watching the defendant commit the crime can give you excellent reason for believing that he committed it. Put differently, good reasons are not the only thing that can confer justification: sensory evidence can too.[22] Reasoning comes to a nonarbitrary end with perceptual beliefs: that, in a nutshell, is empiricism.

But does this really paint an accurate picture of the architecture of knowledge? Empiricism, it turns out, is more problematic than it appears. For one thing, it's often appropriate to question perceptual judgments. In fact, it can be irresponsible not to. Consider the defense attorney who fails to question the otherwise damning testimony of a nearsighted eyewitness who claims to have spotted the defendant at the scene of the crime, even though the vantage point and light were poor. More generally, our senses can deceive us. We sometimes see things that aren't there, and quite often fail to see things that *are* there. Thus perceptual judgments can, but need not, bring reasoning to a close. How are we to know when they do and when they don't? Or when they should and when they shouldn't? Empiricists don't say.

Second, perceptual beliefs seem an inadequate basis for the full breadth of our knowledge—a corpus that includes not just matters of empirical fact, but also mathematical truths (e.g., the Pythagorean theorem), counterfactuals ("If average global temperatures rise two degrees, sea levels will rise"), causal laws ("Smoking causes cancer"), things about the near future ("I will go to the store tomorrow"), ethical knowledge ("Honesty is the best policy"), basic things about other people's minds ("Joe is happy"), and so on. Indeed, it is exceedingly difficult to give a convincing account of how causal knowledge, knowledge of the future, knowledge of right and wrong, and knowledge of other minds are grounded in empirical evidence. When doubts are raised about the reliability of the senses, even knowledge about objective facts becomes hard to redeem.

Empiricism has not yet articulated a standard that is both expansive enough to explain how we can know all these things and strict enough to exclude patently irrational belief. Indeed, by suggesting that only perceptual beliefs are basic, it tends to promote skepticism about these other classes of knowledge. Historically, this has weakened the rationalist enterprise. Thus, Hume could manage only a "skeptical solution" to the problem of causal knowledge, and twentieth-century empiricists had to write off moral knowledge as mere expressions of preference.[23]

Even today, science deniers flog the "correlation doesn't prove cause" idea to deny climate change. When they do this, they exploit the exact same loophole in empiricism that Hume himself discovered and was unable to patch. (Philosophers call this loophole the "problem of induction.") Moreover, the empiricist picture continues to paint value judgments as fundamentally subjective—as relative to an essentially arbitrary set of preferences. This idea sows real confusion about the scope of reason's authority. It promotes moral relativism, and resignation about the possibility of using reason to resolve our deepest differences. Consequently, unaccountable moral and political talk flourishes, giving rise to ideological thinking. Some of this dysfunction is traceable to empiricism.

Finally, perceptual judgments are not uniquely suited to bringing reasoning to a close. Indeed, our actual deliberations frequently turn on judgments of other types. For example, you might remind me that today is Friday, and thereby persuade me to stay for a beer. Or use words to direct my attention to a problem with the logic of my argument. Or remind me of commitments I've made. The premises that decide arguments, it turns out, come in many different forms; when it comes to the premises that prove decisive, direct observation reports are just the tip of the iceberg. In this sense, empiricism is not so much wrong as incomplete. It gives us only a partial solution to the problem of basic belief.

And why should we accept Hume's assumption that a questioner is within his rights to demand support for everything *except* direct perceptual judgments? The reflexive, mechanical use of why-questions doesn't represent the epitome of rigor; it's fundamentally lazy and represents bad epistemic policy. (By analogy, the Platonic conception is also bad policy, for it is nothing but the abstract embodiment of the annoyingly persistent regress skeptic.)

Empiricism, in other words, fails to articulate what we might call a normatively adequate standard—a standard that squares with considered judgments about how reasoning ought to go. If we don't endorse the indiscriminate, mechanical use of why-questions (or the insufficiently discriminating policy of asking "why" whenever the claim isn't directly perceived), we shouldn't endorse empiricism. In fact, empiricism's uncritical acceptance of the Platonic model probably warps the fragile sensibilities that make for competent reason-giving practice.

The point can be put in economic terms. The epistemic economy is shaped by both supply and demand. Competent reasoners don't demand reasons for everything. Nor do they demand reasons for everything other than the facts immediately before their eyes. Their taste for reasons is far more discriminating. The trouble with empiricism is that it gives us a cartoon depiction of how reasoning ought to go. Yes, empiricism is more nuanced than radical skepticism, but compared to educated common sense, it's terribly *in*discriminate. Were we to adopt it and allow it to govern our actual reasoning, our mental immune health would probably *decline*. Absent significant caveats, empiricism is a cognitive immune *disruptor*.

Empiricism gives us a nice, clear example of how reasoning can end. It explains how some knowledge is possible. To its credit, it steers a course between dogmatism and all-corrosive skepticism. As a programmatic exhortation to observe and reason carefully, it's a fine thing. For all these reasons, empiricism represents a huge step forward. But if we want a truly practical standard of reasonable belief— one that will educate mental immune systems and nudge us down the path to wisdom—we need to look elsewhere.

## Clifford's Evidence-Based Picture

The ethic of belief that prevails across much of the world today is a variant of empiricism. It centers on the notion of *evidence*, so philosophers call it "evidentialism." The core idea is simple: to be genuinely reasonable, a belief or claim must be backed by sufficient evidence. The quality and quantity of supporting evidence are what set truly reasonable claims apart. So if you want to know whether a claim is worth accepting, examine the body of evidence that supports it; if it proves to be enough, accept it; if it doesn't, don't. (This is the same idea W. K. Clifford defended, so the Western tradition's "Big 4" pictures of reasonable belief are, on my telling: the Socratic, the Platonic, the Humean, and the Cliffordian.)

The last of these is now hugely influential. It gives today's sciences their distinctive character. It's central to the culture that prevails on many college campuses. It's highly regarded among the well educated. It motivates "data-driven" problem-solving in business. It propels an influential movement for "evidence-based medicine." In a way, Cliffordian evidentialism has gone mainstream.

But the view remains misunderstood and contested. For example: What *is* evidence, exactly? And what does "sufficient" really mean? How much evidence does a claim need? Is the criterion meant to apply in all domains, or only some? Can a religious experience count as evidence? What about anecdotal evidence? Do our moral intuitions deliver evidence? What weight if any should the apparent badness of suffering, or the seeming virtue of kindness, have in our moral deliberations? Is it even possible to properly evidence claims about what and who matters? If so, how? If not, what follows?

An influential strain of Christian philosophy claims to have refuted evidentialism. Emboldened fundamentalists increasingly flaunt evidential standards. New-age spiritualists chafe at what they experience as an oppressive constraint. Conspiracy theorists bend the rules of evidence and succumb to confirmation bias. Propaganda outlets manipulate powerful emotions to undermine evidence-based reasoning, and right-wing ideologues challenge evidence-based public policies. These phenomena receive varying explanations, but few seem to realize that they share a root cause. The truth of the matter is this: unresolved questions feed a growing unease with the "sufficient evidence" standard. The resulting anxiety emboldens unreason. A backlash is forming, and it promises to get ugly.

Why are so many pushing back against the expectation that we only believe well-evidenced things? If we wish to understand our predicament—and the reactionary forms of unreason that haunt it—we must come to terms with evidentialism. We need to understand its origins and virtues, but also its blind spots and limits.

Let's begin with the view's origins. Where did evidentialism come from? Empiricism, I think, matured into evidentialism. In a way, it's just empiricism generalized. For why should we limit ourselves to just *sensory* evidence? Hume held that perceptual beliefs are uniquely capable of bringing the regress of reasons to a satisfactory close. He was right that such beliefs can serve as unargued "first" premises, but there's nothing particularly special about such beliefs. Yes, the senses are channels that admit information about the world, but there's no need to fixate on the boundary between self and world. When Hume was writing—the early 1700s—Western philosophy was plagued by the Cartesian fear that the world outside of our minds might be radically different than it appears. This made the self-world boundary seem especially significant, and caused Hume, and many others, to stress the role of the senses. Eventually, though, philosophers lost interest in external world skepticism and turned to more tractable questions.

We now understand that evidence comes in many forms: a clear sensory impression is a fine thing, but so, too, is a distinct and accurate memory. There's nothing wrong with a retinal image of a tree, but invisible-to-the-naked-eye background radiation can also have evidential import. Evidence can take the form of a data table, a spectrometer reading, or a bundle of field notes. A chemical residue in a test tube can be evidence, as can a bag of fossils. A signature on a contract is a kind of evidence, and so is the beep of a state trooper's radar gun. Indeed, almost any reliable indicator of something can count as evidence. Notice that a computer model can generate evidence that a storm is coming without human sensation playing much of a role at all. In fact, scientists are constantly devising ways to *bypass* the senses: think of the way seismographs take human subjectivity out of the earthquake measurement equation. The truly important thing is to gather reliable indicators, and the senses are not the only indicators available to us. Nor the most reliable.

So empiricism has matured. More precisely, its concept of basic belief has expanded. On Hume's original formulation, only the direct observation of a fact, or a distinct memory of a fact, could produce a basic belief. In the 270 years since, though, we've recognized that many other cases are relevantly similar. Nowadays, pretty much any well-evidenced claim may be put forward as an unargued premise. The resulting view—evidentialism—is more theoretically satisfying and better aligned with competent reason-giving practice.

The central features of empiricism live on in evidentialism. Its baseline skepticism—"don't believe it unless"—remains in force. Both views build on the Platonic picture's universal demand for backing and insist that reasons *and* evidence can provide such backing. Both find that the phenomenon of evidence gives them a solution of sorts to the problem of basic belief. In this way, each paints a picture of knowledge as resting on evidential foundations.

Evidentialism also improves on empiricism. It generalizes beyond sensory evidence, and provides knowledge with a broader and more stable foundation. Its picture of how reasoning should go more closely resembles what we recognize as skilled reasoning. In this way, it helps to bring theory into better alignment with practice. It dissolves some of empiricism's perennial difficulties and makes better sense of actual scientific methodology.

Like its predecessors, though, evidentialism faces challenges. Chief among these is the strident backlash it's generating. We're coming to understand that this backlash is real and capable of reversing centuries of progress. Let's see if we can comprehend its conceptual roots.

## Legitimation Crisis

Evidentialism entails the *illegitimacy* of beliefs *not* supported by sufficient evidence. It's not hard to imagine this standard working well to sort responsible from irresponsible claims about what *is*. Indeed, it has a long and distinguished track record of doing just that. Unfortunately, we can't say the same about its treatment of claims about what *ought to be*. In fact, it's quite hard to see how evidence alone can license any claim about right or wrong, good or bad. Remember,

Hume's concept of evidence involved the direct observation of a state of affairs, and the formation of a belief *describing* that state of affairs. On this picture, the foundations of our knowledge are made up entirely of descriptive claims.

Now add to this modern skepticism about inferences from "is" to "ought." Hume had pointed out that people often argue, quite uncritically, from the one to the other. He urged us to examine such inferences carefully. Well and good. Hume's insight, though, was taken up in an unexpected way. Philosophers began glossing it with slogans like *You can't derive an "ought" from an "is."* We began picturing the world of facts and the world of values as wholly distinct realms. We imagined these two worlds separated by a yawning chasm. Attempts to argue from descriptive premises to normative conclusions were labeled "the naturalistic fallacy," and ridiculed as a sophomoric mistake.

Combine these elements and the conclusion is all but inescapable: beliefs about right and wrong are illegitimate. In fact, all judgments about what's good or bad, better or worse, turn out to be unreasonable. Want to say something about rights or responsibilities? Sorry, that goes beyond what the factual evidence warrants. Think kindness is better than cruelty? Sorry, "better" is just a subjective valuation, with no evidential validity. Have convictions about the need to respect human dignity? Sorry, evidentialism exposes such convictions as involving an irrational leap. Want your life to matter in some way? Sorry, but "mattering" is just an illusion. Ready to take a stand against hate? Sorry, that would compromise your obligation to be rational and objective.

If you really immerse yourself in the evidentialist picture, all kinds of normative judgments start to appear unjustifiable. Can any normative claim be properly evidenced? It appears not, so evidently, responsible agents abstain from value judgments. Many people, I think, have reached conclusions along these lines. Why is it that "the best lack all conviction"? Perhaps it has something to do with evidentialism.

In this way, evidentialism spawns a pervasive skepticism about responsible normative judgment. The resulting view is akin to nihilism: the belief that it's all meaningless, that nothing really matters. There's a legitimate worry, I think, that people will really take these conclusions to heart and become cynics, misanthropes, or callous hedonists. Our genetic programming ensures that relatively few will end up outright psychopaths, but for all we know, evidentialist ideas nudge us all in the direction of callous indifference. Or apathy.

Most of us can't reconcile ourselves to outright nihilism. We might conclude that cosmic purpose is an illusion, but even then, we cling to the conviction that our mundane needs and interests matter. Normativity is woven into the way we experience things, and that's not going to change. Nor should it: ceasing to see anything as good or bad would not be liberating. It wouldn't bestow perfect equanimity, true wisdom, or sterling character. It would make us apathetic and indifferent. A certain critical distance from our knee-jerk valuations is a fine thing, but an outlook completely untouched by valuation of any sort? That, as Nietzsche said, would "castrate the intellect."

So how do those in the grip of the evidentialist picture reconcile themselves to the value-skepticism that flows so readily from their epistemological premises? Usually, they keep double books; they move back and forth between two accounting systems. They say things like: "Well, nothing is really, objectively right or wrong, but things can be right or wrong relative to our subjective goals and preferences." Or: "Given a set of preferences, we can use reason to work out what's right and what's wrong." Reason, they say, is competent to address questions of *means*, but structurally incapable of addressing questions about *ends*.

Note that this view appears to license a Machiavellian hedonism, where desire fulfillment is the end, and the ends justify the means. Note also that it follows quite directly from the Platonic picture of reason: for if reasoning is fundamentally a matter of appealing to something *more* basic, then reason can have nothing to say about our *most* basic ends and values. Our core ends and values, it seems, must be determined by something utterly nonrational: preference, desire, faith, or the like. In this way, the Platonic and Humean pictures promote moral relativism. Indeed, it flows with uncomfortable directness from the evidentialism that prevails today.

And here I must agree with evidentialism's detractors. There's a real problem here. For one thing, the double accounting move is intellectually shaky at best. You can't say that nothing is really right or wrong, then turn around and insist that Republicans really are wrong about climate change. You can't say that nothing really matters, then turn around and say Black lives matter. Second, the idea that morality is fundamentally relative is profoundly corrosive of reason-giving discourse. It entails that, when the discussants have different ends, reasoning is pointless. It delegitimates value inquiry before it can even begin.

Evidentialism as I've defined it invalidates a great deal. It tells us to give up all beliefs, attitudes, and behaviors that can't be redeemed with evidence and logic. It places what amounts to a burden of proof on anyone who would believe, say, or do anything. Add the idea that evidence is, by its very nature, evidence of factual states of affairs, and it's not clear that values of any kind can be properly redeemed. It even appears to delegitimate the idea that *we* matter. That, I believe, is a deal breaker for many. Hence the backlash.

Some will say: "Real mattering isn't important; it's enough that we *seem* to matter. Our nervous systems generate the illusion of mattering, and that's all we need." Sorry, but that's not going to cut it. People need to believe that they really do matter, and any concept of reason that denies them that belief is not going to be well functioning.

In 1973, the German philosopher Jürgen Habermas published a book titled *Legitimation Crisis*. I think he was on to something. Only the roots of the phenomenon go deeper than Habermas imagined. For the moment you buy into the Platonic picture of reason, legitimacy becomes something that must be demonstrated. Nothing is legitimate by default: legitimacy must in every case be inferred. Or at least *con*ferred. Moreover, its blanket "nothing is reasonable unless" ensures that justifying premises are similarly in need of legitimation: that's why reason appears to regress.

No wonder people are anxious about evidentialism. It has deeply unsettling implications. Apparently, it saddles us with the conclusion that nothing really matters: not even ourselves. For many (me among them), this is too much to stomach. Evidentialism, it seems, is in serious need of repair. It fails to illuminate the foundations of sound moral judgment and, in the process, threatens to invalidate everything we care about.

For all its virtues, evidentialism is a formidable mental immune disruptor.

## Is Evidence a False God?

No. Evidence is not a false god. It's not a false ideal either: evidence really is a key ingredient of responsible belief. I'll argue as much shortly, but first we need to understand more fully why people are turning away from evidentialism.

We've seen that social and emotional commitments are a big part of the story: people often build their identities around cherished beliefs and refuse to rethink them in the light of new evidence. Such refusals, it turns out, are profoundly corrosive of reason's fulcrum. Hence, we need to help everyone build an identity where *the will to find out* predominates over *the will to believe*.

We've also learned that there are legitimate questions about the sufficient evidence standard's suitability for evaluating normative judgments. For example, "Human beings have rights" is extraordinarily useful, but it's not known to be evidence-based. (Its validity appears to derive from downstream implications, not upstream evidence.) Nor is it clear that we'll ever be able to demonstrate, on evidential grounds, that kindness is a virtue, or that recreational cruelty is wrong. Should we reject these propositions, then? Or suspend judgment until a demonstration is produced? Surely not.

Evidentialism, then, is hard to square with perfectly ordinary value judgments. And it's not clear that, if forced to choose, we should give up the latter. Perhaps the evidentialist scruples should give way instead—or at least be more limited in scope. This objection cuts deep—far deeper than is commonly supposed.

In recent years, opponents of the sufficient evidence standard have sought to tear it down. An influential school of Christian apologetics flatly asserts that nothing makes sense unless we presuppose God, and evidence be damned. On this view, nonbelievers are dismissed in advance as incapable of making sense. Advocates for this view (so-called presuppositionalists) then imply that failures to presuppose His existence amount to a blameworthy kind of faithlessness. On this view, mere open-mindedness to the possibility that God *might* not exist represents a sort of betrayal. Needless to say, the view is blatantly coercive: it wields the threat of divine punishment to lock minds in a closet of fear. It prevents people from entertaining alternative possibilities. Ideas like this are profoundly destructive of reasoned dialogue and common sense.

A related argument merits closer scrutiny. For some years, the philosopher Alvin Plantinga has been arguing that, in many cases, rational belief simply doesn't require evidence. Or, for that matter, *any* supporting argument. A God-believer like himself, Plantinga asserts, is "entirely within his intellectual rights to believe as he does even if he doesn't know of any good theistic argument . . . even if no such argument exists."[24]

This represents a very direct challenge to evidentialism. It's the kind of challenge that can do real damage to the evidentialist ethos. If arguments like this go unanswered, the evidentialist ethos will eventually wither and die. Plantinga's case, though, is presently *gaining* influence: it's anthologized in popular introduction to philosophy textbooks, and is routinely taught to thousands of undergraduates. Sadly, it's often taught as the final word on the subject. (I teach it myself, but help students see that it's not the final word.) Indeed, it's important that undergraduates not walk away from the debate with the idea that the sufficient evidence standard is bankrupt. But that's precisely the impression Plantinga creates: that we're not obliged to believe in ways that are accountable to evidence.

Here's Plantinga's argument: Consider the belief that 2+1=3. Or the belief that the world has existed for more than five minutes. Both beliefs are rationally permissible despite appearing to lack an evidential basis.[25] Plantinga proposes that we call such beliefs "properly basic": basic because they aren't based on anything more basic, and proper because they're rationally permissible even so. It turns out there are many such beliefs. Under suitable conditions (e.g., standing before a tree in good light), "I see a tree" can be properly basic. The same can be said of "There's a mild pain in my knee" and "I had breakfast this morning." Again, notice two things about these propositions. First, we'd be hard-pressed to demonstrate any of them to the satisfaction of someone who harbored serious doubts. Second—and this is important—we appear to be within our intellectual rights to believe them even so.

Plantinga's point is that, if we were really serious about withholding assent from everything that hasn't been evidentially demonstrated, we'd have a hell of a time recovering even a fraction of what we ordinarily, in our saner moments, consider reasonable. Religious skeptics seem eager to wield the sufficient evidence standard against religious beliefs, but more reluctant to apply it to everyday articles of common sense. But why the double standard? Shouldn't they have to apply it consistently, rather than selectively? And why should theists feel obliged to apply it to their own religious convictions, when rationalists are reluctant to apply it to many secular convictions?

Plantinga presses the point by asking whether evidentialists have succeeded, yet, in producing an evidence-based derivation of the standard itself. It's a fair question; for if no such derivation is forth-coming, the criterion is self-undermining. Shouldn't evidentialists practice what they preach? Plantinga then points out (correctly, in my view) that "no one has yet developed and articulated . . . reveal-ing necessary and sufficient conditions for proper basicality."[26] His point, stripped of jargon, is simple: no one has yet spelled out what may properly be deployed as an unargued premise. Rationalists seem to owe us such an account, for they propose an argument-centered standard of rational permissibility. To function capably as rational beings, we need to know when it's okay to treat a claim as admissible, yet not in need of further argument. Rationalists, though, have yet to provide such an account.

Plantinga's case is not without intellectual merit. There really do seem to be reasonable claims that are not evidenced in any straight-forward way. With this, he draws attention to something many epistemologists have missed: despite all our progress, we still need a better account of basic belief. Our grasp of reason's requirements remains tangled in confusion.

Can evidentialism be repaired? Can we resolve the quandary of basic belief, and revive the rationalist project? The answer, it turns out, is yes. But only if we make a clean break from the Platonic pic-ture of reason.

## How Rationalism Lost Its Way

The tale of philosophy's search for a mind vaccine deserves a thumb-nail telling. Here's mine: about a hundred generations ago, some self-styled lovers of wisdom thought to ask: What is it that distinguishes truly wise judgments? A guy named Plato hypothesized that ground-edness is the essence of reasonable belief. The hypothesis proved en-trancing, for it implied that their favorite pastime—philosophical questioning—was of surpassing significance. A conceit formed: such questioning doesn't just debunk foolish opinions, it reveals the true, objective foundations of knowledge. This conceit would mesmerize many generations of philosophers.

As we've seen, the hypothesis had some unintended consequences. It made beliefs and claims unreasonable by default. Just as the doctrine of original sin painted all humans as in need of redemption, Plato's hypothesis painted all *judgments* as in need of redemption. On both orthodoxies, everything is *tainted unless*. The guiding presumption was and is: guilty until shown to be innocent.

This global presumption didn't reveal the deep structure of knowledge, it created an artificial cognitive economy, one where indiscriminate demand rigged the reasoning game against claimants and believers. Cognitive immunology allows us to see what went wrong: theoreticians fell in love with an immune-disruptive picture of reasonable belief.

The rest, as they say, is history. As the centuries rolled by, rationalist sentiment would wax and wane: the critically inclined (usually progressives) would seize on some variant of the Platonic picture and press for a more thoroughgoing rationalism. Others (mostly conservatives) would intuit that the implied standard would invalidate much that we cherish. This would stoke a low-level fear and motivate anti-intellectual backlash. Sometimes, pushback would take the form of accountability-defying faith. Other times, it would manifest as superstition, ideological tenacity, gullibility, or science denial. And so, we've vacillated from uncritical to hypercritical: from immune deficiency to autoimmune hyperactivity. In all that time, a cognitive standard that makes for robust mental immune health never materialized. As a result, we made only fitful progress toward collective wisdom. The search for wisdom had lost its way.

# CHAPTER 12

# The Mind Vaccine

## Rethinking reason's requirements

The important thing is to never stop
questioning. —Albert Einstein

Welcome back to the mind-vaccine lab! You've arrived at a good time. I'm about to mix up a batch of our most promising serum. Stick around and I'll share my recipe; you'll learn how it fared in preliminary trials and why its properties have cognitive immunologists intrigued. You'll pick up the basics of vaccine development, and lend a hand, I hope, with testing. If all goes well, our work will yield a general-purpose mind vaccine: a cognitive standard that reduces susceptibility to bad ideas.

## From Questions to Challenges

Years ago, I was searching the dusty reaches of the lab's storage closet. High on a shelf at the back, behind three sets of Plato-inspired proposals, I came across Socrates' *example*. In it, I found the notion that an idea must *withstand questioning* to merit acceptance. I knew that Socrates had inspired millions to think critically, so I dusted the idea off and began studying its properties. I found that, as a cognitive standard, it imparts an impressive level of resistance to bad ideas. Internalize it, practice the art of asking questions, and your mental immune health can improve dramatically. Long story short, I made this "off-the-shelf" inoculant the primary ingredient of my mind vaccine.

I then set out to enhance it. A first step involved purifying my sample. For many questions don't contribute in any direct way to competent idea-testing. Indeed, some divert us from it. The trick is to ask the *right* questions—the ones that directly illuminate the idea's merits and defects. Now clarifying questions (such as "What exactly do you mean by that?") play an essential role in this process. The idea is to fine-tune your understanding of what a claim is saying before you consider its pros and cons. This is wise practice, for a little clarifying can prevent a lot of fruitless argumentation.

Clarifying questions have other virtues. When you ask one, you show that you're concerned to understand another's point of view. They make people feel heard. They postpone the tricky business of disputing the point of view and give conversation a collaborative vibe. They build trust and let discussants develop a little common ground. These features make clarifying questions wonderfully useful for keeping conversation constructive; as I like to put it, they *turn down the heat* and *turn up the light*. I use them frequently and find that they deepen and enrich my conversations.

The wisest people I know rarely express disagreement. Instead, they ask clarifying questions and give them time to work their magic. The Black blues musician Daryl Davis has de-converted hundreds of Ku Klux Klansmen. His secret? He asks questions and listens.[1] A similar approach can de-convert conspiracy theorists and science deniers.[2]

All this is true, but clarifying questions don't so much *test* ideas as set them up for testing. Their role is to prepare the hypothesis to be tested. Once I'd achieved a little clarity about this, I turned my attention to what happens next—and noticed that questions like "How do you know?" can nudge a conversation into a new phase. They're typically used to *take issue* with a claim: to challenge its merits and initiate a process of joint review. Conversational gambits like *that*, I realized, are the real catalysts of idea-testing. So I gave them a name: *challenges*.

As I conceive it, a challenge is a move in the reasoning game. A challenge often requests information, but it also conveys information. In effect, a challenge says: "Hang on; I'm not comfortable with that claim; I think it might be a mistake to rely on it. Can you show me that it's worth accepting?" I here express the subtext of a challenge with deliberate politeness. Because challenges can feel threatening, it's almost always a good idea to express them in a friendly manner. "Bullshit!" is also a challenge, but it tends to make conversation adversarial. You get the idea: a challenge signals that the challenger isn't on board with something the claimant has said; it flags a lack of shared understanding, and it informs the claimant that she shouldn't take the claim for granted. At least not yet.

Studying challenges, I came to see that they have a special effect on the conversational situation: according to the norms of reason-giving dialogue, they *suspend the claimant's right to rely on the claim*. Philosophers have a useful phrase for this effect; we say that challenges *suspend entitlement* to the claims they target. The point here isn't complicated: in the wake of a challenge, a claimant isn't supposed to turn around and rely on the claim. If you indicate that you have a problem with X, and I act as if I'm entitled to it anyway, I've essentially brushed off your concerns. That's not kosher: until the issue has been resolved, we should each refrain from assuming right of way.

Entitlement suspension—the ban on taking challenged things for granted—is also meant to give the ensuing review some measure of impartiality. For if you can rely on the very thing at issue, it becomes trivially easy to establish anything. So our reasoning practices evolved to disallow it. When someone relies on an idea a previous challenge has rendered off-limits, an alert thinker will flag the error as "question begging." This is a bit like a judge telling a prosecuting attorney to stop referring to the defendant as "the culprit": since the whole point of the exercise is to determine whether the defendant really is the culprit, you can't, as a prosecuting attorney, pretend that that question has already been settled. Skilled thinkers play with challenges and develop an essential habit of mind: the habit of suspending judgment and seeking out non-question-begging evidence—the kind of evidence that doesn't beg the question.

A challenge also invites the claimant to try to *redeem* the claim: to provide it with an adequate defense. Ideally, this leads to a dialogical give-and-take: an exchange that resolves the issue to the satisfaction of both parties. The idea is to forge shared understanding, and properly conceived, the norms of reason-giving dialogue serve this end.[3] I call a challenge's impact on the players' rights and responsibilities its "force."

Challenges, it turns out, aren't just moves in a game. They're also extraordinary cognitive microbes. They're like antibodies: when a mind is working properly, they swarm to the scene of a bad idea and attempt to neutralize it. They're the mind's first responders: the security detail that shows up to confront suspicious ideas. In this regard, they're like the white blood cells scientists call "lymphocytes." Immunologist David Bainbridge describes lymphocytes as "about the cleverest little cells in the whole body."[4] What makes them so impressively clever? The science writer Bill Bryson channels Bainbridge's answer: "Their ability to recognize almost any kind of unwanted invader and mobilize a swift and targeted response." Challenges are the lymphocytes of the mind.

About thirty years ago, I concluded that it's a good idea to stimulate the production of these clever little buggers. So I took the Socratic standard and plugged in the concept of challenges. That yielded what we might call the "New Socratic" standard: *The true test of a good idea is its ability to withstand challenges.*

This standard is designed to stimulate the production of cognitive antibodies. I hope that, right now, it's having that effect on you: that in your mind, questions of clarification are forming, and doubts— nascent challenges—are lining up behind them. This is healthy: let them form. Give voice to them. Refrain from accepting the proposal until you're satisfied that the challenges can be addressed.

By the way, you're permitted to employ challenges in the mean- time. For in no way does using them beg the question against my view. Or show illicit bias toward it. Quite the opposite, in fact. If someone were to challenge the permissibility of breathing, you'd be within your rights to continue breathing while you consider the mat- ter, right? The same holds here. So challenge away: when it comes to new and potentially disruptive ideas, it's the right thing to do.

## When Challenges Arise

Now that our serum stimulates the production of cognitive antibod- ies, let's add an ingredient to prevent their *overproduction*.

Our last chapter showed that the overproduction of cognitive antibodies is a real problem: philosophical proposals routinely pro- mote incessant challenging. That's why they're haunted by the spec- ter of skepticism, and why they tend to provoke dogmatic backlash. Culture wars are the predictable outcome: factions afflicted with hy- peractive immune systems face off against factions with underactive ones. Why do challengers to the status quo tend to align on dozens of political issues, and defenders of the status quo congregate around equally complex but opposing political platforms? Because political fault lines are shaped by differences in cognitive immune function.

Culture wars are strikingly similar to a well-known class of bodily immune disorders, where the immune system is "perpetually acti- vated" yet "fails to clear infections."[5] In cases like these, it's not that the immune system fails to activate; it's that it activates continually but fails to do the job. It's like seasonal allergies: pollen triggers an over-the-top immune response, and it's the system's *response* that makes your nose run, eyes itch, and you miserable. The system fails to rid your world of pollen but churns away anyway, adding insult to irritant.

Another example is chronic stress: environmental stressors trigger the release of neurochemicals designed to induce fight-or-flight behavior—in the apparent hope that such behavior will put an end to the stress. But sometimes, the stress doesn't abate and the brain ends up on high alert for days, weeks, or months at a time. In the body, this is linked to high cortisol levels, tissue inflammation, and poor health outcomes.

The final sections of the last chapter essentially show that the body politic is vulnerable to similar ailments. The "perpetual activation" of cultural immune systems can fail to "clear" a culture of ideological thinking. This kind of double whammy immune failure— where immune deficiency and immune hyperactivation are found side by side—can be found, then, in bodies, minds, and cultures.

So let's see what we can do to *modulate* mental immune response: to promote the *judicious* rather than the *indiscriminate* use of challenges.

What if the applicable standard required us to consider not every conceivable challenge, but only the sensible ones? I mean those that genuinely *arise*, as opposed to those that merely happen, for accidental reasons, to be *posed*. To clarify: as I use the term, *arises* is a normative notion. To say that a challenge arises is to say that it makes good sense to raise that concern. It's to say, roughly: "That's a good question—I think it deserves an answer." It implies that the challenge *succeeds* in suspending the claimant's right to use the claim. To say that a challenge has been *posed* is comparatively noncommittal: it says nothing about the quality or worthiness of the challenge, and implies nothing about the resulting standing of the claim. Importantly, a challenge can *arise* even though nobody in the community of inquiry thinks to *pose* it.

In "The Adventure of Silver Blaze," Sherlock Holmes solves a murder by pondering the curious fact that the dog *didn't* bark. I think we can unravel a profound philosophical mystery by looking at the challenges that *don't* arise.

You'll readily grasp the question that I am now obliged to answer: How do we know whether a given challenge arises? Is there some objective—that is, nonarbitrary—way to decide such questions? I studied this question as a graduate student and discovered something interesting: it turns out there is. The solution involves distinguishing two kinds of challenge. One kind seeks to invalidate a claim by presenting *reasons against* the claim at issue: by offering what I call "grounds for doubt." For example, you can challenge a claim by saying: "Really? You're claiming C? How do you reconcile that with G?" (G here represents a ground for doubt; to function well in this capacity, it must weigh against claim C in a telling way.) Challenges like these essentially take on the burden of proof. Or more precisely: the burden of *disproof.* That's why I call them "onus-bearing" challenges.

Onus-bearing challenges arise when, but only when, circumstances offer up suitable grounds for doubt. You can confirm this yourself via thought experiment. Imagine showing that a challenge's grounds for doubt are tenable. Doing this reinforces the entitlement-suspending force of the challenge, does it not? Conversely, showing that a challenge's grounds for doubt are *untenable* drains the challenge of its force. That's how the game is played: show that a challenge rests on shaky assumptions and you show that it doesn't really suspend entitlement. Simply put, you show that it doesn't arise.

Note that the availability of grounds for doubt in a situation is not a private, subjective thing: it's a public, intersubjective condition. For example, our modern context affords many grounds for doubting Flat Earth theory, among them photographs that reveal our planet to be stubbornly globular. Such grounds for doubt are in no way arbitrary or subjective: they're truly *there*—part of the cultural ethos, well established, and publicly available for premising. (And yes, they thoroughly debunk Flat Earth theory.)

Sometimes, though, the world doesn't afford *any* tenable grounds for doubt. For example, I know of no grounds for doubting that "Rutabagas exist," and no grounds for doubting the Pythagorean theorem. The same goes for "Spring follows winter," "Napoleon was defeated at Waterloo," and "Poseidon doesn't exist."

In cases like these—and there are many—we can say that onus-bearing challenges *don't arise*. Our instinct to issue onus-bearing challenges is in this way modulated, in a very natural way, by the supply of grounds for doubt—a supply that tends to be limited.

The other sort of challenge is simpler. Sometimes, a challenger offers no reasons *against* but instead just asks the claimant to provide reasons *for*. "How do you know?" usually accomplishes this neatly. As does "What makes you say that?" These simpler challenges are naked of grounds for doubt, so I call them *bare*. Like onus-bearing challenges, bare challenges mean to suspend entitlement: they present the claim as in need of redemption.[6] Note that these features make bare challenges a powerful move in the reasoning game: for when they're successful, they place a redemptive burden on the claimant, and do so without entangling the challenger in any comparable commitments. By contrast, an onus-bearing challenge commits the challenger to defending its grounds for doubt.

The persistence of regress concerns in epistemology underscore an important point: it's not enough to modulate our use of onus-bearing challenges; we must also modulate our use of bare challenges. For it is bare challenges—the iterated application of "Why?" or "How do you know?"—that drive the regress. The modulating must be done carefully, though, so we don't sanction closed-mindedness or otherwise create a poorly functioning reasoning game.

In the movie *Spider-Man*, the hero's uncle delivers a memorable line: "With great power," he says, "comes great responsibility." He meant the kind of power that superheroes possess, but the principle applies to economic, social, and political power as well. It also applies to the kind of power that challengers possess. For the right to suspend entitlement to ideas cannot be unlimited. Any reasoning game worth playing, in other words, will regulate the use of bare challenges. Like claimants, challengers—even the purveyors of bare ones—must be held accountable. But how?

## The Subtle Art of Challenge Regulation

It's easy to assume that a challenger is always within his rights to issue bare challenges. In fact, countless philosophers have assumed just this. This is understandable, given that interesting and controversial claims—the sort that need backing—occupy the foreground, while uncontroversial claims keep a lower profile. But philosophers who make the incautious generalization invariably find that reason regresses. Remember Agrippa and Sextus Empiricus? Entire schools of ancient philosophy managed to convince themselves that iterated bare challenges undermine all claims to knowledge. They became indiscriminate critics and lost the support of more pragmatic thinkers. It's hard to imagine, but these profoundly corrosive skepticisms persisted for centuries. In fact, they gave philosophy a reputation as thoroughly impractical and set the stage for a crushing anti-intellectual backlash. Ignorance, superstition, and moral disorientation then ruled Europe for a thousand years.

Even the estimable David Hume convinced himself that bare challenges may be iterated *almost* indefinitely. You'll recall his words: "If I ask why you believe any . . . matter of fact, which you relate, you must tell me some reason; and this reason will be some other fact, connected with it. But as you cannot proceed after this manner *in infinitum*, you must at last terminate in some fact, which is present to your memory or senses; or allow that your belief is entirely without foundation." I'd like to challenge Hume on this point: Is it really okay to mindlessly iterate the question "Why?" and expect it to saddle the claimant with a burden of proof each time? Or every time the claim fails to assert a "fact present to your memory or senses"? Or is such indiscriminate questioning the opposite of wise?

Is it true that a challenger is always (or almost always) within his rights to issue a bare challenge? No. Take any perfectly sensible and unproblematic claim; "I have two eyes and a nose," say. (Philosophers call such claims prima facie true, after the Latin for "on the face of it.") In cases like this, the burden of proof doesn't lie on the claimant; instead, a burden of disproof falls on the challenger. The evident fact that I have these facial features is part of the reason why, but sensory evidence is by no means the only circumstance that can have that effect. For example, "We should treat each other kindly" is by no stretch of the imagination a "fact present to the senses." Nor is it a "fact present to memory." (Most philosophers don't even consider it a fact.[7]) It's plainly true, though, and those who assert it are under no obligation to prove the point.

Imagine a kindness skeptic issuing a bare challenge to "We should treat each other kindly." A kindness *advocate* would be within her rights to reply, "Why do you doubt it?" This deft reply (to a daft challenge) puts the onus back where it belongs. To confirm this, just ask yourself whether the counter-challenge ("Why do you doubt it?") "undoes" the entitlement-suspending force of the bare challenge ("How do you know that we should treat each other kindly?"). Perform this thought experiment carefully, and you'll find that it does.[8]

To access the relevant evidence here, you need to consult your sense of propriety. But that's no bar to its being admissible or decisive, for normative judgments are not invariably suspect.[9] Nor is it out of bounds to employ normative concepts (such as "arises") to explain a normative concept (such as "reasonable"). For it is not theory's job to reduce normative concepts to nonnormative ones. Nor is it theory's job to relieve us of responsibility to exercise normative judgment. A useful account will direct our attention to the relevant features of context, but it needn't supplant the judgment of situated thinkers. Theory must know its place.

If that argument doesn't persuade you, try another. Imagine a reasoning practice that *always* permitted a claimant to defend a claim with a counter-challenge such as "Why do you doubt it?" Imagine this rule empowering claimants to dismiss bare challenges at their whim. Surely that would be a degenerate, ill-functioning game—one rigged against challengers. Why then do so many philosophers imagine that bare challenges are always permitted? Wouldn't *that* rule empower challengers to undermine claims at *their* whim? If the former rigs the game, so does the latter. The conclusion is plain: neither rule makes for a well-functioning reasoning game. Hence both must be set aside. I call this the "argument from symmetry."

The point can be made yet another way: when you issue a bare challenge, you presuppose that the burden of proof is on the claimant. The fact that bare challenges are relatively noncommittal (compared to onus-bearing challenges) makes them appear presuppositionless. But this turns out to be an illusion. To see this, reimagine our kindness skeptic employing a bare challenge to question the virtue of kindness. Imagine him demanding a proof, say, that wanton cruelty is bad. Could we not reply to this demand by questioning his supposition that the burden of proof falls upon us? And wouldn't such a reply "undo" the purportedly entitlement-suspending force of his demand? More generally, you can counteract a misplaced bare challenge with "But is the burden of proof really on me?" This *shows* that bare challenges really do make the supposition in question.[10]

## Presumptions

Can we say more about when bare challenges arise, and when they don't? We can. In law, the plaintiff's burden of proof is codified in something we call the defendant's "presumption of innocence." "Burden of proof" and "presumption" in other words, are correlated notions; they're two sides of the same coin. Let's adapt this fact to our purposes. Specifically, let's call claims for which the challenger bears the burden of disproof "presumptions" (an example would be "Birds exist"), and claims for which the claimant bears the burden of proof "nonpresumptive" (example: "Ghosts exist"). We can then say things like: "It's up to the claimant to secure a nonpresumptive claim, but up to the challenger to show that a presumption is problematic." Put simply, bare challenges *arise* against nonpresumptive claims, but *don't arise* against presumptive claims.

Here's the takeaway: *presumptive claims are effectively immune to bare challenge.* They're immune to bare challenge because (by definition) the burden of disproof is on the challenger, and in such cases, a bare challenge *shouldn't* suspend entitlement. Plato's picture of reason, it turns out, gave the rationalist project a blind spot: an inability to "see" presumptions, or properly understand the role they play in sound reasoning. Plato inadvertently banished presumptions—and hamstrung the rationalist project.

A few points are worth stressing. First, presumptiveness is a context-sensitive property. A claim can be presumptive in one situation, but nonpresumptive in another. Thus, "I see a tree" tends to be presumptive in the presence of a tree, but not otherwise. Similarly, "The rich should pay more in taxes" might be presumable in a conversation with a liberal but not presumable in a conversation with a conservative. A claim can be presumptive at the start of a conversation, be undercut by a telling challenge, and remain nonpresumptive thereafter.

Remember Alvin Plantinga's examples of what he called "properly basic belief"? Beliefs like "2+1=3," and "The world has existed for more than five minutes"? They're all presumptions. Indeed, presumptions constitute Plantinga's evidence that properly basic beliefs exist. In fact, the categories of presumption and properly basic belief match up perfectly.[11] The point is that the concept of presumption answers the practical question "What are we within our rights to treat as an unargued premise?" It also answers the theoretical question "What are the true foundations of knowledge?" More on this in a bit.

Third, presumption is a weak and easily overridden status. A valid objection can flip a claim from presumptive to problematic, and a valid counter-challenge can flip it back. For example, "But it's going to rain" can transform "The picnic is on" from presumptive to nonpresumptive, and "Actually, the National Weather Service is now forecasting perfect weather" can restore its presumptive status. This sort of thing happens all the time—sometimes several times in a single conversation.

It follows from all this that philosophers shouldn't bother defining the class of presumptions precisely. For folks are constantly bringing relevant considerations to light, and thereby moving claims from the presumptive to the nonpresumptive side of the ledger. And vice versa. This is as it should be: authority should rest, ultimately, with the persuasive considerations themselves, and the dialogical processes that bring them to light. It's entirely appropriate, then, to accord presumptive status to the claims that have survived past inquiries. Dialectical history matters, and should matter in just this way. Again, theory must know its place.

Theory *can* propose a sensible starting point for those just learning the ropes. For example, we can instruct novice reasoners to begin by treating as presumptive anything that, to them, seems likely to be true. This proposal has the merit of encouraging young thinkers to argue and inquire from wherever they happen to be. It says, in effect: "Have the courage to argue from the convictions you have." This will tend to get "prior" convictions out there, where reason-giving dialogue can begin sculpting them.

Of course, personal convictions aren't the final arbiter of interpersonal disputes. If you and I are trying to work through our differences, it's not my personal beliefs, but our shared situation, that should decide where the burden of proof lies. For such purposes, we might say that the beliefs we have in common should count as presumptive. This proposal has the merit of requiring the party with additional information (above and beyond our common beliefs) to share it. As one matures intellectually, it makes more and more sense to treat as presumptive what the community of responsible inquirers takes to be likely. It's the challenger to *that* status quo that should shoulder the burden of proof.

So there are different ways to define the class of presumptions. We could say that shared background beliefs should be treated as presumptive. We could nominate the elements of the prevailing worldview, or current scientific consensus. We could accord presumptive status to whatever the relevant experts attest. Each of these proposals merits consideration.

I'm partial to proposals that promote dialectical engagement, idea-testing, and the refinement of shared understanding. We should be encouraged to hazard our convictions (that is, put them forward as presumptive) and see how they fare. Of course, we must also let "better reasons" change our minds. Chapters 3, 8, and 9 explain why.

Perhaps you can see a better way to define the class of presumptions. If so, do share it. Show me that the result is yet better functioning, and I'll thank you for enlightening me. In the meantime, we can celebrate the fact that all the proposals mentioned above represent a significant advance over the Platonic picture, which inadvertently banished presumptions altogether. Truly, the bar on an adequate theory has been set that low.

We've just seen that the distinction between bare and onus-bearing challenges allows us to modulate mental immune response. It can help us regulate the activity of powerful cognitive antibodies. Burden of proof considerations turn out to be more than a legal nicety; they're an integral feature of the reasoning game, and essential to cognitive immune health. The everyday notion of *presumption* (the idea that some claims are reasonable by default) and the counter-challenge "Why do you doubt it?" help to preserve this fundamental, immune-modulating insight. By all means: voice the challenges that make sense to you, and answer them as you think best; just understand that you might encounter considerations that require you to rethink them. There's wisdom embedded in our pre-theoretical grasp of how reasoning should go, and any theory that hopes to strengthen mental immune systems must take account of it.

## The New Socratic Model

Our mind vaccine is nearly complete. The next step is to preserve the serum. We do that by introducing a bit more terminology and curing the resulting understanding. To that end, take one more look at the question "Why do you doubt it?" I've called it a "counter-challenge" because, under certain conditions, it can blunt the force of a bare challenge. This illustrates a significant fact about the reasoning game: you can sometimes ward off a challenge without answering it. There are moves in the game that instead allow you to show that a challenge *doesn't need answering*.

Nullifying "How do you know?" with "Why do you doubt it?" is an edge case. Successful counter-challenges more often neutralize onus-bearing challenges. They do that by showing that the challenge's grounds for doubt are untenable. For example, you can counter the challenge "But that never happens!" by showing that "that" *has* happened. Let's call moves of this general type "indirect defendings." For they represent the possibility of defending a claim, not *directly* (with a justifying reason) but *indirectly*, by negating the instigating challenge. Where a *direct defending* accepts a challenge as well posed (and goes on to present one or more supporting reasons), an *indirect defending* tries to show that the challenge was never a threat to the claim's standing in the first place.

The difference here is akin to the difference between divorce and marriage annulment. Divorce dissolves the commitment at the heart of a marriage but supposes that the commitment was in fact duly made. By contrast, an annulment declares that the commitment was never properly undertaken. Yes, the difference can seem academic—the marriage *is* dissolved either way—but sometimes subtle differences make a big difference. Henry VIII didn't divorce his first wife Catherine of Aragon; he had their royal marriage annulled. Why? Because divorce was a grievous sin in the eyes of God, and back then, annulment was the work-around for the well connected. When the pope refused to annul the marriage, the conniving king made a momentous decision: he renounced papal authority, nationalized the Church of England, and secured his annulment that way. He then married his sweetheart Anne Boleyn and tried again to sire an heir. Later, he grew tired of Anne, too, and had her head removed. A sordid business to be sure, but the point stands: a pedantic distinction helped to change the course of history. A major religion split off from its parent, Boleyn's daughter Elizabeth became one of England's most revered monarchs, and England went on to become a global superpower. All this because an academic distinction compelled a philandering king to take extreme measures!

The distinction between direct and indirect defendings is every bit as useful (but without being creepy). In fact, it's a game changer. Here's why: it can give players clarity about how the game is unfolding. Discussants often need to examine a challenge together, then return to the main issue with a shared sense of where the digression leaves them. The direct/indirect distinction helps here. More broadly, the bare/onus-bearing and direct/indirect distinctions can help us keep track of our conversational rights and responsibilities, thereby making us more capable reasoners.[12] They illuminate the structure of knowledge systems and clarify the kind of open-mindedness required of rationally responsible thinkers. (We'll see in a bit that they unravel an influential excuse for closed-mindedness and strengthen mental immune systems.)

A last bit of terminology: a defense that disarms a challenge is said to *meet* it. A challenge can be met directly, with supporting evidence, or indirectly, with a demonstration that the challenge doesn't truly destabilize the claim after all. In either case, the point is to show that the claim survives the challenge (as opposed to merely saying so).[13] A claim successfully defended in one of these two ways is said to *withstand* the challenge.

And with that, we've defined the last important concept we need. The pieces of the puzzle then fit together neatly:

> The true test of a good idea is whether it can withstand the challenges that arise.

Only now we've defined the concepts of *challenge* and *arising*, and know what it means for a claim to *withstand* challenging. We've detailed the kinds of challenges that need to be considered and understand a claimant's options for defending claims. All this adds up to a detailed understanding of how the reasoning game is supposed to be played. (In the appendix, I've spelled out the rules of this game in just a few pages.)

I can now deliver the long-awaited mind vaccine:

> A belief is reasonable if it can withstand the challenges to it that genuinely arise.

To be clear: challenges can be bare or onus-bearing, and anyone in the extended community of inquirers may pose one. (To a first approximation, anyone who *does* pose a challenge should, by that very deed, be considered a member of the community of inquiry.[14]) The believer may employ direct or indirect defendings but only the ones that (can) withstand scrutiny provide genuine closure. I call this the "New Socratic Model" of reasonable belief. My philosopher friends will pick at it. That's okay: it's more a heuristic than a fully worked-out theory, and I welcome efforts to refine it. But some detractors will demand criteria for deciding whether, say, a given defense successfully wards off a challenge. I'm going to push back against demands of that type by insisting that it's not for *me* to *say* what these criteria are. Instead, it's for *us* to *show* what they are.

More precisely, this is not a job for high-level theory. We're unlikely to specify definitive criteria in the abstract. I'm saying that relevant considerations—those churned up by engaged reasoners in concrete contexts—should decide. There's nothing wrong with trying to understand the reasoning game in the abstract, but to settle concrete issues, you must immerse yourself in the relevant particulars—and let *them* settle the matter. Don't think, *look*: play the idea-testing game and *see* what happens. Then follow the better reasons where they lead. Theory only takes us so far. From that point on, it's about practice.

## A Passel of Virtues

I'd like to show that this New Socratic Model has several desirable qualities. I'll start with its *practical* virtues: the ones likely to improve our capacity to think and reason well.

Take a careful look at the New Socratic Model. Notice that it doesn't direct us to look for supporting reasons. Not like the Platonic picture does. Instead, it advises us to do what the world's most skilled thinkers do: ask questions. This is a hugely consequential difference. For where the Platonic picture nudges us into the "How do I validate this?" mindset of those prone to confirmation bias, the Socratic nudges us into the "What should we make of this?" mindset of the genuinely curious. One primes us to rationalize; the other, to inquire.

When you look for confirmatory reasons, you tend to find them. The New Socratic Model, then, offers a better "choice architecture" for everyday thinking.[15] I see this as the model's primary virtue.

You'll recall that confirmation bias is our tendency to look for evidence that might *validate* a favored belief, while overlooking considerations that might *invalidate* it. Experts agree that this bias is widespread, tenacious, and consequential. And these days, many assume that it's innate. And perhaps it is—to a degree. But it may also be culturally conditioned. After all, we live in a world where the Platonic picture exerts a powerful grip on the popular imagination. Mightn't people trained to think Socratically diverge from the confirmation-biased norm? The question deserves to be investigated empirically.

For all we know, it's possible to substantially mitigate confirmation bias. Imagine a world where everyone learned the art of Socratic idea-testing early. Imagine moving the needle on this just a little (rendering ourselves 10 percent less prone to confirmation bias, say). Might this not affect much larger changes? Remember, confirmation bias plays a major role in ideology formation; the shift to a Socratic conception of reasonable belief, then, could mitigate, not just confirmation bias, but our proneness to ideological derangement. Let's call this *virtue 2*.

*Virtue 3*: The New Socratic model also implies that it's not enough to mindlessly repeat the question "Why?" It tells us that lazy regress questioning is for pikers; that real critical thinkers employ bare *but mostly onus-bearing* challenges (and each as appropriate). Those inoculated with the model, then, are constantly rubbing elbows with grounds for doubt. They're compelled by their habits of mind to consider *reasons against* as well as *reasons for*. I'm saying *real pros make a habit of weighing cons*. If that doesn't mitigate confirmation bias, it's hard to see what would.

*Virtue 4*: Notice next that the model directs us to consider both upstream evidence and downstream implications. For when a bare challenge arises and someone offers a direct defending, we end up examining upstream evidence. When an onus-bearing challenge arises, we generally end up exploring downstream implications. Since a challenge can call attention to an idea's problematic *effects*, we're also enjoined to examine *causal* implications. (Recall that chapter 6 highlighted the need to examine ideas from both *epistemic* and *pragmatic* perspectives: comprehensive assessment looks at both truth *and* usefulness.) The New Socratic model, then, compels us to consider pros *and* cons, upstream evidence *and* downstream implications, logical *and* causal properties, *epistemic* and *pragmatic* fallout. Here's the plain truth: When you scrutinize ideas in this fashion, you're more likely to spot the bad ones. And send them packing. *That*, I think, is what higher-order cognitive immunity looks like. And clearly, the New Socratic Model promotes it.

*Virtue 5*: The model *modulates* mental immune response. In fact, it's carefully designed to temper the impulse to question and criticize. It regulates the production of cognitive antibodies, and even tells us how to spot and counteract overweening challenges. Unlike exhortations to "think critically," it doesn't exhort us to dwell ceaselessly on the negative, or constantly find fault. It's therefore less likely to exacerbate negativity bias. It recognizes that hypercritical individuals are hardly paragons of cognitive virtue. (Indeed, they're poster children for cognitive autoimmunity.) Instead, the model deliberately levels the dialectical playing field. In so doing, it restores balance to our reasoning practices—the same balance that makes for mental immune health.

*Virtue 6*: The New Socratic Model promotes the growth mindset. For it primes us to *learn also from challenges*. It says: it's not enough to learn from findings that compel *additions* to your belief system (reasons to form new beliefs), we must also learn from those that compel *subtractions* from it (reasons against existing beliefs). A truly growth-oriented mindset stands ready to make adjustments of either kind, and the model encourages us to seize both kinds of opportunities. Embrace it, and you can master both additive and subtractive learning. And more fully embody the growth mindset.

*Virtue 7*: The model sanctions open-mindedness and scientific humility. For no matter how well you understand an issue—no matter how familiar you become with the challenges that arise in a domain—it's always possible that a new challenge will arise and upset the applecart. It follows that it's not okay to make up your mind and refuse to consider new challenges. The need to keep an open mind thus flows directly from the model. As does the need for epistemic humility.

*Virtue 8*: The model also tells us what we must do to merit the courage of our convictions: become intimately familiar with the challenges to a claim that arise in a domain, and make sure that you can successfully address them. Where the world simply fails to produce worthwhile challenges to "The sun rises in the east," you're allowed to assert it with confidence. The same goes for more controversial claims: you've earned the right to confidently assert "Abortion should be safe, legal, and rare" when you know how to defend it against all the standard challenges.

*Virtue 9*: The model points to more effective ways to teach critical thinking. Here's an example: we currently tell students to argue for their claims. But this is a confusing mandate. It applies to their thesis statement, and to some supporting claims they might be tempted to invoke, but it doesn't apply to *every* premise they might employ. (Premises are claims too, after all.) Some claims are properly treated as presumptive—as *unargued* premises. And students should know this. So we're better off instructing them to write persuasive essays that marshal presumptive premises in support of interesting and surprising (that is, nonpresumptive) conclusions.

What currently passes for good critical thinking instruction leaves students confused: it makes them defensive and leaves them with a distinct impression that we apply our standards haphazardly. The concept of presumption, however, allows us to give them real clarity: more transparent guidance about how to write a good persuasive essay, more insight into the process of building new understanding, and greater clarity about how to think critically. Adept critical thinkers understand this: *good argumentation is fundamentally a matter of marshaling presumptive premises to defend nonpresumptive conclusions.* Critical thinking is all about finding claims that happen to sit on the wrong side of the ledger, and showing why they need to be moved to the other side.

The model also lends critical thinking instruction something it has long lacked: a useful picture of what a good idea looks like. Instead of telling students one hundred ways that arguments go bad, and have them play at faultfinding—a formula that often leaves them floundering—we can now give them a handy standard: good ideas stand amid challenges yet manage to ward them off. Convey this to students, and simply invite them to test ideas. Show them that the process is a ton of fun, turn them loose on issues they care about, and you'll watch their critical faculties bloom.

*Virtue 10*: The model expands the purview of science. For the machinery of challenge-and-response allows us to treat *any* claim as a hypothesis. Almost any conversation can become a quasi-scientific inquiry: an illuminating exploration of an idea's pros and cons. Now imagine the ubiquitous use of conversational idea-testing. Suppose we divert, say, 1 percent of the world's daily supply of waking person-hours. (In practice, this amounts to your average person spending an additional ten minutes per day conversing philosophically.) The output? That would be 1.25 billion person-hours spent filtering bad ideas from the meme pool. And that's just day one. Then another 1.25 billion person-hours spent on day two. And so on. Here's the point: together, we can uproot a lot of mental weeds.

Now imagine this done with ever-increasing skill. Imagine a more critical sensibility becoming normal. Imagine habits of mind shifting as a result. Could this not strengthen mental immune systems around the globe? Could it not boost our immunity to substandard political ideas? And dissolve stagnant ideologies? Imagine such measures putting an end to egregious forms of science denial and expanding the influence of good ideas. None of these outcomes strikes me as the least bit implausible, for small reductions in the influence of bad ideas accelerates the pace of fruitful inquiry.

Arguably, the model can mitigate groupthink, foster dialogical engagement, and promote fair-mindedness too. But that's enough for now. Now, let's look at whether the New Socratic Model has the qualities needed to spark a cognitive revolution.

## Closure Without Closed-Mindedness

The New Socratic Model neatly resolves an ancient philosophical puzzle. I'm talking about the quandary of basic belief—the utterly fundamental question of what (if anything) makes up the foundation of our knowledge. When perspectives on issues this fundamental shift, paradigms quake. This makes me hopeful that the New Socratic Model can bring about an overdue philosophical reckoning: a new Enlightenment, if you will. But I'm a player, not an impartial referee, and like everyone else, I'm prone to wishful thinking. So let's revisit the puzzle and see what *you* think.

The quandary at the heart of philosophy's long struggle to make sense of reason's requirements can be framed like this: Should we regard everything as open to question (Option 1), or instead treat some things as *not* open to question (Option 2)?[16]

We've seen that both options prove devastating to rationalist hopes. Consider Option 1: it treats everything as open to question, even our purportedly foundational "first principles." If we allow such questions, even our basic beliefs appear to need justifying. Produce such justifications, though, and our basic beliefs don't appear so basic. Indeed, they become derivative. And there's the rub: What kind of foundation recoils at the touch of a question? Apparently, the not-very-solid kind.

We philosophers express this problem in an abstract way; we say that, on Option 1, reason "regresses." The abstract language, though, points to a real danger: mightn't systematic questioning consume the very ground we stand upon? Mightn't it leave us in cognitive free fall, unable to say or believe anything with confidence? It seems that, to function at all, we must treat some things as *not* open to question.

I have religious friends who see unwavering faith as the answer: the backstop to a life that might otherwise lack meaning. Another friend, a fellow freethinker, draws this lesson: "If you open your mind too wide, your brains will fall out." It bothers me that both religious and secular thinkers make such concessions to closed-mindedness.

Which brings us to Option 2. This horn of the dilemma requires us to concede that some things are *not* open to question. To embrace this option is to sanction a certain limited closed-mindedness. And it gets worse: for if you're entitled to accept X without question, why can't I accept Y without question? This path throws open the gates to arbitrary forms of irrationality. Moreover, the resulting picture paints reason as *relative* to one or another set of dogmatic commitments. Such relativism isn't just a theoretical problem: it does real practical damage. For it implies that reasoning is powerless to adjudicate between belief systems built on rival commitments. I've spoken with hundreds of highly educated people who have this depressingly limited picture of reason's powers, and time and again, I've watched it derail reason-giving dialogue. It's profoundly immune-disruptive.

Taken together, these two options make up what I call the "dilemma of ultimate commitment."[17] It seems we must choose, and we hobble the rationalist project either way. It seems that closed-mindedness is the only path to cognitive closure.

Fortunately, the New Socratic Model dissolves the dilemma neatly. The key insight is this: a premise needn't be immune to *all* challenges to function as basic; it's enough that it be immune to *bare* challenge. Presumptions, in other words, are the key to halting the slide into regress skepticism.

Here's how it works: you're a skilled reasoner, so you build your argument on presumptively reasonable premises. Presumptions are immune to bare challenge, so any would-be challenger must shoulder the argumentative burden. It's up to them, in other words, to find grounds for doubt. If they can't find any, you win that round of the reason-giving game. Put differently, it's possible to bring reasoning to a satisfactory close without being the least bit closed-minded: just remain open to onus-bearing challenges, and bare challenges where and when they arise.

The key point merits emphasis: an important kind of closure can be had without closed-mindedness. You can argue from presumptive premises, shift the onus onto challengers, and redeem disputed claims—all while remaining 100 percent open to the possibility that an onus-bearing challenge might come along and shuffle the deck. New grounds for doubt might turn up and undermine your premises. They could invalidate core beliefs, even turn your worldview upside down. The whole time, though, you can have the courage of your convictions *without obstinate tenacity*. Just be ready to yield to any telling onus-bearing challenge that might arise.

The solution clarifies what it means to be truly open-minded: we *do* need to be forever open to *onus-bearing challenges*, but we needn't assume that everything is vulnerable to *bare challenge*. We must do the first to avoid rigging the reasoning game against challengers; we must do the second to avoid rigging it against claimants. The epistemological solution engenders a salutary attitude: one that's forthright yet open, strong but resilient. This very attitude, it turns out, is the secret to cognitive immune health.

Here's the thing to see: this kind of openness doesn't cause the bottom to fall out. Presumptively reasonable beliefs continue to abound, so reason doesn't regress, and skepticism, cynicism, and nihilism remain at bay. You enjoy the courage of responsibly held convictions, but needn't resort, ever, to dogmatic inflexibility. That article of faith you cling to so tightly? Let it go. At the very least, contemplate onus-bearing challenges openly and honestly, and learn from them. Let grounds for doubt whittle away at problematic beliefs, even the cherished kind. You'll find what millions of others have found: there's truly nothing to fear. You'll only fall as far as the nearest presumption. Thinking isn't like free solo rock climbing; it's like top-roping.

I once went rock climbing with fellow epistemologist Alvin Plantinga; he free-soloed a rock face that petrified me. His Christian faith, I concluded, is impressively real.

## The Ratchet of Progress

The path to deep understanding gets steeper here, so I offer two options. Option 1: prepare yourself for the final ascent. Rest, fortify your resolve, and buckle your safety harness. When you're ready, we'll proceed upward. Slowly. Patience is needed to scale this summit. Option 2: skip the rest of this chapter. Backtrack, study the arguments of the preceding chapters, and try again later.

There's no shame in the latter. Here's why: the air is thinner up there. Just as climbers must gradually acclimate their bodies to higher altitudes, philosophers must gradually acclimate their minds to environments where deep and subtle challenges are taken seriously. (That's why this treatment of cognitive immunology has four stages: to scaffold aptitude for higher-order thinking.) If you find the next several pages too abstract for your tastes, don't sweat it: just skip the rest of this chapter. I'll rejoin you at base camp (the start of the next chapter) for the final—and far gentler—climb.

Presumptions have just the qualities needed to function as basic. They can *provide a basis* because they're presumptively reasonable but don't themselves *need a basis* because it's up to any challenger to present grounds for doubt. "Basic," in other words, is a functional status: a belief or claim can function as basic in one context because, given background conditions, it doesn't need justifying. It can function properly as an unargued premise even if, under other circumstances, its validity would need demonstrating. Presumptions, then, are *contextually* basic.

With this, we steer a path between skepticism and dogmatism. We avoid skepticism because many claims are presumptive and immune to bare challenge. Presumptions prevent cognitive free fall.

Meanwhile, we avoid dogmatism by treating everything, presumptions included, as forever open to onus-bearing challenge. *This very balance is the key to cognitive immune health.*

This solution also gives us an insightful answer to the question of what knowledge ultimately rests upon: our knowledge rests on presumptions. Presumptive foundations, it turns out, are as good as it gets. Even in mathematics, we build theorems atop presumptively reasonable axioms.[18] The same is true in the sciences. we build our knowledge atop presumptions: premises that are forever open to undermining by onus-bearing challenge yet, for all that, stand (contextually) immune to bare challenge. "There is a real world outside of my mind," for example. Again, many of these presumptions are empirical and can be regarded as evidence-based. We're under no obligation, though, to treat them as forever needing and getting evidential support. Indeed, many of them don't need evidencing *now* precisely because they were sufficiently evidenced *then*. We accord the findings of earlier inquiries presumptive status so that later inquiries can build upon them.

Presumptions, in other words, are a bit like the "click" or "pawl" of a ratchet—the spring-loaded finger that prevents a ratchet's gear from unspooling. Presumptions, like pawls, catch forward movement, preserve it, and prevent backsliding. We need presumptions to conserve dialectical progress.[19] Yes, we sometimes need to challenge and rethink presumptions, just as we sometimes disengage a ratchet's pawl and allow the gear to unspool a bit. But you can't banish presumptions altogether and expect reasons to function properly: that's the lesson of the last chapter.[20]

By welcoming presumptions back from their lengthy epistemological exile, we "unrig" the reason-giving game and allow it to function properly. We restore a kind of balance to our mental models and make theory relevant again to ordinary epistemic practice. In fact, we open the possibility, again, of theory *strengthening* those practices: of theory fortifying mental immune systems.

Meanwhile, the distinction between bare and onus-bearing challenges allows us to show why tenacious commitment is unnecessary. It can help us impart the scientific attitude and promote critical thinking. It can help us cultivate the growth mindset. It can help us inoculate minds.

A nice feature of this solution is that it doesn't really restrict the scope of critical questioning. In fact, it expands it. It does this in two ways. First, it leaves all beliefs—even "basic" beliefs—open to critical scrutiny. This undermines an influential excuse for closed-mindedness (the one that says: "Everyone takes things for granted, so I'm entitled to take my cherished beliefs for granted").

Second, the limited bare challenge immunity that presumptions enjoy is properly seen as an *expansion* of the purview of criticism. For in effect, we've built a model of reasoning that allows us to question questions. We've shown, specifically, that it's sometimes possible to defend a claim *indirectly*—by challenging a challenge rather than answering it. If an unscrupulous skeptic wants to level bare challenges at everything, fine, but he can't expect us not to counter, in suitable circumstances, with counter-challenges like "Why do you doubt it?" That's the beauty of it: we *expand* the right to issue challenges and still halt the slide into regress skepticism. We turn criticism on itself and restore balance to our picture of reason.

The New Socratic picture, then, has theoretical as well as practical virtues. Flaws will probably come to light, but let's pause to appreciate the advance it represents over the Socratic, Platonic, Humean, and Cliffordian pictures.

First, the Platonic picture lives on as a special case of the New Socratic picture. For wherever a bare challenge arises and is met directly, justification is had by virtue of supporting reasons. The New Socratic model thus subsumes the Platonic model the way relativity theory subsumed Newtonian physics. The New Socratic conception represents a more encompassing truth.

Where the Platonic model struggled to account for basic beliefs, though, the New Socratic model accounts for them easily and elegantly: they are "contextually basic" when, in the context in question, sensible challenges to them don't arise.[21] Basic beliefs, in other words, are just the special case where "All arising challenges can be met" is trivially satisfied. (For where *no* sensible challenges arise, it follows that *all that do* can be met.) The standard is satisfied, not because supporting reasons are *available*, but because supporting reasons aren't *needed*.

This doesn't mean that supporting evidence doesn't exist, only that it's not up to the believer or claimant to produce it. It's for this reason, and this reason only, that "Spring follows winter," "Happiness is good," "The sun will rise tomorrow," "Emeralds are green," "The Earth has existed for more than five minutes," and countless other claims are properly treated as basic. The New Socratic model handles basic belief without breaking a sweat.

These two features of the New Socratic model—its subsumption of the Platonic model, and its straightforward handling of basic belief—bode well. For as historians and philosophers have noted, successor paradigms are generally constrained by the need to cast a coherent narrative explaining their predecessor's successes and failures.[22] And this is precisely what the New Socratic Model provides: a compelling account of why the Platonic picture could have seemed so natural and intuitive, and a clear view of where and why that picture breaks down. The Socratic Model duplicates the successes of the Platonic paradigm, while also addressing the anomalies that have long distressed that paradigm.

This means we don't have to regard the generations of thinkers who operated within the Platonic paradigm as deluded: they were captivated by a picture of reason that makes excellent sense of the cases we tend to foreground: the cases where a bare challenge arises. At the same time, the New Socratic Model allows us to move beyond the Platonic paradigm and revitalize the rationalist project.

## How Presumptions Encode Evidence

Is sufficient evidence the hallmark of responsible belief, or not? Of the criteria that enjoy significant currency, the evidentialist standard may be the best known. It is certainly among the most salutary, as judged by its implications and historical effects. It encourages people to look for indications of a belief's truth and recommends a skeptical attitude when such indications are lacking. The idea helped rid the world of demons, witches, and evil spirits, and it deserves credit for freeing us from countless imagined fears. Where it has taken hold, the sciences have flourished, and worldviews have become dramatically more accurate and enlightened.

We've seen, though, that the evidentialist standard raises vexing questions. Among these are questions of clarification: What counts as evidence, exactly? And how much is enough? There are also troubling allegations of self-referential incoherence: Is the standard *itself* properly evidence-based? If so, why has no one yet succeeded in deriving it from empirical data? Is it even possible for such a derivation to span the is/ought gap (as it clearly must)? There are questions about the attitudes the standard engenders: Is it really a good idea to treat *every* conviction as invalid until evidentially validated? Or is such an attitude too indiscriminate to be well functioning?

There are questions about its logical implications: What if the standard proves too corrosive? Didn't Hume discover that, taken seriously, it wipes out causal knowledge? And what about *moral* knowledge: weren't twentieth-century empiricists compelled to dismiss moral claims as mere expressions of preference? Finally, there are questions about the standard's pragmatic implications: Does the sufficient evidence standard leave enough room for beliefs that serve our social and emotional needs? What about our needs for purpose, connection, and belonging? What about our need to matter? Does it allow us to believe in human rights?

And do any of us apply the evidentialist standard consistently?

Alvin Plantinga showed that we all believe things we don't have the first idea how to evidence. Plantinga has concluded that evidentialism is bankrupt, and others are following suit. The prospects of humanity forming a robust consensus around the evidentialist standard seem bleak.

The New Socratic model, though, allows us to rescue evidentialism. For it is not the standard itself that generates the difficulties: it's the Platonic construction we place upon it. Philosophers smitten by the Platonic picture interpret the requirement as assigning a kind of default "unreasonable" to every judgment that has not yet been properly evidenced. It's precisely this indiscriminate baseline presumption, though, that is causing our legitimation crisis.

Practicing scientists don't wipe the belief-slate clean, then painstakingly populate it only with evidence-based conclusions. Like all of us, they take many things to be presumptively true, and reason from them. (Without these presumptions, they wouldn't get very far.) Science isn't special because it starts from scratch and builds everything from evidence and logic alone; it's special because it's resolutely committed to countenancing cogent challenges and making necessary revisions. And it's not just its conclusions that are fair game for challengers: a good scientist will entertain cogent challenges to any ingredient in their reasoning: premises, assumptions, intuitions, conjectures, presuppositions, estimates, hunches, and conventions—all of these are grist for the challenge-and-response game.

Practicing scientists, in other words, give evidentialism a Socratic rather than a Platonic spin. They grow into a community of inquiry that takes many things as presumptively true, and for the most part, they accept those presumptions. That's part of the process of becoming a scientist. Sometimes, a scientist will challenge elements of the scientific consensus and succeed in overturning one or several of them. But they never discard all their discipline's presumptions, and start from scratch. If they did, they'd be doing something like Cartesian epistemology, not science.

The New Socratic picture of reason, then, doesn't require us to abandon the sufficient evidence standard. Instead, it urges us to enrich our picture of how reasoning and inquiry work. Inquiry yields findings, which are then presumed, for the most part, to be true. These presumptions become available for premising, and a spur to new inquiries. Often, these presumptions summarize accumulated evidence or otherwise encode hard-won insights. In this way, the evidence and insight they contain become the "basis" of new knowledge. In this sense, it remains true that empirical knowledge is "based" on evidence. (In another, perfectly straightforward sense, of course, that very same knowledge is based on presumptions.)

So in a sense, presumptions are repositories of evidence. As I use the term, to presume something is to adopt something like this attitude toward it: "My past encounters with various indicators make me reasonably confident that X is true, so for now, I will treat it as true—provided you have no objection." Responsible believers, I think, take this attitude toward *all* their beliefs.

There are several reasons to prefer the Socratic to the Platonic construal of evidentialism. To begin with, it sidesteps all the difficulties that plague Platonic conceptions: it avoids self-referential incoherence and resolves the quandary of basic belief. It doesn't cause reason to regress, or flirt with radical skepticism. It untangles our legitimation crisis.

In a way, the New Socratic Model helps us get a handle on the meaning of "sufficient evidence." For one, it gives us a more recognizable picture of what evidence typically looks like. Evidence takes indefinitely many forms—data tables, scatterplots, hoofprints, gathering clouds, a fingerprint at the scene of the crime—but in conversation, we usually encounter it in the form of presumptive claims: claims that distill evidential indications into a simple, dialectically useful form. That's what (many) presumptions do: they take evidence and make it available for premising.

Arguably, the model also helps us get a handle on "sufficient."

How do you know if the accumulated evidence is enough? Well, formulate the corresponding presumptions and feed them into the reason-giving game. Use them to challenge and defend the claim at issue, and see what happens. If they prove adequate to the task of defending the claim, then you have enough evidence. If not, not.[23]

Socratic evidentialism also proves friendlier to normative conviction. Because it's Socratic, it doesn't start with the Platonic picture's blanket presumption of epistemic guilt. Instead, many normative claims—such as "We should treat each other kindly"—are presumed innocent. And rightfully so: there are excellent reasons for treating claims like these as default rational.

Nor is the Socratic evidentialist obliged to conceive of evidence as a thin veneer of sensory indications. Instead, we can understand evidence more broadly, as any (reliable) indicator of the truth of something. We can even understand common normative presumptions— behavior-guiding maxims that have proven useful in the past, and have thus far survived critical scrutiny—as a kind of evidence. "Try not to harm others," "Don't cheat," and "Slavery is wrong" strike us as self-evident, but not because they confer rational legitimacy on themselves. Instead, they're self-evident because each one distills a wealth of experience and insight into a maxim that is presumptively reasonable—available for premising, and likely to prove useful.

Here's the point: the New Socratic picture is a friendly complement to the "sufficient evidence" standard of reasonable belief. Indeed, it seems to elaborate that standard in a useful way. But this leaves two important questions: Can this view be defended against objections? What onus-bearing challenges arise here, and can they be addressed?

## Objections and Replies

Shakespeare loved tales of villains who fell into their own traps. He even coined a phrase for the phenomenon: schemers, he implied, were apt to get "hoist(ed) on their own petard." The expression has since gained wide currency in the English-speaking world. It reached my ears when I was about ten. Assuming that a petard was something like a unitard, or maybe a leotard, I envisioned a sharp upward yank on a tight-fitting bodysuit. It seemed the grown-ups were referring to some sort of karmic wedgie.

Silly me: a "petard," it turns out, is a small bomb: Shakespeare was referring to a then-common fate of military engineers: they'd invent a diabolical device, and often manage, in building it, to blow themselves to bits. Incidentally, the word *petard* also refers to a violent expulsion of *intestinal* gas, which means the esteemed Bard was influencing posterity by cracking wise about flatulence. Any cosmos that grants immortality to a purveyor of fart jokes has got to be fond of existential wedgies.

Epistemologists, it turns out, are often hoisted on their petards. They propose standards of reasonable belief meant to correct humanity's uncritical tendencies of thought, and find that those standards prove self-undermining. For example, "Accept only what is empirically provable" turns out to be anything but empirically provable. Similarly, "Believe only what you can derive from self-evident premises" turns out not to be derivable from self-evident premises. Nor are these isolated cases: unexpectedly explosive epistemological standards are more the rule than the exception. Like petards, they're astonishingly prone to self-demolition. In epistemology, getting hoisted on your petard is something of an occupational hazard.

So, does the New Socratic model share this defect? Or does it meet its own standard and thereby qualify as self-consistent? Let's find out.

By its own lights, the New Socratic model merits acceptance only if it can be properly defended against the challenges to it that genuinely arise. So let's examine these challenges and see if they can be met. The bare challenge "Why should I take this model seriously?" really does arise, I think. More precisely, it *did* arise at the start of this inquiry, which is why I assumed the burden of proof. I've since worked to lift that burden, offering many reasons why we should prefer the New Socratic conception. I like to think that, in the process, I've managed to *shift* the burden: that a burden of *disproof* now rests on the model's critics. If you grant this much, we can turn our attention to a set of concerns usually expressed as onus-bearing challenges.

I've shared this model with many and made note of the concerns they tend to express. Some worry that the proposal could sanction dogmatism. Others worry that it makes rationality subjective. Some argue that it courts relativism. Still others object that the account deploys unexplained normative language, and thereby fails to fully explicate the concept. It's also sensible to wonder whether the model is unacceptably vague or indeterminate. Let's examine these challenges in turn, and see whether the model holds up.

I've urged a retreat from the Platonic paradigm's assumption that every candidate for rational acceptance requires validation. It's natural to wonder whether such a retreat yields an insufficiently critical mindset. I've also argued that some claims are presumptively reasonable, and therefore immune to bare challenging. Some feel that it sets a very bad precedent to treat anything as immune to *any* kind of questioning, and worry that the proposal could inadvertently sanction dogmatic tenacity. So does it?

In answer, let me clarify the proposal. I share the conviction that insulating claims against critical scrutiny is a bad idea. For this reason, I insist that all claims are, and forever remain, open to onus-bearing challenges. We should never close our minds to the possibility that telling grounds for doubt might come along and invalidate a belief. Nor should we be unwilling to yield to such grounds when they *do* come along. My point is that bare challenges must be handled differently. For if we treat bare challenges as always and everywhere appropriate, we allow challengers to suspend entitlement at their whim. That's the lesson of the regress problem: the right to issue bare challenges must be circumscribed, or we rig the reasoning game against claimants.

It's one thing to recognize the situational impropriety of bare challenging and another to exempt cherished beliefs from critical scrutiny. The latter really *is* ethically problematic, but that in no way makes the former so. Acknowledging the reality of presumption isn't tantamount to endorsing tenacious closed-mindedness. In fact, we must acknowledge presumption to achieve what William James called "skeptical balance"; it's needed to level the dialectical playing field. (Notice, by the way, that if a skeptic is always within his rights to suspend entitlement with a bare challenge, claimants can abuse that very privilege to undermine any grounds for doubt a challenger might put forward: both claimants and challengers need presumptions.) I think this reply fully addresses the concern that the New Socratic model somehow sanctions dogmatism.

Others worry that it's a mistake to yoke reason to the challenges that happen to arise. For a particular person or community might never consider the important challenges. Suppose no one in Nazi Germany thought to challenge the party's policy of exterminating Gypsies. Would that have made the policy reasonable? Of course not. More generally, it's a mistake to make a normative concept (like "reasonable") a simple function of de facto questioning habits. Why? Because it's easy to imagine scenarios where the relevant parties just don't ask the important questions.

This challenge is based on a failure to understand the proposal. For I've distinguished between a challenge's arising and its being (de facto) posed, and I've carefully linked reason to the former rather than the latter. To elaborate: there's a difference between a question seeming (subjectively) to arise, and a question's really (objectively) arising. There are two sides to this; first, a challenge can be *posed* without really *arising*. (A case in point is the very objection I'm addressing, for it is based on a misapprehension. The fact that clearing up the misapprehension drains the challenge of its entitlement-suspending force *shows* that it doesn't really arise.)

Second, a challenge can *arise* without being *posed*. Indeed, the Nazis had to ignore many such challenges to proceed with their genocidal plans. Challenges based on the notion of human rights, for example. *Where* were these challenges, exactly? Well, they were "in the air" at the time. The idea is that they really were part of the epistemic situation, even if many Germans were too scared to voice them. (These unvoiced challenges existed, at the very least, as real dialectical possibilities.)

The account's notion of a challenge's being *met* is similarly objective: it's one thing to voice a reply to a challenge, and something else to issue a reply that *rationally suffices* to disarm it. (So a reply's de facto rhetorical influence is one thing, and its true rational force could be something else.) The point is that I anticipated the objection and employed language and distinctions meant to address it. It's easy to hear talk of challenges arising (or talk of challenges being met) and overlay it with a subjective interpretation, but with a little practice, you can understand such talk in the way I intend.

Some worry that the New Socratic Model makes rationality *relative*. It's certainly true that I've urged an understanding whereon reason turns out to be highly sensitive to relevant features of context. On this account, a claim can be reasonable in one context, but not in another; or reasonable at one moment in a dialectical exchange, and not reasonable the next. This much context sensitivity is arguably a good thing, for the presentation of a telling persuasive consideration *should* affect a claim's epistemic standing. You may caricature this sensitivity as "relativist," but that doesn't make it problematic.

The important thing is to explicate the concept in a way that doesn't prevent reasoning from functioning properly in the resolution of differences (or in determinations of what's true). If we make reason relative to the de facto standards of subculture A, then our standard will probably fail to function properly when subculture B challenges the standards of subculture A. Indeed, it will probably beg the question against subculture B. But that's not the situation here. The New Socratic Model recommends scrupulously engaged sensitivity to relevant features of dialectical situation and history, not blind allegiance to de facto standards.

Some philosophers will find fault with my use of normative concepts: for using terms like *arises*, *meets*, and *relevant* to explicate the notion of a belief's being reasonable. This charge, too, rests on an error. For it's not theory's job to reduce normative concepts to nonnormative ones. Nor is it theory's job to relieve epistemic agents of the responsibility to exercise normative judgment. A standard of reasonable belief should direct our attention to the relevant features of context, but leave it to individuals to apply that standard. If applying the standard requires the exercise of normative judgment, so be it.

There's nothing wrong with wanting further clarification of the operative concepts. In the fullness of time, we may be able to explicate them as well, further reducing vagueness. (I assume Bayes' theorem can be used to spell out these ideas more precisely, but I leave that task to others.) The thing to see is that the notion of a *complete* explication is a false ideal. For all explanations end somewhere. Nor does an account's incompleteness render it incorrect. If you'd like to see the New Socratic standard explicated more fully, have at it: further development of the idea would be most welcome.

Some might fret that I've not demonstrated the correctness of my proposed criterion of proper basicality. Why, they might ask, should they have to accept my spin on what counts as presumptive? Who gets to define what's basic?

It's true that I have not provided such a demonstration. What I have done is mention several possibilities that make for a suitably well-functioning reasoning game. "Treat elements of the prevailing scientific consensus as presumptive," for example, essentially tells us to pick up the discussion where previous scientific inquiries left off. For scientific purposes, this seems about right. Alternatively, interlocutors A and B could treat their common beliefs as presumptive. That way, the party who wants to assert something the other party doesn't accept is asked to shoulder the burden of proof.

Again, I think that seems about right: reasonably fair, and reasonably truth-conducive. No, I can't *prove* that this is *the* correct account, but I can point out that, in friendly dialogue, a burden of proof is often a small thing, requiring no more than a minute or two, and a couple of good reasons, to shift. For most purposes, then, a standard like this is good enough. I can also point out that proposals like this represent a significant advance over the presumption-denying Platonic status quo in academic epistemology. In science, a theory must explain the phenomena better than its competitors; shouldn't a similar, better-than-the-alternatives-on-offer standard prevail in a newly "scientized" epistemology—that is, one freed of its Platonic misconceptions?

To sum up: I think that challenges to the New Socratic Model can be met. Properly understood, the view can be defended against common challenges. I've tried to *show* this. In my eyes, the model survives such criticism and merits acceptance. If it's a petard, it hasn't detonated yet.

Of course, I may be overlooking cogent challenges—challenges that would compel any rational person to revise or abandon the model. The model itself compels me to acknowledge that possibility. Indeed, the challenge-and-response game generates a great many possibilities, and I can't examine them all. That's why it's so important to inquire together.

It was Hamlet who spoke of hoisting military engineers on their own petards. In fact, he reckoned it great "sport" to "delve one yard below their mines, and blow them at the moon." That martial mindset, imported into the reasoning game, sparks culture wars. So here's my plea: by all means, explore the space of possible challenges, and give voice to those I've missed. Delve deeper than I have, and bring overlooked challenges to my attention. But don't make sport of hoisting my petard; be a friend, and lead me away before it blows.

Better yet, guide us all to a better alternative.

# Propagating Enlightenment

## *How to bend the arc of history*

For millions of years, mysterious afflictions visited our ancestors. Diseases spread through populations, bringing illness, suffering, and death. Loved ones fell to pox or the plague, and speculation swirled among survivors. Are we being punished for our sins? Whose sins? Will placating the gods bring relief? Or has a deadly miasma descended from the heavens? No one knew. They didn't understand the microbial origins of disease, and the not knowing added to the terror. And century after century, our ancestors remained largely powerless to halt contagion.

Then in short order, everything changed. Science validated the germ theory of disease. Virologists identified the deadliest pathogens. Epidemiologists demystified transmission. Immunologists revealed the immune system's role in resistance and recovery. These disciplines developed solutions that saved literally billions of lives. Why are smallpox and the Black Death unknown to us? Because scientists went to great lengths to secure badly needed understanding.

These sciences transformed the human condition. They did this, in part, by weaving a story: a narrative replete with heroes and villains, conflict and life lessons. Clinical language downplays the drama, but at bottom, it's a morality tale:

> *Manipulative bugs (pathogens) are constantly invading the home-land (our bodies), but microscopic defenders (antibodies) rally to our cause. Responsible citizens support the resistance (by getting inoc-ulated), cut enemy supply lines (quarantine the ill, wash hands), and steer clear of invaders (avoid exposure). We slow the enemy's advance (practice social distancing, "flatten the curve") and hang on until munitions experts (medical professionals) can deliver the weapons (antibiotics, vaccines) that yield decisive victories.*

Important prescriptions (such as "Wash your hands" and "Get your kids vaccinated") became common knowledge in part because they fit neatly into this mobilizing narrative. If stories like these hadn't rallied large populations to participate in public health efforts, some of the greatest success stories of the modern sciences wouldn't *be* success stories.

Now imagine our descendants telling a comparable tale:

> *Humanity was once visited by mysterious mental afflictions. Mind pathogens proliferated across social networks, rendering worldviews strangely resistant to evidence. They aggravated par-tisan divisions, corrupted moral sensibilities, and sparked point-less culture wars. And then, in the early decades of the twenty-first century, root causes came into focus. We awoke to the parasitic nature of bad ideas and overcame our reluctance to take on divi-sive ideologies. We grasped that minds have immune systems and learned that willful believing corrupts them.*

This story—the one our descendants might someday tell—might continue:

*In short order, our understanding coalesced into know-how. We learned to test claims with a certain kind of question: to seed minds with ideas that can withstand such questioning and weed minds of those that can't. In effect, our forebears modified an ancient inoculant, produced a mind vaccine, and administered it widely. In this way, they curtailed the outbreaks of unreason that once terrorized our ancestors. They learned how to cultivate mental immune health, and transformed humanity's prospects.*

Will this be the story our descendants tell? That depends. It depends, mostly, on what *we do* in the coming years. Here, then, is my question for you: Which tale would you rather our descendants tell? The tale of how we clung to comforting beliefs and wrung our hands as unhinged thinking spread across the Internet, tearing cultures apart? Or the tale of how our generation got serious about mental immune health, developed and administered a mind vaccine, and brought about a second Enlightenment?

We have it within us to choose the wiser path. And now, we have the tools to make it happen. The cognitive immunology revolution *will* happen—if each of us does our part.

## What You Can Do

If anything deserves to be called a miracle cure, it's a vaccine. For all that, they're not magic wands. You can't just wave a vaccine, mutter an incantation, and expect things to change. Nor are they really miraculous: in each case, the disease had to be studied, and the vaccine had to be designed, refined, and developed, tested, mass-produced, and distributed. The process is invariably painstaking, and success depends on billions of people participating in the solution.

I've done what I can to develop a general-purpose mind vaccine. My collaborators and editors have helped to refine it, and my students have helped test it. HarperCollins is doing what it can to mass-produce it. Booksellers will do their part to distribute it. You can help: Recommend this book to others. Loan your copy to a friend. Discuss its ideas. Share them. Above all, put the investigation's findings to work.

The other day, a no-nonsense friend asked if I could sum up cognitive immunology's practical implications. "What exactly should I *do* differently?" she asked. She wanted clear, simple instructions. It was an excellent question, but it put me in a bind. You see, we philosophers tend to dislike such direction. To us, imperatives feel authoritarian; we prefer to ponder underlying facts and make up our own minds, thank you very much—without anyone having to issue imperatives. In this way, we're a bit like headstrong teenagers. Bottom line: our discipline leaves us mildly allergic to advice giving (and advice taking)—especially advice that feels "self-helpy."

But perhaps our aversion to prescriptive language is an *over-reaction*. Many of us have bodies that overreact to allergens; perhaps philosophers have minds that overreact to directive language. So let's get practical.

In chapter 2, I asked readers with a practical bent to indulge my clarifying; here at the end, I turn the tables. I want to get prescriptive for the implementers among us, and ask my fellow clarifiers to cut me some slack. If the directive language makes you bristle, too, just translate my prescriptions into friendly suggestions, and take from them what you will. Or don't. Either way, own your response.

Here, then, is a kind of "12-Step Program" to cognitive immune health. Each step is meant to produce a certain inversion, or shift in perspective. Together, I think, they induce a kind of paradigm shift . . .

*Step 1*: Play with ideas. Test them. Ask questions. Pose challenges. Explore unsettling notions without fear. But also handle them with care. Remember, ideas aren't inert; they're self-replicating agents capable of remaking minds. Unassuming insights have re-made cultures, and toxic ones have torn them asunder. Ideas can inspire, connect, and enlighten; they can also distract, disorient, and delude. Treat them as the active agents they are. More gen-erally, don't let the trendy concept of informational "content" fool you: information is rarely passive, obedient, and well behaved; of-ten, it takes on a life of its own. Information is profoundly *unruly*.

*Step 2*: Understand that minds are not passive knowledge recep-tacles. They're infection-prone contraptions cobbled together by natural selection. Willful belief is an especially dangerous form of folly, for an ideology can hijack a mind and warp it beyond recognition. Treat your mind like a bucket full of precious stones, and it will become little more than a repository for random, over-confident opinions. Instead, treat it as a searchlight and use it to cast light into darkness.

*Step 3*: Get past the self-indulgent idea that you're entitled to your opinions. What you believe affects the well-being of others, so believe responsibly. If you find yourself relying on controversial convictions, stop to ponder whether you're really entitled to them. Do you *know* them to be true? How? Is your method of know-ing them truly reliable? Suppose someone else applied the same method to arrive at a conclusion you deplore; would you be okay with that? If not, rethink.

*Step 4*: Distinguish between good and bad faith. By all means, honor the quasi-religious insight that it's not just "upstream" ev-idence that matters: the "downstream" consequences of mental states matter too. There's a world of difference, though, between resolute hopefulness and tenacious dogmatism. Work to promote pro-social attitudes but don't excuse willful irrationality. We can have the faith that sings to our better angels, and do it without summoning our inner demons. To get there, though, reason and resolute hopefulness must lead. Belief must follow.

*Step 5*: Give up the idea that learning is merely a matter of *adding* to the mind's knowledge stockpile. Yes, it's important to learn new facts, but it's also important to unlearn "alternative facts." Install good information, but work also to uninstall bad information. Notice an inconsistency in your beliefs? Take time to address it.

*Step 6*: New information is like a puzzle piece; you must find where it fits and how it connects. True wisdom requires you to *clarify* and *order* your thoughts. Examine your convictions; bounce them off others. Strive to reconcile them. Give challenges their due. When your opinions don't add up, have the courage to admit it. Take your worldview apart and reassemble it. Try out new and interesting configurations. Find the truth in dissenting voices. Internalize their lessons and adjust your confidence levels. Deep learning isn't just additive: it's clarifying, constructive, and coherence enhancing. If you want a worldview worth sharing, *craft* one.

*Step 7*: Don't use "Who's to say?" to cut short unsettling inquiries. If you hear someone else employ these words, reply: "Clearly, *we're* to say: who else will take responsibility?" In the same vein, don't let "It's all relative," "It's all subjective," or "Objectivity is a false ideal" dissuade you from taking on the hard questions. It's not okay to keep kicking the hard questions down the road. Here's the truth: there are more and less responsible ways of thinking about *everything*, and we all need to seize opportunities to refine our understanding. (Besides, value inquiry is *fun!*)

*Step 8*: Let go of the idea that value judgments can't be objective. Kindness *really is* a virtue, and cruelty *really is* a vice: these truths are as certain as any mathematical theorem. Slavery really *is* an abomination, and homosexuality really *isn't*. The idea of human rights *really has* improved human well-being. The notion that we can't develop responsible shared understanding of what's good and right is mistaken: it's a vestige of a dysfunctional orthodoxy. Let it go.

*Step 9*: Treat challenges to your beliefs as opportunities rather than threats. Those beliefs, assumptions, and ideas of yours? They aren't you. A challenge to them in no way diminishes your worth. So don't get defensive; instead, think of your challenger as bringing a learning opportunity to your attention. Seek first to understand it. Find the insight or truth in it, and acknowledge it. Honor efforts to enlighten you, even if they prove, in the end, to be misguided. De-escalate. Turn down the heat, and turn up the light.

*Step 10*: Satisfy your need for belonging with a community of *inquiry* rather than a community of *belief*. Join a "big ideas" discussion group, a secular congregation, or a Unitarian church. Create a meet-up dedicated to the exploration of controversial ideas. Team up with others to debunk harmful illusions. Celebrate reason. Promote dialogue over dogma. Afford your children identity options that encourage open-mindedness in all things: *freethinker, humanist, rationalist,* and *skeptic* all do nicely.

*Step 11*: Upgrade your understanding of reasonable belief. The idea that a good reason can fully secure a belief is a myth. Something's *seeming* reasonable after *some* consideration is never a guarantee that it's *truly* reasonable, all things considered. A healthy mind is always open to the possibility that a new question or countervailing reason will upset the balance. The best-supported hypotheses are in principle open to unanticipated challenges. Has your conviction undergone vigorous questioning? If so, it may merit *provisional* assent.

*Step 12*: Don't underestimate the value of ideas that *have* survived scrutiny. They may not be "proven," but often, they're better than the alternatives and worth relying on. Have the courage of well-tested conviction. Rely on presumptions, and boldly go where no one has gone before. But be ready, when needed, to reexamine and discard them. Think, then put your values into action.

## What We Can Do

As the principles of cognitive immunology spread, we'll become more aware of cognitive immune disorders and begin to see over-looked remedies. We'll devise cognitive inoculants and take a more systematic approach to achieving mental immune health. Universities will launch cognitive immunology departments, and researchers will share their findings in new journals. Psychologists and philosophical counselors will practice new forms of cognitive immunotherapy, and teachers will skillfully cultivate the growth mindset.[1] Intellectual historians will tell previously untold tales: of how good ideas rewired human brains for cooperation, and how bad ideas sowed chaos and division.

Leaders will apply the principles of cognitive immunology to make their organizations more effective. Religions will initiate "accountable talk" reforms. Some will renounce bad faith. Governments will develop systems for promoting cognitive immune health. We'll design highly deliberative environments, erect safeguards against ideological corruption, and consciously work to mitigate known forms of bias. Trained mediators will de-escalate ideological conflicts and help avert culture wars. And over time, outbreaks of ideological thinking will become less frequent.

Together we can take the art of critical thinking to new heights.

We can neuter rabid ideologies, and free people to think for themselves. We can think more clearly and responsibly and dialogue in ways that bridge ideological divides. Stick with it, and the art of collaborative inquiry will flourish; sciences of right and wrong will emerge, and moral progress will accelerate. We'll deepen our understanding of what truly matters and connect in ways that satisfy our primal need for purpose and belonging.

Martin Luther King once said that "the arc of the universe is long, but it bends towards justice." To this I would add: where we uphold reason's fulcrum, it bends the faster. And you can help bend that arc: all you need is information that others have overlooked, the expectation that others take account of it, and the will to change minds. Of course, you must be willing to let others change *your* mind. That's the price of admission: the willingness to learn.

We merit the courage of our convictions only when we have the courage to part with them.

# Acknowledgments

Authors get their names printed on book covers; those who enable them have their names mentioned on pages like these. I used to think this a just arrangement; now I know better. This project taught me the truth: producing a book is a huge and hugely collaborative undertaking, and a book is rarely better than its author's support system. To all those who encouraged, enabled, supported, and contributed to *Mental Immunity*, I wish I could recognize you properly.

Bad ideas find their way into all kinds of books, and I'm sure this book is no exception. I'm supposed to say that the fault for this is 100 percent mine and in no way a reflection on others. That, of course, would be the gracious thing to say; but were I to write such a thing, I'd be guilty of deliberately introducing yet another bad idea. For gracious untruths are a species of bad idea—in fact, they're an especially insidious type. If the argument of this book is sound, they pave the way for more problematic modes of thought. So here instead is the ungracious truth: idea filtering is also a team sport; the things our minds produce are always a function of the things connected minds produce. Hence responsibility must be shared, just as credit must be shared. Still, as a practical matter, you might bring your issues with the book to me and lay them at *my* feet.

To my extraordinary agent, Dan Lazar: thanks for seeing this project's potential and guiding me down the path from writer to author. To my editors, Karen Rinaldi and Rebecca Raskin: thanks for believing in my vision for the book and helping me realize it more fully. It was a genuine pleasure working with you, and I hope we'll do it again. To Lee McIntyre, you're the best friend and role model an aspiring public philosopher could want; your support has been constant, and your "tough love" early feedback was crucial in making this book what it is. To Steven Pinker: your encouragement, your writings, and your example have shaped me in ways I can scarcely describe. You're a mensch, and I was in your debt even before you contributed this book's foreword.

Other thinkers have inspired me time and again, or had an out-sized influence on the way I see the world. Among these I include: Carl Sagan, Rebecca Goldstein, Daniel Dennett, Robert Wright, Yuval Noah Harari, Jonathan Haidt, Richard Dawkins, Sam Harris, and Rutger Bregman. Mark Lance also belongs in this category, as do my graduate advisers Arthur Fine and Michael Williams.

For reading and providing feedback on manuscript drafts, a heartfelt thank-you goes out to: Reece Norman, Liane Norman, Lee McIntyre, Clay Farris Naff, Eric Lotke, Scott Morgenstern, Eve Wider, Tom Juring, Mary Crossley, Mateo Arevalo, Christie Dixon, Leslie Wright, Don Matlack, and Justus Hibschman.

For providing encouragement, a sounding board, or other form of aid: Bart Campolo, David Canary, Tom Canfield, James Croft, Mike Dickey, Tasha Eurich, Bob Faw, Tom Flynn, John Helgerson, John Hooper, Mickey Maudlin, Dana Morganroth, Erin and Dave Nine-houser, Marie Norman, Tony Norman, Richard Scheines, Michael Shermer, Lowell Steinbrenner, Andrea Szalanski, Ariel Tan, Jeffrey Tayler, Michael Tomasello, Dennis Trumble, Aaron Watson, Matt Weiss, David Sloan Wilson, and Sarah Bolling. Also, I must thank the Pittsburgh Freethought Community, First Unitarian's Ideas Fo-rum, and the ever-lovin' Squirrel Hill Swine. (Skyduck, Truckstop, and Pain: you bear special responsibility for the person I've become.)

To my parents, Bob and Liane: I'll always be grateful for your wisdom and unflagging love. Mom, your courage and integrity are an inspiration. Dad, thanks for teaching me to do a job right. If only every kid got the kind of support you provided Emily, Marie, and me.

To my sons, Reece and Kai, who each contributed a marvelous tale to the overall story this book tells. I'm so proud of the young men you've become, and I ardently hope that this book helps your generation build a sustainable future.

And last but not least—in fact, last because most—my wife, Heidi: You married into my lifelong dream and got more than you bargained for. You endured my obsessive commitment to this project and did it without complaint. You've done more than I ever could have asked and always done it with patience and grace. I love you and can't express the extent of my gratitude. Our dreams were never perfectly aligned, but maybe now we can rent that shack by the beach and sell burritos.

# How to Play the Reason-Giving Game

Inquiry can be modeled as a reason-giving game. What follows is a simple, two-player version of the game.

## Claimants, Challengers, and the Spirit of the Game

The game begins when one player ("the claimant") makes a claim or assumption that the other player ("the challenger") calls into question. The object of the game is to find out whether the questioned claim is worth accepting, given what both players know. On the surface, the game is adversarial and *zero-sum*: the players take opposing sides, and one must lose for the other to win. Approached in the right spirit, though, the game is decidedly *non-zero-sum*: both players win as they learn together, deepen shared understanding, and move together toward the (whole) truth. The reason-giving game should always be played in this collaborative, "win-win" spirit.

## Commitments, Entitlements, and Game Trees

To play the game well, you need to recognize the different move types and understand how they affect the distribution of rights and responsibilities (here called "entitlements" and "commitments"). The concept of a *game tree* is useful here. Picture a tree with branches that represent the different ways the game might play out. As players make actual moves, they steer the game out onto one or another of the tree's branches. You orient yourself within the game by knowing which branch the game is on; by keeping track of the moves made so far, categorizing them correctly, and understanding how these moves shape the space of permissible moves that lie ahead (that is, how the limb you're on continues to branch).

## Claims, Presumptions, and Burden of Proof

A *claim* is a move in the game that puts forward as true something that has the structure of a sentence. When a player makes a claim, she undertakes a commitment to defend that claim with reasons. If unable to succeed in this, she is expected to *retract* the claim.

| PRESUMPTIONS: | NONPRESUMPTIONS: |
|---|---|
| reasonably likely | not reasonably likely |
| available for premising | not available for premising |
| challenger bears burden of disproof | claimant bears burden of proof |

The game's first branching is determined by the initial status of the claim at issue. It can be *nonpresumptive* or it can be *presumptive*. Claims that are not reasonably likely (given common background knowledge) are properly treated as *nonpresumptive*, which means they need to be redeemed before they can be used. With nonpresumptive claims, the claimant bears the burden of proof. On the other hand, claims that *are* reasonably likely should be treated as presumptive. This means they count as default entitlements: players are entitled to use these claims, unless or until they are called into question.

When a presumption is challenged, the burden of disproof lies on the challenger.

## Challenges, Bare and Onus-Bearing

A *challenge* is a move in the game that *takes issue* with a claim or assumption. It is said to *target* that claim or assumption, and it has the effect of *suspending entitlement* to it. In effect, challenges "bracket" the claims they target, making them temporarily unavailable for premising. Challenges also initiate a collaborative inquiry into the target's worthiness to be accepted, with entitlement to the contested claim hinging on the outcome.

The second branching concerns the type of challenge issued. Challenges can be *onus-bearing* or *bare*. An onus-bearing challenge presents *grounds for doubt*—one or more reasons meant to count against the target claim. The issuer of an onus-bearing challenge undertakes a commitment to defend his grounds for doubt. If it turns out she or he is unable to do this, he is obliged to *withdraw* his challenge. A bare challenge takes issue with a claim without offering grounds for doubt. In effect, it calls the claimant to account by demanding that she provide supporting reasons *for* her claim. The question "How do you know?" often has the force of a bare challenge.

## Defendings, Direct and Indirect

A *defending* is a move in the game that attempts to redeem (or partially redeem) a claim at issue. A defending is *direct* when it responds to a challenge by providing supporting reasons for the claim challenged. A defending is *indirect* when it responds to a challenge by attempting to show that the challenge misfires in some way: that it relies on questionable grounds for doubt, for example, or that it mislocates the onus of proof. For example, a bare challenge to a presumptive claim can be met indirectly by pointing out that the claim is fine as it stands, that it is not the claimant but the challenger that has reason-giving work to do. (Presumptions are immune to bare challenge but are always open to being undermined by grounds for doubt.) An indirect defending of either sort is successful when it "undoes" the entitlement-suspending force of a challenge.

## The Common Ground

In general, players should attempt to draw their premises (both claimants their supporting reasons, and challengers their grounds for doubt) from the *common ground* represented by the intersection of their belief sets. As issues are resolved and contested claims are redeemed (and thus jointly embraced) or undermined (and jointly rejected), the common ground expands, and mutual understanding grows.

## Retractions and Withdrawals

A *retraction* is a move that reverses a commitment to defend. It involves taking a claim (or assumption or ground for doubt) "off the table." This gets the player off the hook for defending it but typically involves conceding nonentitlement to the claim retracted. A player can also reverse an earlier challenge by *withdrawing* it. This usually involves *conceding* the claim that had been challenged, rendering it something the claimant *is* entitled to use and/or act upon.

## Embedded and Embedding Issues

In the simplest cases, a challenger takes issue with a claim, the claimant provides good supporting reasons (a successful direct defending), and the challenger withdraws his objection, conceding the claim. Things get more interesting, however, if a second challenge is played before the issue raised by the first challenge gets resolved. This can happen, for example, when the challenger challenges, in turn, a claimant's supporting reasons. (Note that a challenger may also challenge the implication that the reasons offered suffice to redeem the original claim—in effect putting the defender's *suppressed premise* at issue.) In another scenario, the claimant opts to defend his claim indirectly by questioning the cogency of the original challenge. In both cases, we say that the issue raised by the second challenge is *embedded* in the issue raised by the first. This means that the initial (embedding) question is put on hold while a resolution of the second (embedded) issue is taken up. Later, if the inquiry yields a resolution of the embedded issue, the embedding issue can be taken up again, now with better odds of success.

# Notes

## Introduction: Tree of Life, Seeds of Death

1. Jonathan Haidt, *The Righteous Mind* (New York: Random House, 2012).
2. To gain clarity about the deep philosophical issue here, consider the case of web servers. They "host" the bundles of information we call websites, yet seem to slavishly serve the "interests" of those bundles. When prompted, a web server will jump to the task of serving up a copy of a web page. Who's serving whom in this case? If the host server is in charge, why do we call it a "server"? When a mind serves up an idea—as I am doing now—it can be equally unclear where the agency lies. The philosophical issues raised by such talk were thoroughly explored in the wake of Richard Dawkins' *The Selfish Gene*. Daniel Dennett may have said it best: we need to treat microbes and genes and memes *as if* they had (some sort of) agency to describe and understand important natural systems. Sometimes, you have to stretch words beyond their customary use-cases to develop a better understanding of the universe. The moral of the story? Don't resist the implication of distributed agency. Instead, revel in it.
3. Maarten Boudry and Steije Hofhuis, "Parasites of the Mind," *Cognitive Systems Research* 53 (2018): 155–67.
4. "How to Fight an Infodemic," *The Lancet*, February 29, 2020.
5. "Inoculating Against Misinformation," Sander van der Linden et al, *Science* 358, no. 6367 (December 2017): 1141–42, https://science.science mag.org/content/358/6367/1141.2.
6. A Thomas Friedman Op-Ed in the *New York Times* on May 5, 2020, brought the concept of cognitive immunity to a wide audience. It seems

he got the idea from a Palo Alto think tank called the Institute for the Future (IFTF).

7. Boudry and Hofhuis, "Parasites of the Mind."

8. Ibid.

9. C. Betsch and P. Schmid, "Effective Strategies for Rebutting Science Denialism in Public Discussions," *Nature Human Behavior* 3 (2019): 931–39, https://www.nature.com/articles/s41562-019-0632-4. I learned about William McGuire's inoculation theory as this book was going to press. See https://en.wikipedia.org/wiki/Inoculation_theory.

10. Jonathan Haidt and Michael Tomasello have each argued persuasively that the human capacity to forge shared outlooks was critical to the evolution of human consciousness. Language, culture, technology—all of these appear to build on our capacity for mindsharing. See Haidt's *The Righteous Mind* (New York: Pantheon, 2012), 204ff.

## Chapter 1: Beyond Critical Thinking

1. John Cook and Stephan Lewandowski, "Neutralizing Misinformation Through Inoculation: Exposing Misleading Argumentation Techniques Reduces Their Influence," *PLOS One*, https://doi.org/10.1371/journal.pone.0175799. See also Sander van der Linden and Jon Rozenbeek, "Bad News: A Psychological 'Vaccine' Against Fake News," *International Forum for Responsible Media Blog*, July 9, 2019.

2. Plato, *Theaetetus* (148e-151d).

3. Thomas Hobbes, *Leviathan* (Indianapolis: Hackett, 1994), chapters 13–15. The science I have in mind is evolutionary game theory.

4. In *The Scientific Attitude* (Cambridge, MA: MIT Press, 2019), Lee McIntyre shows that science's success isn't due to its possession of a distinctive method. Instead, it's the flexible attitude that scientists bring to the task of understanding the world.

5. A full treatment of the subject would take us beyond the scope of this book, but chapter 7 provides a down payment on such an argument. To learn more, see my contribution to *Free Inquiry*'s symposium on mattering theory, vol. 37, no. 2 (February/March 2017), and my online addendum to that symposium: https://secularhumanism.org/2017/02/cont-a-different-mattering-theoretic-take-on-the-is-ought-problem/.

6. For example, college graduates are less likely to become anti-vaxxers,

science denialists, and Trump voters. See, for example: https://www
.washingtonpost.com/politics/as-trump-slumps-his-campaign-fixes-on
-a-target-women/2020/06/22/8bed7cda-af1b-11ea-8758-bfd1d045525a
_story.html and https://www.nytimes.com/2020/06/24/us/politics/trump
-biden-poll-nyt-upshot-siena-college.html?referringSource=article
Share. Similar evidence is commonplace.

7.  "Exclusive Test Data: Many Colleges Fail to Improve Critical Think-
ing Skills," *Wall Street Journal*, June 5, 2017. See also Richard Arum and
Josipa Roksa, *Academically Adrift. Limited Learning on College Campuses*
(Chicago: University of Chicago Press, 2011).

8.  Richard W. Paul, Linda Elder, and Ted Bartell, "California Teacher Prepa-
ration for Instruction in Critical Thinking: Research Findings and Policy
Recommendations" (Sacramento, CA: Foundations for Critical Thinking,
1997).

9.  https://www.pewresearch.org/fact-tank/2016/11/09/behind-trumps
-victory-divisions-by-race-gender-education/.

10. These ideas are often associated with the intellectual fad known as post-
modernism. I won't attempt to litigate the matter here, for others have
done plenty to demonstrate the movement's intellectual shallowness. The
Alan Sokal affair is a noteworthy example: https://en.wikipedia.org/wiki
/Sokal_affair.

11. Paul Kurtz and Tim Madigan, eds., *Challenges to the Enlightenment* (Am-
herst: Prometheus Books, 1994).

12. See Appendix A for a two-page summary of the rules of this game.

## Chapter 2: The Cognitive Immunology Toolbox

1.  Maarten Boudry and Steije Hofhuis, "Parasites of the Mind," *Cognitive
Systems Research* 53 (2018)

2.  Philip Tetlock, "Thinking the Unthinkable: Sacred Values and Taboo
Cognitions," *Trends in Cognitive Science* 7, no. 7 (July 2003):

3.  Other uses of the word *ideology* have gained currency in political science,
and my usage may disrupt the discourses built on them. A friend suggests that I coin another term—perhaps *malology*—for belief systems that
are fundamentally problematic. This may be the wiser course, but I have
trouble imagining *malology* catching on. Readers who need *ideology* for
other purposes may read *malology* where I write *ideology*.

4.　I borrow the analogy from Matt Richtel's *An Elegant Defense* (New York: William Morrow, 2019).

5.　Note that both axioms are normative and nonarbitrary: neither is "merely subjective." Again, don't be fooled by the rhetorical question "Who's to say?" People use it to avoid value inquiry and postpone difficult conversations, but its underlying premise—that we have no standing to make tough value judgments—is false. No perfect objectivity or godlike omniscience is going to filter out the bad ideas for us. It is *we* who must do this. *We're* to say. This doesn't mean we may do this on arbitrary grounds, of course. Personal preferences, ideological leanings, and faith orientations are not the final arbiters of value questions. Instead, responsible thinkers employ patient, collaborative inquiry: they attend to the facts, reason carefully, and try to avoid arbitrary commitments. A conceptual revolution is coming that will render moral sciences a recognized phenomenon.

## Chapter 3: The Widening Gyre

1.　Katherine Stewart, *The Power Worshippers: Inside the Dangerous Rise of Religious Nationalism* (London: Bloomsbury, 2020); and Andrew Seidel's *The Founding Myth* (New York: Sterling, 2019).

2.　"The Evangelicals Who Pray for War with Iran," Sarah Posner, *The New Republic*, January 9, 2020.

3.　This definition of "growth mindset" represents my gloss on Dweck's idea; it may differ in subtle ways from her own.

4.　Carol Dweck, *Mindset: The New Psychology of Success* (New York: Ballantine Books, 2006).

5.　David Chakranarayan and Ken Ham, "Disciplining Children God's Way," Answers in Genesis website (July 19, 2013).

6.　Elizabeth T. Gershoff, "More Harm Than Good: A Summary of Scientific Research on the Intended and Unintended Effects of Corporal Punishment on Children," *Law and Contemporary Problems* 73, no. 2 (Spring 2010): 31.

7.　Dan Kahan, "Misinformation and Identity-Protective Cognition," *Understanding and Addressing the Disinformation Ecosystem* (Philadelphia: Annenberg School of Communication, 2017), pdfs.semanticscholar.org.

8.　https://www.pewresearch.org/global/2020/07/20/the-global-god-divide/. See also Greg Epstein's *Good Without God: What a Billion Nonreligious People Do Believe* (New York: William Morrow, 2010).

9. For example: Thomas Edsall, "The Whole of Liberal Democracy Is in Grave Danger at This Moment," *The New York Times*, July 22, 2020. See also Max Boot, "Foes of Science Faced Ridicule at the Scopes Trial: We're Paying the Price 95 Years Later," *The New York Times*, July 8, 2020.

10. Thomas Friedman, "Make America Immune Again," *The New York Times*, May 5, 2020.

11. Paul Krugman, "A Plague of Willful Ignorance," *The New York Times*, June 23, 2020.

12. Gordon Pennycook et al., "On the Belief That Beliefs Should Change According to Evidence: Implications for Conspiratorial, Moral, Paranormal, Political, Religious and Science Beliefs," *Judgment and Decision Making* 15, no. 4 (July 2020).

## Chapter 4: Six Immune-Disruptive Ideas

1. The AIDS epidemic was never a purely American phenomenon, of course. Many of the 35 million fatalities occurred outside of the Reagan administration's jurisdiction. Nor can the administration's inaction be attributed to religious beliefs alone. Some historians think homophobic attitudes also played a role.

2. Notably in *Republic* and *Protagoras*.

3. Alvin Plantinga, "Religious Belief Without Evidence," *Introduction to Philosophy: Classical and Contemporary Readings*, 4th edition, ed. Louis P. Pojman and James Fieser (Oxford: Oxford University Press, 2008).

4. Something like this occurred recently in the wake of a tweet by author J. K. Rowling. Social justice warriors took offense and tried to "cancel" Rowling.

5. I borrow the concept of "accountable talk" from learning researcher Lauren Resnick. Her idea is that we can hold children to high standards of accountable talk and thereby facilitate important kinds of growth. In immunology-speak: mental immune health grows in communities that encourage accountable talk.

6. Gary Abernathy, "What's Really Behind Republicans Wanting a Swift Reopening? Evangelicals," *The New York Times*, May 20, 2020.

7. In 1996, physicist Alan Sokal exposed the lack of accountability in postmodern discourse by publishing a spoof article in a journal devoted to postmodern cultural studies: https://en.wikipedia.org/wiki/Sokal_affair.

## Chapter 5: Fighting Monsters

1.  Brendan Nyhan and Jason Reifler, "When Corrections Fail: The Persistence of Political Misperceptions," *Political Behavior* 32 (March 2010), 303–30.
2.  Carol Dweck, *Mindset: The New Psychology of Success* (New York: Ballantine Books, 2006).
3.  Built by former students, *Socrates Jones: Pro Philosopher* was popular for a time; I'm currently working with them on a sequel. I have anecdotal evidence that the game sparks enthusiasm for idea-testing and grounds for thinking that game play deepens dialogical sensibilities. But I've yet to amass hard evidence of the learning outcomes. I invite game designers, critical thinking experts, and learning scientists to help evolve this approach. A capsule version of the reason-giving game can be found in an appendix.
4.  Rutger Bregman, *Humankind: A Hopeful History* (New York: Little, Brown, 2020).

## Chapter 6: The Ethics of Faith

1.  The data on war deaths suggests that this is a conservative estimate: https://en.wikipedia.org/wiki/List_of_wars_by_death_toll.
2.  The argument for this claim can get a little technical, but it's mostly a matter of definition. Pragmatists like James and C. S. Peirce argued that belief is nothing other than a disposition to behave as if the belief were true.
3.  Daniel Dennett, *Breaking the Spell* (New York: Viking, 2006), 200ff.
4.  To understand this phenomenon, reflect on Antony Flew's classic "invisible gardener" parable in A. Flew and A. McIntyre, *New Essays in Philosophical Theology* (London: SCM Press, 1955).
5.  Gregory Paul, "Cross-National Correlations of Quantifiable Societal Health with Popular Religiosity and Secularism in the Prosperous Democracies, *Journal of Religion and Society* 7 (2005).
6.  https://www.pewresearch.org/fact-tank/2016/02/29/how-religious-is-your-state/?state=alabama.

## Chapter 7: Thought Police Need Not Apply

1.  Dan Ariely, *Predictably Irrational* (New York: Harper Perennial, 2010).
2.  The fact that we have names for different specialties within science should

not distract us from the key fact: science writ large is a single, unified effort to understand our world.

3. https://en.wikipedia.org/wiki/Replication_crisis.

## Chapter 8: Reason's Fulcrum

1. The literature on illusory superiority is vast. See Ethan Zell et al., "The Better-Than-Average Effect in Comparative Self-Evaluation: A Comprehensive Review and Meta-Analysis," *Psychological Bulletin* 146 , no. 2 (2020): 118–49.

2. I develop this argument and detail the empirical evidence for what I call the Intention Alignment model of reason's evolutionary functioning in Andy Norman, "Why We Reason: Intention-Alignment and the Genesis of Human Rationality," *Biology and Philosophy* 31, no. 5 (2016): 685–704.

3. Ibid.

4. Jonathan Haidt, *The Righteous Mind* (New York: Random House, 2012). Haidt rightly credits Michael Tomasello for the basic insight and research in this space. Michael Tomasello, *The Origins of Human Communication* (Cambridge: Bradford Books, 2010). There are some differences in the way Tomasello, Haidt, and I characterize the key development. Tomasello points to "intention sharing" and Haidt speaks of "moral matrices." I emphasize reason-giving, but the three of us seem to agree on this: the capacity to weave complex webs of mutual understanding probably paved the way for language, culture, and technology.

5. Rutger Bregman, *Humankind: A Hopeful History* (New York: Little, Brown, 2020), chapter 3.

6. Chip Walter, *Last Ape Standing* (New York: Bloomsbury, 2014).

7. See also the evidence compiled in B. Hare and V. Woods, *Survival of the Friendliest* (New York: Random House, 2020). Hare and Woods argue that the emergence of friendliness was the key development that propelled *Homo sapiens* to dominance. Perhaps, but this, too, was key: our ancestors' facility with reason allowed for a hugely advantageous kind of mind synchronization.

8. Some philosophers think that Bayes' theorem gives us an algorithm for aggregating reasons. In principle, the disciplined application of the laws of probability could approximate such an algorithm. I remain agnostic about the stronger claims of Bayesian epistemologists.

9.  The dialogue is called *Euthyphro*. Plato, *Five Dialogues* (Indianapolis: Hackett, 2002).

10. There are now many important and accessible books on the natural origins of morality. See especially Robert Wright, *The Moral Animal* (New York: Vintage, 1995).

11. Clay Farris Naff and Andy Norman, "Getting Real About Right and Wrong," *Skeptic* 23, no.3 (2018).

12. Hugo Mercier and Dan Sperber, "Why Do Humans Reason?" *Behavioral and Brain Sciences* 34, no. 2 (2011): 62–63; and Jennifer S. Lerner and Philip E. Tetlock, "Accounting for the Effects of Accountability," *Psychological Bulletin* 125, no. 2, 255–75.

13. Steven Pinker, *The Better Angels of Our Nature* (New York: Penguin, 2011), chapter 4.

14. Consider questions of the form: "What grounds could we possibly have for denying blacks/women/gays equal protection?" When we pause to examine the excuses people give for preserving unearned privilege, the attitudes that prop up unjust systems begin to crumble. Reasoning in this fashion has in this way been instrumental to moral progress. See Andy Norman, "The Machinery of Moral Progress: An Interview with Rebecca Newberger Goldstein," *The Humanist* (August 2014).

15. John Locke, *Second Treatise on Government*, and Jean-Jacques Rousseau, *The Social Contract*. Hobbes came close to doing the same in *Leviathan*.

16. Robert Axelrod, *The Evolution of Cooperation* (New York: Basic Books, 2006).

## Chapter 9: Reason Unhinged

1.  You'll find useful overviews of this research in Dan Ariely, *Predictably Irrational* (New York: Harper Perennial, 2010); D. Kahneman, *Thinking Fast and Slow* (New York: Farrar, Straus & Giroux, 2011), and Jonathan Haidt, *The Righteous Mind* (New York: Random House, 2012).

2.  I'm trying to paint a picture of the "physics" of rational belief change. On this picture, an interesting argument does nothing more than juxtapose premises and conclusion in a way that shows that one or more minds need to change. Reconciliation can involve embracing the conclusion, discarding a premise, questioning the logic, or adjusting the likelihoods we attach to one or more of the claims involved. The argument itself doesn't

settle the question of which of these expedients makes the most sense; that requires background knowledge and perspective.

3. Thomas Friedman, "Make America Immune Again," *The New York Times*, May 5, 2020.

4. Paul Krugman, "A Plague of Willful Ignorance," *The New York Times*, June 23, 2020.

5. Katie Rogers and Kevin Roose, "Trump Says QAnon Followers Are People Who 'Love Our Country,'" *The New York Times*, August 19, 2020.

6. Will Storr, *The Unpersuadables: Adventures with the Enemies of Science* (New York: Harry N. Abrams, 2015).

7. Lindy West, "What Are Trump Fans Really 'Afraid' to Say?" *The New York Times*, March 16, 2016.

8. Eve Peyser, "The Summer's Hottest Trend Is Owning the Libs," *Rolling Stone*, July 26, 2018.

9. Gordon Pennycook et al., "On the Belief That Beliefs Should Change According to Evidence: Implications for Conspiratorial, Moral, Paranormal, Political, Religious and Science Beliefs," *Judgment and Decision Making* 15, no. 4 (July 2020).

10. Dan Kahan, "Misconceptions, Misinformation, and the Logic of Identity-Protective Cognition," Kahan, Dan M., Cultural Cognition Project Working Paper Series No. 164, Yale Law School (May 24, 2017).

11. Goldstein planted the seeds of mattering theory in her novel *The Mind-Body Problem* (New York: Random House, 1983). Others picked up on her idea of "mattering maps," and she returned to the subject years later. She and I worked out the basics of mattering theory in a symposium for *Free Inquiry* 37, no. 2 (Feb/March 2017).

12. Inga Jasinskaja-Lahti and Jolanda Jetten, "Unpacking the Relationship Between Religiosity and Conspiracy Beliefs in Australia," *British Journal of Social Psychology* 58, no. 4 (February 1, 2019).

13. Ibid. See also James Gibson, "The Political Consequences of Religiosity," *Religion and Democracy in the United States: Danger or Opportunity?* ed. Alan Wolf and Ian Katznelson (Princeton: Princeton University Press, 2010).

14. Antoine Marie, "Moral Rigidity Evolved to Strengthen Bonds Within Groups," *The Evolution Institute* (June 8, 2020), https://evolution-institute .org/moral-rigidity-evolved-to-strengthen-bonds-within-groups/.

15. Philip Tetlock, "Thinking the Unthinkable: Sacred Values and Taboo Cognitions," *Trends in Cognitive Science* 7, no. 7 (July 2003): 320–24.

16. Alex Olshansky, "Conspiracy Theorizing and Religious Motivated Reasoning: Why the Earth 'Must' Be Flat (master's thesis, Texas Tech University, 2018), 45, https://ttu-ir.tdl.org/handle/2346/82666. When a fellow philosopher of science went undercover at a Flat Earth convention, he was astonished by the prevalence of Christian evangelicals among the attendees: Lee McIntyre, "Flat Earthers and the Rise of Science Denial in America," *Newsweek*, May 14, 2019. See also McIntyre's *How to Talk to a Science Denier*, forthcoming from MIT Press.

17. Many commentators have expressed astonishment that 81 percent of Christian evangelicals voted for the manifestly immoral Donald Trump in the 2016 election. The damaged fulcrum model, though, suggests that facts like this are a predictable consequence of faith-based believing. Proneness to science denial and conspiracy thinking also correlate with religiosity. Joseph E. Uscinski et al., "Why Do People Believe COVID-19 Conspiracy Theories?" *Misinformation Review* (April 2020), http://misinforeview.hks.harvard.edu/article/why-do-people-believe-covid-19-conspiracy-theories/.

18. Thomas Edsall, "The Whole of Liberal Democracy Is in Grave Danger at This Moment," *The New York Times*, July 22, 2020, and the study it cites: Gordon Pennycook et al., "On the Belief That Beliefs Should Change According to Evidence: Implications for Conspiratorial, Moral, Paranormal, Political, Religious and Science Beliefs," *Judgment and Decision Making* 15, no. 4 (July 2020).

19. I borrow this distinction from Clay Farris Naff's *Free God Now* (Scotts Valley, CA: Createspace Independent Publishing, 2012).

20. Several philosophers at my university study the costs and benefits of conducting science under different conditions. Some even model scientific practices, and run simulations. Can tweaking the incentives for scientific discovery yield a more productive institution? Can we modify prevailing evidentiary norms, and thereby reproduce findings more reliably?

21. Carl Sagan, *Pale Blue Dot* (New York: Ballantine Books, 1997).

22. Richard Sosis and Eric R. Bressler, "Cooperation and Commune Longevity: A Test of the Costly Signaling Theory of Religion," *Cross-Cultural Research* 37, no. 2 (May 2003): 211–39.

23. The philosopher Bertrand Russell once wrote: "William James used to preach the 'will to believe.' For my part, I should wish to preach the 'will to doubt' . . . which is the exact opposite." This pithy observation captures what Peirce found problematic about Jamesian pragmatism.

## Chapter 10: Mind Upgrade

1. In the United States, people and organizations seeking bankruptcy protection file under the law's "chapter eleven." In this way, the phrase "chapter eleven" became synonymous with bankruptcy.

2. Antoine Marie, "Moral Rigidity Evolved to Strengthen Bonds Within Groups," *The Evolution Institute* (June 8, 2020), https://evolution-institute .org/moral-rigidity-evolved-to-strengthen-bonds-within-groups/.

3. Some philosophers accept that moral facts exist, but most deny this. I happen to think that such talk can be useful—a good way to call attention to real features of the human condition that have moral import. For example, kindness is more conducive to shared well-being than cruelty is, and honesty is more conducive than dishonesty. Really: these claims are true in some objective— or at least non-merely-subjective—sense. You might say they state facts.

4. I owe the concept of "mattering maps" to Rebecca Goldstein. Her work paved the way for what I call mattering theory: a systematic way of thinking together about what really matters—and resolving value questions. See our joint symposium on the subject in *Free Inquiry* 37, no. 2 (February 2017), and my online addendum to that exchange: "A Different Mattering-Theoretic Take on the Is-Ought Problem."

5. Technically, you need to look at the way *attributions of reasonableness* function: at what's supposed to *follow from* a determination that something is reasonable or unreasonable. The criteria for making such attributions, and the upshot of making such attributions, need to sync up in a well-functioning whole.

6. I am indebted to Rebecca Goldstein for her wonderful book *Plato at the Googleplex* (New York: Pantheon, 2014).

7. Goldstein dismantles the assertions of "philosophy-jeerers" like Lawrence Krauss, ibid.

8. Steven Pinker, *The Better Angels of Our Nature* (New York: Penguin, 2011). See also his *Enlightenment Now* (New York: Viking, 2018).

## Chapter 11: Seductive Misconceptions: How Rationalism Lost Its Way

1.  Tests like: Does the criterion meet its own standard? Can one accept it without at the same time violating it? Is it too lax? Is it too stringent? Does it handle the obvious cases—the clearly reasonable and clearly unreasonable cases—correctly? Does it prove useful for judging harder cases?

2.  In any complex culture that divides cognitive labor, it must be possible, in some cases, to answer a challenge by citing the authority of relevant experts. So sometimes, someone else's ability to answer the relevant challenges substitutes for your own.

3.  Here's the logic, spelled out step-by-step: Basic beliefs are by definition not underwritten by anything more basic. This means that they're literally *baseless*. According to the Platonic standard, this makes them not reasonable, hence unworthy of our credence. It also makes them incapable of providing a suitable basis. If this argument doesn't move you, don't despair. Instead, try another version of the argument: the Platonic picture forces rationalism onto the horns of a dilemma. Each supposedly basic belief must be either reasonable or unreasonable; if reasonable, it must be supported by reasons—for that is, after all, what the model requires. But that means it isn't truly "first" or "basic" after all! If unreasonable, though, it doesn't deserve to be treated as supportive, or for that matter, acceptable. Either way, basic beliefs can't do the work the Platonic model needs them to do.

4.  Aristotle, *Posterior Analytics*, 72b5–23.

5.  Ibid., 72b5–21.

6.  Julia Annas and Jonathan Barnes, *The Modes of Skepticism: Ancient Texts and Modern Interpretations* (Cambridge: Cambridge University Press, 1985).

7.  Ibid.

8.  Christian thinkers of the Middle Ages took Aristotle's idea of the first cause (the "unmoved mover") and used it to argue that God must have set the universe in motion. Thomas Aquinas developed five variations on this argument.

9.  Technically, faith-enabled "apprehensions of intelligible form." This view shared the defects of Aristotle's epistemology but remained powerfully influential.

10. To regain knowledge of the physical world, Descartes cheated: he posited a God who wouldn't deceive him and argued in a circle to boot.

11. I developed this idea in academic journal articles in the 1990s, notably A. Norman, "Regress and Doctrine of Epistemic Original Sin," *The Philosophical Quarterly* 47, no. 189 (October 1997): 477–94.

12. This didn't prevent philosophers from harboring hopes that "self-evident" beliefs would somehow defy the physics, levitate, and thereby provide a basis for other beliefs.

13. Hobbes, for example, avowed that "there can be no certainty of the last conclusion, without a certainty of all those affirmations and negations, on which it was grounded and inferred." Locke was similarly captivated: "[Do] not entertain any proposition with greater assurance than the proofs it is built upon will warrant." Hume: "If I ask why you believe any matter of fact, which you relate, you must tell me some reason . . . or allow that your belief is entirely without foundation." Leibniz made the idea a cornerstone of his philosophy: "In virtue of the principle of sufficient reason, we assume that no fact can be true or real and no judgment correct without there being a sufficient reason or ground why it is thus and not otherwise." I was surprised to find its simplest expression in the writings of Immanuel Kant: "Every proposition must have a reason." (Kant is notorious for using convoluted sentences.) The list could easily be lengthened, for among modern philosophers, foundationalism was almost universally assumed.

14. Little-known fact: astrology originated in an age when people believed that the planets and stars were locked in crystalline orbs that rubbed against our worldly orb, causing the changes we see here on Earth; within such a cosmology, astrological assumptions have a certain plausibility. But when this picture of the cosmos died, astrology became a vestige of an outmoded worldview—an empty vessel for wishful thinking.

15. Descartes' external world problem was the seventeenth century's version of the question "How do we know we're not in the matrix, being fed a giant simulation of reality?" The question asks for evidence of a kind that would rule out a peculiar possibility. The problem is that it's easy to generate possibilities that are in principle impossible to rule out: any imaginable evidence could be part of the simulation. The deep solution to this sort of skeptical problem, I think—and others, such as the problem of induction—is to adopt the design standpoint, and insist that the rules of the reasoning game shouldn't make it trivially easy for reflexive naysayers to render wide swaths of knowledge indefensible. I shouldn't be allowed

to mention the mere possibility that we're all hallucinating aardvarks on Mars, and thereby frustrate a serious debate on climate change. Nor should the mere possibility of a deceptive demon wipe out all knowledge of the external world.

16. One version of this apparently definitional truth goes like this: to be justified, a belief must be justified *by* something. This makes it look like legitimacy is invariably conferred.

17. Hume essentially concedes failure by acknowledging that his solution to the problem of induction amounts to nothing more than "a skeptical resolution" of skeptical doubts.

18. To those who view the German philosopher Immanuel Kant as the culminating figure in modern philosophy, note this: he inherited the problematic in roughly the state Hume left it, and wondered how knowledge was possible. He concluded that certain innate principles must play an essential role in knowledge formation. Reason's capacity to grasp these principles directly (without the aid of the senses), he argued, is the only thing standing between us and full-blown Humean skepticism. When you realize that innateness is no guarantor of truth, Kant's solution also reveals itself to be a souped-up skepticism.

19. David Hume, *Enquiry Concerning Human Understanding* (Indianapolis: Hackett Books, 1993).

20. Hume treated memories of facts as a one-off: a kind of stored version of the essential phenomenon.

21. Hume understood that mathematical and factual knowledge must be treated differently; for the former seems to be erected on definitions rather than perceptions.

22. According to empiricism, sensory evidence justifies perceptual knowledge *noninferentially*, and perceptual knowledge justifies the rest *inferentially*— that is, by argument of inference.

23. I refer here to logical positivism. See Alfred Jules Ayer, *Language, Truth, and Logic* (Dover: Dover Publications, 1952).

24. Alvin Plantinga, "Is Belief in God Properly Basic?" *The Norton Introduction to Philosophy*, ed. Gideon Rosen, Alex Byrne, Joshua Cohen and Seana Valentine Shiffrin (New York: Norton, 2015), 88.

25. "The world has existed for more than five minutes" is notoriously impossible to evidence because the hypothesis one is supposed to rule out—that the entire universe came into existence five minutes ago, complete with

misleading memories, misleading fossilized remains, etc.—is engineered to be in principle impossible to rule out! Many forms of extreme skepticism are built on alternative hypotheses like these. See this chapter's note 15.

26.   Alvin Plantinga, "Is Belief in God Properly Basic?" ibid, 89–93.

## Chapter 12: The Mind Vaccine: Rethinking Reason's Requirements

1.   Daryl Davis, *Klan-destine Relationships: A Black Man's Odyssey in the Ku Klux Klan* (New York: New Horizon, 2005).

2.   Lee McIntyre, *How to Talk to a Science Denier*, forthcoming from MIT Press.

3.   I mean for the concept of shared understanding to exclude shared *mis*understanding. It matters that the issue be resolved, but it also matters that the joint conclusion be true.

4.   Quoted by Bill Bryson in *The Body: A Guide for Occupants* (New York: Doubleday, 2019).

5.   Immunologists tell us that "a large number of immunodeficiency syndromes [combine an] inability to clear infections with perpetual immune system activation." I take the language from Wikipedia, but the fact itself is a commonplace of immunology.

6.   Sometimes such questions simply request information, without intending to contest the claim. In such cases, I don't classify them as challenges. If it calls the rightness of the claim into question, though, it counts as a challenge.

7.   Philosophers call the idea that there are moral facts "moral realism." It's a minority position.

8.   When performing this thought experiment, you'll likely come across this consideration: it would be decidedly unwise for all of us to treat "We should treat each other kindly" as invalid until proven. Instead, we should treat it as prima facie true.

9.   To assume otherwise is to beg the question and betray a residual attachment to the very Platonic picture I am challenging. For I am questioning the whole idea that certain skeptical challenges successfully problematized huge swaths of knowledge in the first place. I'm arguing that those challenges were and are illicit, for reasons many overlook.

10.  This follows from a sensible account of presupposition; something like this: X presupposes Y just in case showing that Y is false undermines (the force of) X. Incidentally, this is a subtle argument; to really feel its force,

you might need to refresh your understanding of the concepts involved and go over it a few times. The trick is to let the concepts direct your attention to the indicated phenomena and *see for yourself* that the argument holds. Yes, the argument invites you to consult your moral intuitions and take what they indicate as a kind of evidence.

11. Elsewhere, I argue that Plantinga errs in treating "God exists" as properly basic. See Andrew Norman, "Understanding Basic Belief: An Evidentialist Reply to Alvin Plantinga," *Think* 16, no. 47 (October 2017): 57–78, doi:10.1017/S1477175617000215. "God exists" may have been presumptive at one point in history. The problem of evil, the advance of the sciences, and the development of naturalistic ethics, though, have rendered it nonpresumptive—or so I would argue.

12. Some logicians call this "deontic scorekeeping." The idea is that dialogue runs more smoothly if participants keep a running tally of the claims they're committed to redeeming, and keep track also of the claims they are and aren't entitled to invoke. To a first approximation: when you make a claim, you undertake a commitment to defend it, and when a certain subset of your ideas is challenged, your right to invoke those ideas as premises is suspended. Justifying reasons are supposed to be non-question-begging.

13. A challenger's grounds for doubt, of course, should be held to the same standard: the question is always "What can you *show*?"

14. This generalization admits of exceptions, of course. Serious researchers shouldn't have to take the challenges of quack scientists seriously—not always, at any rate.

15. In their 2008 book *Nudge*, Richard Thaler and Cass Sunstein discuss cases like the following to argue for the thoughtful application of "choice architecture." In countries like Austria, laws make "organ donor" the default option: citizens are presumed to be donors but can opt out if they wish. Still, about 90 percent remain donors. As a result, the Austrian health-care system is awash in lifesaving organs. By contrast, people in the United States are presumed *not* to be organ donors. We're given the chance to opt in, but fewer than 15 percent do. Consequently, the American health-care system is chronically short of lifesaving organs. Every day, about eighteen Americans die for lack of a donated organ. A simple adjustment to the default enshrined in law could save more than sixty-five hundred lives a year—and improve the lives of many more.

A "choice architect" is someone who applies defaults (among other things) to "nudge" people in the direction of better decisions. Another example: a human resources professional in a large company makes enrollment in a well-designed retirement plan the default, thereby helping employees save money. Employees remain free to opt out, but few do, so more of them save enough for retirement. Some worry about the "paternalism" inherent in such efforts, but Thaler and Sunstein point out that every decision situation has a choice architecture, and there's no particular reason to prefer the choice architectures served up by historical accident.

The choice architectures created by intelligent, well-meaning designers, of course, are importantly different. Take the American legal system's presumption of innocence. This convention assigns citizens a default status—innocent—thereby placing a burden of proof on prosecutors and plaintiffs. The framers of our Constitution were quite deliberate about this: they wanted to make it hard for the state to deprive people of their freedoms. It's easy to appreciate the forethought that went into this choice architecture, and we all benefit from the wisdom it embodies. I've yet to meet the person willing to dismiss it as paternalism run amok. Why not do our best to enhance other choice architectures?

16. I liked this puzzle because it threatened my very identity. It pitted my core convictions against one another. I wanted to believe in reason, dialogue, and open-mindedness, but here was this cursed puzzle, showing that I couldn't have all three. It made my entire life project look silly. So in 1990, I made it the central problem of my dissertation research. The concepts and definitions presented earlier in this chapter all derive from this early work. (I figured out at the time that they're needed to restore balance and fairness to the reason-giving game. Years later, I realized that they also modulate mental immune response.)

17. I borrow the phrase from William Warren Bartley's *The Retreat to Commitment* (Chicago: Open Court, 1991). The book did a lot to shape my thinking.

18. It's easy to imagine that mathematics must employ axioms that are more than merely presumptive, but this isn't so. For one thing, much of mathematics is a matter of stipulating a set of presumptions and seeing what can be derived from that set. For another, if you show a mathematician that one of his axioms is untenable, she'll cease treating it as an axiom.

19. Take note, conservatives, of the word *conserve* here: presumptions are our

friend and are key to conserving the progress we've made. Progressives need to take note, also, and honor the moderate conservatism inherent in the concept of presumption. In practice, this amounts to the burden of proof initially falling on the (progressive) challenger of the status quo.

20. It's one thing to help a curious child understand why we treat X as presumptive—i.e., *explain* a presumption—it's another to yield every time a skeptical science denier claims to saddle us with a burden of proof.

21. In these cases—cases of basic belief—onus-bearing challenges fail to arise because grounds for doubt happen to be unavailable, and bare challenges fail to arise because the claim is presumptive.

22. Thomas S. Kuhn, *The Structure of Scientific Revolutions* (Chicago: University of Chicago Press, 2012); and Alasdair MacIntyre, "Epistemological Crises, Dramatic Narrative, and the Philosophy of Science," *The Monist* 60, no. 4 (October 1977): 453–72.

23. I'm under no illusion that this formula magically simplifies such determinations. It doesn't. Nor is it meant to supplant the more mathematically rigorous Bayesian updating. The model is more of a pragmatic supplement: a useful, dialogue-conducive heuristic for gauging the worthiness of claims.

## Conclusion: Propagating Enlightenment

1. For thousands of years, philosophers used questions to help people think through practical life problems. Then the professionalization of philosophy rendered much of it abstract and hard to relate to the everyday challenges of living. Today, the pendulum is swinging back: professional philosophers are encouraging one another to do "public philosophy"— philosophy that speaks to more than specialists. Also, certified philosophical counselors like myself provide a question-driven form of life coaching you can't get from traditional providers of mental health services. To learn more, check out the American Philosophical Practitioners Association, the National Philosophical Counseling Association, and the Public Philosophy Network online.

# Index

# About the Author

**Andy Norman** directs the Humanism Initiative at Carnegie Mellon University. He's done research on the evolutionary origins of human reasoning and the norms that make dialogue fruitful. He works to clarify the foundations of responsible thinking about what matters, writes for national magazines, and helps organizations develop next-level critical thinkers. He likes to engage audiences on topics related to science and human values.